Looking at the Renaissance

ESSAYS TOWARD A CONTEXTUAL APPRECIATION

Charles R. Mack

THE UNIVERSITY OF MICHIGAN PRESS
ANN ARBOR

Published in the United States of America by
The University of Michigan Press
Manufactured in the United States of America
♾ Printed on acid-free paper

2008 2007 2006 2005 4 3 2 1

A CIP catalog record for this book is available from the British Library.

Library of Congress Cataloging-in-Publication Data

Mack, Charles R., 1940–
Looking at the Renaissance : essays toward a contextual appreciation / Charles R. Mack.
p. cm.
Includes bibliographical references and index.
ISBN 0-472-09890-X (cloth : alk. paper) — ISBN 0-472-06890-3 (pbk. : alk. paper)
1. Art, Renaissance. 2. Renaissance. I. Title.

N6370.M235 2005
709'.02'4—dc22 2004019089

For my students, past and present:
This is what I really meant to say.

&

For my granddaughter, Gabriele Nicole Daniels,
whose arrival brought me a Renaissance.

Acknowledgments

This book of interrelated essays is the product of more than three decades of active engagement with the artistic language of the Italian Renaissance. During the course of my involvement with this cultural era and the artworks coming out of it—as I introduced my survey classes to the beauty of Renaissance painting, sculpture, and architecture and investigated the accomplishments of the period at greater depth with my graduate students—I began to think more and more about how and why the Renaissance came to be and just what actually did determine its period style. Was there, in fact, some common cultural denominator at work that gave a particular character to the era? Was there some sweeping cultural gesture that typified what was, after all, the beginning of our modern age? Gradually, as my questions found answers that seemed to satisfy, my thoughts began to arrange themselves into some semblance of coherence. I finally have arrived at an overall vision of the Renaissance, and this book is the result. Although the pages in it are relatively few in number, the time it has taken to fill them has been long.

Some of my initial thoughts on the subject were first presented at the University of West Florida in 1981 as a public lecture honoring retiring art historian John Carey. Additional ideas were offered in a Columbus Year talk at the Columbia Museum of Art in 1992 and, in more refined form, a year later at my university as the inaugural lecture of my William Joseph Todd Professorship in the Italian Renaissance. Portions of what would become chapter 5, dealing with monastic frescoes, appeared in the 2001 issue of *Arris,* while some of the material in the section concerning Botticelli's *Venus* in chapter 4 was published in 2002 as an essay in *Explorations in Renaissance Culture.* The second chapter of this book also incorporates a version of an article on Brunelleschi's use of proportions in his design for the Hospital of Innocents that appeared in *Studies in Iconography* in 1979.

Despite these scattered public outings, it was always my intent and hope that my interpretation of the Renaissance would find eventual expression in book format. It was to that end that I devoted much of a sabbatical leave in fall 2000, with the completion of what could pass for a first draft being accomplished in the following spring. The maturation process certainly has been slow, delayed by several other projects along the way, by encounters with new and thought-provoking publications, and by my own unfolding and often changing perceptions.

Throughout the course of this evolving endeavor, I have profited from the knowledge and advice of many. Thrice, in teaching a graduate seminar on Renaissance methodologies, I have inflicted this manuscript (in varying stages of unreadiness) upon my students. Upon each occasion, I have benefited greatly from their comments and criticisms, made both publicly and privately. Several graduate students (Diann Montigue, Lisa Harris, and Alecia Harper) who have held my university's William Joseph Todd Graduate Research Assistantship in the Italian Renaissance have graciously read and critiqued versions of the text. Their recommendations as to content and presentation proved most helpful in making the final revisions. Ms. Harper's fortuitous background as a copy editor also was of considerable assistance as I prepared the manuscript for publication, and I am deeply grateful for her labors.

In addition to the assistance of my students, I have received useful advice from a number of others. Among the mentors to whom I am most indebted for helping to shape my attitudes concerning the Renaissance, I must record my especial appreciation to Professor John W. Dixon III and to the late Professors Clemens Sommer and Philipp Fehl. I have gained much from their perception and just as much through their example. The late Professors Ulrich Middeldorf and Howard Saalman also were liberal in sharing their considerable knowledge of the Florentine Renaissance. Among the colleagues at various institutions from whose advice and conversations I have benefited, several have been particularly generous: Charles Burroughs, Liana De Girolami Cheney, Bruce Cole, Andrew Ladis, Norman Land, William Levin, Henry Millon, Vernon Hyde Minor, Perri Lee Roberts, Barbara Watts, and Carroll (Bill) Westfall. Here, at the University of South Carolina, I especially am indebted to Jerry Hackett of the Department of Philosophy, who offered advice on matters pertaining to his discipline. Susan Hogue guided me through a software problem, and I appreciate her expertise and patience. A thorough revision of the text was undertaken during the course of an informal fortieth reunion of members of the Berlin 513th INTC unit held in August 2003 near Charlottesville, Virginia, and I thank Dean Wilder for his hospitality on that occasion.

Once the proposal for this book reached the University of Michigan Press, I received encouragement and guidance from acquisitions editor Christopher Collins, editorial assistant Sarah Mann, and some most helpful and constructive criticism from two anonymous readers. The final version of my manuscript has been much improved by their intervention and assistance. John Benicewicz and Ryan Jensen at Art Resources facilitated the procurement of illustrations. Finally, throughout the long process of writing and revision, I have enjoyed the support of my wife, Ilona, to whom I always will remain in debt.

> If I have failed to satisfy my readers, let them not abuse me, but rather consider that I had the temerity to tackle such a subject. If my talent has proven insufficient to complete what I attempted, credit should still be due me for having made the attempt. There is nothing that can be both initiated and made perfect simultaneously. Perhaps someone will come along to make right the errors I have committed.
>
> *Paraphrased from book 3 of Leon Battista Alberti's* On Painting, *completed and dated 17 July 1436.*

Contents

Illustrations

Introduction

"The pleasant word 'Renaissance' recalls to lovers of beauty only the advent of a new art and the free play of the imagination. For scholars, it is the renewal of classical studies, while for jurists, daylight begins to dawn over the confused chaos of our ancient customs."[1] To these descriptive phrases, Jules Michelet then added, "Is this all?" The question posed by the French historian in the 1860s continues to be asked today. The responses come back with increasing complexity.

In formulating my own interpretation of the Renaissance, I have tried to avoid a deliberate and restrictive methodology. Some three and a half decades ago, when I was in graduate school at the University of North Carolina at Chapel Hill, its art history program eschewed rigid positions; although, as I look back, I suppose most of us did follow what now might be called formalist, object-oriented, and iconographical approaches. But no particular position was enunciated or mandated. It has been in this same spirit that we have approached the teaching of art history at my present institution. Although, in keeping with the current emphasis upon theory, we do make our students aware of theoretical positions, we have embraced no specific one collectively and have deliberately built a faculty representative of a wide variety of viewpoints and approaches. While we now explain and compare the various current methodological approaches, we still believe that our students (and colleagues) should be free to mix and match ideas as their current opinions direct them or as the particular problems they confront dictate. This essentially pragmatic attitude is in sharp contrast to the doctrinaire positions taken by those who shape their view of the history of art around a specific and controlling premise. The danger in that approach lies in the temptation to project ourselves into the past and to impose our attitudes and theoretical assumptions upon previous cultural situations where they do not apply. The writings, for example, of Frederick Antal (a perennial whipping boy) make, in my view, inappropriate art history despite the fact that his provocative Marxist cultural interpretations do create great social commentary (for his time but not for that of Giotto, however).

Frankly, I have found little use for the terminologies or agendas that, during the past couple of decades, have inundated the humanities.[2] All these isms—deconstructionism, Marxism, feminism, Freudianism, Derridaism, poststructuralism, the various permutations of the so-called new historicism, postmodernist criticism, and their ilk—hold little practical meaning for me, despite the fact that I have been told that traces of several of these approaches may be found in my own research and writings. If so, so be it. In any case, I prefer to be empirical. Although, as the subtitle of this book indicates, I do have a strong interest in the context of things, I remain an art historian, and, no matter where I wander, I must end up back at the object. It is that "objective" approach, after all is said and done, that distinguishes my discipline and defines its unique character.[3] Art history is both less and more than anthropology and history.

I have taken up the task of presenting this treatment of the Renaissance with some trepidation, mindful of the cautionary words of Renaissance historian Denys Hay concerning the sheer impossibility of absorbing the vast quantity of pertinent literature. "Here," Hay cautioned, "only someone foolhardy would venture on the task of integrating the cultural history with the political and social history."[4] What was true for Hay in 1960 is even more true as, more than forty years later, I try to address a number of the same issues. My choice of inspiration and bibliographic stimulation is, perforce, idiosyncratic; the selected list of references and readings appended to these essays points to prominent (and remembered) sources; yet many more opinions and viewpoints have been absorbed over the years.

At the start of my art historical studies, while still an undergraduate, I was stimulated by reading Wylie Sypher's *The Four Stages of Renaissance Style.* This now-aging volume was decried by many when it first appeared in 1955 then was eventually ignored. Sypher was accused of oversimplification, of trying to see too much too broadly, of being unmindful of the ifs, ands, or buts of true scholarship. That he chaired a broadly composed

Division of Language, Literature, and Arts at Simmons College pointed ominously to his eclectic approach. Certainly, his unquestioning embrace of the Wölfflinian doctrine was sufficient to alarm many an art historian, and other offenses were found by scholars in his own discipline of English literature.[5] Sypher was too much the synthesizer for most. Yet it was this very effort to homogenize the cultural events of the Renaissance that fascinated me.

My own research (primarily archival ferreting and documentary nut-gathering) has been largely the product of what my wife aptly has called "a greengrocer's mentality." At the same time, Sypher's encyclopedic and eclectic approach continues to have much alternative appeal for me. And I still admire his daring. He attempted to find common denominators linking together the entire cultural history of an age and to see the commonality of the movements within it: similar concerns, according to Sypher's argument, linked art and literature into a common early Renaissance or High Renaissance or mannerist mood. I have held on to that thought, encouraged by the fact that Sypher's holistic, zeitgeist approach to an appreciation of Renaissance cultural creativity rested upon the synthetic interpretations of two great nineteenth-century German scholars, Georg Voigt and later Jacob Burkhardt, whose seminal cultural study of the Italian Renaissance was first published in 1860.

Unity, I am convinced, *is* the hallmark of the Renaissance, and our perception of the period should be guided by seeing the age with a sweeping gesture. The Renaissance's urge to unify defines not only the overall style of the period but also each of its contributions and contributors. The nature of the individual trees is better seen, I believe, if the totality of the forest is understood.

I have been particularly drawn to the ideas of John Stephens, among the more recent interpretations of the Renaissance that have appeared. Although I had formulated most of my own ideas prior to my tardy reading of his book *The Italian Renaissance: The Origins of Intellectual and Artistic Change before the Reformation,* I was encouraged by several parallels in our approaches and have been able to refine some of my positions in light of his insights.

Generally, it has been the beginnings of things that fascinated me more than the ends—archaic more than Hellenistic Greece, the early Roman Empire more than the late, colonial more than post–Civil War America. That is why, I suppose, my specialty is the early Renaissance and not the high or late phases of that era. A beginning assumes an ending, so the late

Middle Ages must be ever present in my Renaissance thoughts. In fact, as I have addressed early Renaissance issues over the years—primarily the architecture of central Italy—I have found myself inching ever farther backward in order to gain a better visual focus upon the picture of the birth of the Renaissance.

When most of us think of those long centuries that preceded the Renaissance, what we call (and Renaissance man also called) the Middle Ages, we generally think of the church. We feel that it was in the medieval period that Christianity was in its heyday—when it was the matrix of both spiritual and temporal existence. I quickly admit that any medievalist so inclined could pick that statement to pieces, yet I am convinced that the general impression still would remain: medieval society and the church as tightly woven together as the interlacings of a Romanesque manuscript illumination.

Medieval art is a decidedly and most obviously religious art. It places its overwhelming emphasis upon otherworldliness. Medieval art is antiphysical and highly subjective, filled with swaying and abstracted images, expressionistic draperies, the soaring arches of great cathedrals and heavenly rays of light filtered prismatically through glorious windows of stained glass. It is transcendent; it is radiant. No matter how much distortion there is in this view, this is what one thinks of when one hears the word *medieval.*

By contrast, the art of the Renaissance seems this-worldly. In the visual arts, the Renaissance appears to rejoice in the physical beauty of man and his earthly surroundings. A comparison between the *Expulsion* panel from the Bronze Doors that Bishop Bernward commissioned (ca. 1015) for his church of St. Michael's at Hildesheim, Germany (fig. 1), with a similar scene painted by Masaccio (ca. 1426) in the Brancacci Chapel in Florence (fig. 2) seems instructive (although perhaps unfair, in light of time, place, and medium). Bernward's sculptor clearly found his inspiration in a manuscript-illumination tradition stemming from such Carolingian works as the *Utrecht Psalter* and, ultimately, from the energetic and dehumanized imagery of the zoomorphic artists of the Migration period. For Bishop Bernward, man could provide no adequate measure by which the biblical story could be visually narrated. In fact, had the Ottonian sculptor even been able to conceive it in a more physical fashion, it would have been an inappropriate effort. Original sin, perforce, has stripped Adam and Eve of perfection—of both body and soul—even while clothing them in a new sense of shame. Our two forebears waver into desolate damnation with but the merest corporeal identity. For the Florentine painter four centuries later such an abject retreat from physicality has become impossible. Masaccio's Adam and Eve stride into the Unknown endowed with a despairing mind but with a godlike beauty. Clearly Masaccio has utilized both actual observation and classical exemplars as his guides. Since the cleaning of his *Expulsion* in 1988, these noble ancestors possess an even greater sense of virile power. Light, shadow, anatomy have all been called into dramatic play and are further animated by psychological insight. Masaccio was not alone in his innovative humanity. Jacopo della Quercia's two renditions of the expulsion scene for the public fountain in Siena (ca. 1418) and for the portal of San Petronio in Bologna (ca. 1430) offer just as dramatic a contrast with the medieval conception of Bernward.

In short, while the art of the Middle Ages seems mystical, the art of the Renaissance seems fundamentally realistic. Renaissance art is an art, we feel, of this world and not of the other. Renaissance feet appear to be planted firmly, with an ever-increasing weight, upon the soil of this earth.

Despite this initial reaction, I do not mean to say that the importance of Christianity diminished during the Renaissance. It most assuredly did not. The longer I study the art and culture of the Renaissance, the more aware I become of the underlying religiosity of the age. The nineteenth-century English critic John Ruskin was mistaken in believing that the Renaissance should be equated with a revival of heathenism.[6] In much the same way, and much more recently, the noted architectural historian Nicholas Pevsner left an erroneous impression when he wrote that, in the Renaissance, "the religious meaning of the church [building] was replaced by a human one."[7] I do not believe that at all. It is not that theological concerns were replaced by secular ones but that something new (or, rather, revived) was added; it was not a case of either/or but of *more.*

Actually, the Christian religion was every bit as important for those who happened to live during the period of the Renaissance as it had been for their grandparents. One has only to look at the bulk of Renaissance art: its subject matter is still predominately religious. Renaissance masters continued to deal primarily (and sincerely) with portrayals of Old Testament prophets, images of the Holy Family, the life and passion of Christ, the legion of his saints, and with the miracles of the faith and the like. The new and classically inspired naturalism available to the Renaissance artist only served to heighten the spiritual moment.

Even such apparently pagan themes as Sandro Botticelli's *Primavera* have been shown to have had a deeply spiritual significance.[8] Marsilio Ficino, who chaired the Medicean Platonic Academy, was both priest and Neoplatonist, devoutly committed to reconciling the seemingly irreconcilable polarities of Christian theology and pagan philosophy. Marsilio spoke of "following the footsteps of Socrates and Christ by philosophizing in action as well as in disputation," and, with perfect conviction, he could declare that "religious feeling is as natural to humanism as barking is to dogs."[9] Yet, that he felt compelled to defend what seemed obvious may also be instructive.

No matter. The religious art of the Renaissance is, nevertheless, quite different in form and presentation from the religious art of the Middle Ages. The way in which the Christian message was received and the artistic interpretation of that message did change. Despite the fact that few Christians, if any at all, during the Renaissance ever dreamed of renouncing the traditional concepts of their faith, the Renaissance did put aside quite firmly the life-styles and artistic procedures of the Middle Ages that Christianity had been instrumental in formulating.

How this all came to pass and what, in fact, really did come to pass forms the theme of this particular group of essays. I begin my inquiry into the causes and character of the Renaissance by posing those six fundamental questions familiar to even the novice journalist: Who? What? Where? When? How? and Why? But I shall reorder them to suit the line of my inquiry. Accordingly, in the following chapters, I shall be dealing with these issues in roughly the following sequence: when? where? what? how? why? and intermittently a word about who? (and who not?). Obviously, these issues are not discrete ones, and there is, of necessity, much overlap, especially as I approach the truly difficult issues of what, how, and why. In fact those latter issues are so interrelated that it is practically impossible to disentangle them.

CHAPTER I

When & Where

> We are too apt to treat of history in parcels, and to attempt to draw lessons from detached chapters in the biography of the human race. To observe the connection between the several stages of a progressive movement of the human spirit, and to recognize that the forces at work are still active, is the true philosophy of history.[1]

In general, I would agree with this warning given more than a century ago by John Addington Symonds. Yet, perhaps his words have been taken too much to heart of late. In fact, the whole concept of historical periods has come under attack.[2] Not so very long ago, that there was a Renaissance period with its unique set of distinguishing cultural characteristics would not have been questioned. Now, however, many of the meanings traditionally associated with the word *Renaissance* have been subjected to reappraisal. Age-old questions thought to have been explained and put to rest have been raised once again in an era of doubt: When was the Renaissance and where did it take place? Was there, in fact, a Renaissance at all? The age of the Renaissance has been described variously as either a great historical divide or as part of a rather seamless transition from the medieval to the modern, whatever those terms themselves might mean. The problems inherent in defining the nature of the Renaissance are receiving new attention as part of the general "periodization" controversy within the overall context of what has been called the "new art history."

I cannot be oblivious to this challenge to traditional historical organization. It certainly is quite true that the use of historical periods and other such sweeping classifications has limited our vision and has relegated certain artists and movements that did not seem to fit the period pattern to second-class status or even to virtual obscurity—witness the critical fate of such a splendid American sculptress as Anna Hyatt Huntington from the twentieth century and of Pisanello from the fifteenth. On the other hand, the recent effort to deperiodize might itself be interpreted as a part of the current period of diversity and political correctness: a manifestation of the taste of our time.

While I admit that the traditional practice of dividing history into periods does have its limitations, it also offers a chance to step back, gain perspective, and survey the past with a broader vision. To speak of an "age of discovery" or an "age of revolution" or to label a point in time as "art nouveau" or as the "Baroque" is more than a simple convenience. Each of these period-defining labels speaks to general characteristics by which we can comprehend the primary contributions of a time-bound cultural era. And so it is with the term *Renaissance.* Never mind that the philosophical underpinnings of the Renaissance did not reach into the lives of everyone living in Italy during the fifteenth century; they had enough impact to christen the age. Ultimately, whether or not we believe that there really was a discrete period in the flow of European culture that we can label "the Renaissance" is not as important as the fact that those living at the time believed in their special place in history. It may well be true that we will gain a broader vision if we see history as being seamless, but that is beside the real point.

At the same time that some would deny the overall concept of historical periods, other, even more "extreme" scholars are inclined to actually refute the very existence of the social and cultural changes associated with the term *Renaissance.* In fact, this latter group challenges the validity of any unique cultural contribution associated with the word. Almost two decades have gone by since William Hood attempted to sum up the current state of research in the field of Italian Renaissance art in one of those ambitious and valuable topical essays then being published in the *Art Bulletin.*[3] "Over the past twenty years," Hood wrote, "the Renaissance has gradually lost its ancient historiographical identity as a watershed between the Middle Ages and the modern world." He went on to observe that "fewer writers than before seem eager to trace the antique sources of quattrocento and cinquecento art; more would embed it in the political and religious texture of contemporary life. Few write about the classical style at all."

Hood's comments in the *Art Bulletin* would seem to have addressed the lament raised more than forty years earlier by historian Lynn Thorndike in the *Journal of the History of Ideas.*[4] According to Thorndike, "the concept of the Italian Renaissance or Prenaissance has . . . done a great deal of harm in the past and may continue to do harm in the future. . . . It has kept men in general from recognizing that our life and thought is based more nearly and actually on the Middle Ages than on distant Greece and Rome, from whom our heritage is more indirect, bookish, sentimental, less institutional, social, religious, even less economic and experimental."

Today, sixty years later, Thorndike might be pleased, for it has become a matter of fashionable scholarship not only to blur the distinctions between the Middle Ages and the Renaissance but also to play down the significance of a classical revival and even to disavow the fundamental presence of a distinctive Renaissance thought process.[5] Recently, the argument has intensified, bolstered by a number of assaults upon traditional wisdom from art history's sister disciplines of literature, history, and philosophy. Even within the ranks of art historians this has been the case. The late Howard Saalman, always a venturesome scholar, has found the oft-proclaimed father of the Renaissance style, Filippo Brunelleschi, to be decidedly wanting in classical revivalist tendencies. In Saalman's view Brunelleschi was less the harbinger of revolutionary revival than he was a conservative chauvinist with "a personal style . . . deeply rooted in the traditional forms of Florence from the Baptistery to the Cathedral."[6] Yet, this is the same Brunelleschi, who, according to his contemporary, the Florentine banker Giovanni Rucellai, had rediscovered "the ancient building art of the Romans."[7]

Some contend that antiquity, rather than being rediscovered in the Renaissance, was simply flotsam in the ever-flowing medieval current. This claim can be countered by pointing to writers of the period who recognized their age as being a time of rediscovery. Admittedly, although the concept of rebirth was a decided part of the quattrocento consciousness, the actual word *Renaissance,* or *rinascimento,* did not appear until the middle of the sixteenth century. We should not be surprised that the word, or its Italian root of *rinascita,* was first coined to define the artistic events of his age by the artist/art historian Giorgio Vasari back in 1550.[8] It was not until 1855, however, that Jules Michelet picked up Vasari's idea of the artistic rebirth and used the term *La Renaissance* as the title for a volume in his *Histoire de France.* Michelet thus extended the scope and context of the artistic experience recognized by Vasari to the broader cultural event that characterized a general European phenomenon typified by what he defined as "the discovery of the world and the discovery of man."[9] While it is true that Vasari used the word in a limited sense to explain the revolution that had taken place in the art of his country, it is also true that the homogeneity of his age allows us to apply it to the entire reborn culture of the era. It would seem that this particular argument concerning whether or not there was a reawakening of antiquity is all a matter of personal interpretation and one's scholarly agenda.

Additional objections to the entire notion of the Renaissance as a meaningful concept also have been raised by those who believe that the use of such terminology is grounded in elitist assumptions and is therefore misleading at the very least. Those adhering to this position point out that the ideas we commonly associate with the term *Renaissance* affected only a relatively small part of the general population, the ones we might expect to have humanist inclinations: upper-class persons with wealth, position, and connections. Renaissance ideas, according to this interpretation of history, consequently would have made little impact upon the lives of a preponderance of a population consisting of simple craftsmen and laborers. Furthermore, since the Renaissance was an urban phenomenon, it also would have barely touched the workaday patterns of simple country folk. Accordingly, since the term would appear to be so restrictive in its application, it might be better, or so runs this line of thinking, to discard it in favor of a less descriptive phrase such as "early modern."

At first blush, this particular argument against retaining the term *Renaissance* would seem to have much in its favor. I would contend, however, that there is solid evidence to support a belief that the Renaissance spirit was in the air, increasingly pervasive in urban areas, and that it did reach out beyond city confines to impact the countryside.[10] However, even if that had not been the case, the truth of the matter is that the course of cultural development is shaped most often in the urban centers. And it was, of course, in the cities that the spirit of the new age was both broadly felt and made quite visible. In actuality, far from ignoring the development of the new Renaissance style, a large proportion of the population in cities such as Florence, for example, went out of their way to interact with it. Contemporary accounts, for instance, assure us that the majority of Florentines held decided opinions about the construction of the cupola of their cathedral and that almost every inhabitant of the same city turned out to inspect a large *bozzetto* (cartoon) by Leonardo da Vinci for a painting of the Madonna and Child with St. Anne.[11] In fact, one can easily conclude that, as far as the centers of cultural development were concerned, there was greater knowledge of the arts and critical interest in them across a broader segment of society than is now the case. Admittedly, this was in part due to the fact that there were far fewer distractions and forms of entertainment to occupy the attention of the populace than are available today.

Whatever the case, Renaissance thoughts did percolate into the minds of much of Italy's urban population. Certainly the new mood was felt widely, so much so that even as early as the 1430s, a Florentine businessman named Matteo Palmieri could proclaim: "Now, indeed, may every thoughtful spirit thank God that it has been permitted to him to be born in this new age, so full of hope and promise, which already rejoices in a greater array of nobly-gifted souls than the world has seen in the thousand years that have preceded it."[12] In the end, the very fact that the existence of a distinct Renaissance period continues to be debated presents a forceful argument in its favor: why challenge something that did not exist? Accordingly, the existence of a distinct period that can be labeled "the Renaissance" will not be further questioned, at least not in the context I have constructed here. That issue having been put aside, in a somewhat arbitrary fashion, the first two questions of when and where the Renaissance took place can now be addressed.

To begin with, my approach to these questions is conditioned by my bias as an art historian and an American one at that. Certainly my suggestion (really more an assertion) as to an appropriate framework for the Renaissance might be challenged forcefully by historians of philosophy, economics, music, religion, politics, science, intellectual history, and literature. Thus, in responding to the question of just when the Renaissance took place, a historian of Italian literature might say that the period began with the fourteenth-century poet and scholar Petrarch, while at the other end of the geographical and chronological spectrum, a historian of English literature would place the foundations of the period considerably later and would include William Shakespeare among its principals and even, perhaps, John Milton (a full-fledged baroque writer, in my view). Historians of both music and economics might well be tempted to delay the start of the period to the mid- or even late fifteenth century. It all depends on what subject you are concentrating upon, where your vantage point is, and where you direct your gaze (deperiodization proponents can take comfort in this).

As far as the history of art is concerned, however, the term *Renaissance* is now most commonly applied to the two-hundred-year span of time between 1400 and 1600, give or take a few years at either end. Traditionally, the Renaissance is seen as a distinct epoch following the long Middle Ages, preceding the age of the baroque, and acting as a brilliant prelude to what we, presumptuously, call "modern times."

The Renaissance proper was preceded by an introductory period of change during the fourteenth century, often known by the Italian term *trecento.* Among the leading artists in this precursory but still medieval century were Giovanni Pisano, Arnolfo di Cambio, Giotto di Bondone, Pietro Cavallini, Duccio di Buoninsegna, Simone Martini, Pietro and Ambrogio Lorenzetti, and Orcagna. Although they might well be called, from a medievalist's perspective, artists of the Gothic style, they did pave the way for many of the changes that would give renewed direction and cohesion to the next century. Among the literary figures and the philosophers who actually seem much more predictive of the new age were Petrarch, Coluccio Salutati, and Boccaccio (but not Dante, who still is locked into the mind-set of the earlier age). Boccaccio, in fact, in the course of his biography of Dante, credited Giotto with changing painting from an art of symbol into one of thought, from an expression of acceptance into an intellectual provocation.[13] Boccaccio also saw an equation between painting and poetry, thus reviving the ubiquitous *ut pictura poesis* of Horace and later generations of aesthetes.[14]

The Renaissance really got under way shortly after the turn of the century, and its initial phase lasted until about 1495. Among the artists of this early Renaissance, or quattrocento, were its founding fathers, Filippo Brunelleschi, Donatello, and Masaccio, followed by Paolo Uccello, Luca della Robbia, Leon Battista Alberti, Piero della Francesca, Andrea del Castagno, and Andrea Mantegna, and then, toward the end of the era, Andrea Verrocchio, Antonio Pollaiuolo, Sandro Botticelli, Giovanni Bellini, Luca Signorelli, and Pietro Perugino. In literature and philosophy, the period was dominated by the Stoical, Ciceronian, and Neoplatonic branches of humanism represented by such personalities as Niccolò Niccoli, Poggio Bracciolini, Leonardo Bruni, Tommaso Parentucelli (Pope Nicholas V), Flavio Biondo, Aeneas Silvius Piccolomini (Pope Pius II), Cristofero Landino, Marsilio Ficino, Pico della Mirandola, and Poliziano.

The sixteenth century, or cinquecento, embraced two (at least) phases of stylistic development. The artistic High Renaissance, which really began around 1495 (one wonders if the coming of a new century motivates a change in direction or whether centuries simply are points of historical convenience?), represented the mature, or what we might term the classic, stage of the style and lasted but briefly, expiring around 1530. Among its greatest artists were Leonardo da Vinci, Giorgione, Donato Bramante, Raphael Santi, Michelangelo Buonarotti, Tiziano Vecellio (Titian), and Antonio Allegri Correggio. In literature and philosophy, the century began to take on a particularly modern flavor in the writings of Torquato Tasso, Lodovico Ariosto, Niccolò Machiavelli, Giordano Bruno, and Francesco Guicciardini.

The period from just before 1530 to nearly the end of the century was the time of the late Renaissance with its important early subdivision of mannerism. Many of the High Renaissance masters continued to develop their styles during this phase. Mannerism, in particular, represented the dissolution of the principles of the High Renaissance and was typified by experimentation with new sets of often conflicting or ill-defined standards of artistic values. Among the great artists who entered the scene during this final stage of the Renaissance were Jacopo Robusti (Tintoretto), Giulio Romano, Rosso Fiorentino, Francesco Mazzola (Parmigianino), Jacopo Carucci (Pontormo), Giovanni da Bologna, and Andrea Palladio (who, in many ways, would seem to stand apart).

These dates and phases within the artistic and cultural Renaissance are quite loose, of course, and there is considerable and necessary overlap at the borderlines, particularly between the high and the late (and/or mannerist) divisions of the Renaissance. Leonardo may be seen as belonging to both the early and High Renaissance; Titian, during his long life, slides nicely from High into late Renaissance; and Michelangelo, who defies the easy label, displays characteristics of the High and late Renaissance, the mannerist, and even what might be termed the proto-baroque. In any case, all of these terms are matters contrived for our convenience; that fact should be remembered even if we do continue to use them and to find them useful.

All of the names I used here are Italian ones.[15] The overall dates that I have suggested for the Renaissance—1400 to 1600—also apply most easily to the unfolding of artistic events on the peninsula of Italy, and it is about Italian events that comments concerning the Renaissance can be made the most comfortably.[16] I say this fully conscious that, just as many reject the use of periods, there are those who would argue against the nationalistic and ethnic boundaries imposed by tradition. After noting Giorgio Vasari's mid-sixteenth-century effort to make all artistic roads lead to Michelangelo, the historian Michael Levey warned that "what is less pardonable is the continued tendency into our own times to see the Renaissance as primarily an Italian phenomenon."[17]

Attention should be paid to Professor Levey's advice, yet, when all is said and done, I believe the geographical prejudice to be justifiable, for when most of us think about the Renaissance, our thoughts come out with a decidedly Italian accent. The reasons why this is so are many and complex, but few who believe in the Renaissance would deny its Italian origins. "The reason why Italy took the lead," John Addington Symonds wrote, "was that Italy possessed a language, and commercial prosperity, at a time when other nations were still semi-barbarous."[18] Simplistic and overstated as this statement might be, Symonds is essentially correct (not about the barbarism of the others but about Italian leadership). Italy was the birthplace of the Renaissance. It was on the Italian peninsula that the break with the medieval past was the most emphatic, and it is only natural that when we measure the artistic accomplishments of the Renaissance we use an Italian yard (or really a *braccia*) stick.

Thus, in response to the question of where the Renaissance occurred, I would answer that it was, at least for its first century, a peculiarly Italian adventure, taking place first in central Italy, and more precisely in the city of Florence, and then spreading and shifting its foci southward to Rome and Naples and northward to Milan, Mantua, Ferrara, and Venice. The true spirit of the Renaissance did not make its way over the Alps and into the northern regions of Flanders, Germany, and France (the mid-fifteenth-century painter and illuminator Jean Fouquet is the exception who proves the rule) until the very end of the fifteenth century when it finally was given derivative expression in the work of Dürer, Holbein, Altdorfer, Lambert Lombard, Frans Floris, and Jan van Scorel. During the fifteenth century, what is often termed, for chronological (and a college course designator) convenience, "Northern Renaissance Art"—the splendid paintings of Jan van Eyck, Rogier van der Weyden, Hans Memling, and Hugo van der Goes and the glorious sculptures of Tilmann Riemenschneider and Michael Pacher—might be better considered as late manifestations of the medieval Gothic style. This is so despite the fact that these masters share with their Italian contemporaries like interests in space, light, and true-to-life depiction. The essential ingredient—the recognized standard of antiquity—that translated and proclaimed the true meaning of the word *Renaissance* was lacking, however, and, thus, the Renaissance was, at least in its formative stage, and as I will treat it, *una cosa italiana.* In point of fact, it was actually *una cosa fiorentina.*

Key to the whole Renaissance experience, of course, was the conscious rediscovery of Italy's ancient heritage and Roman glory and the intentional attempt to incorporate that past into the present. The assumption that the Renaissance represented a rejection of the medieval in favor of a revival of the classical has been challenged of late. The objection has been occasioned by the very correct recognition that the quattrocento did not renounce the medieval manner in art and culture and return to some purist, Vitruvian form of classicism. Yet, one must remember that the Renaissance humanist patron and the enlightened artist he supported may well have been antiquarian in spirit but were not classically trained archaeologists. What they sponsored and produced was a stylistic blend that looked different from the art of the immediate past and suggested revival. What was rejected in particular was the intrusion of transalpine Gothic tastes into the Italian continuum. The Renaissance began, in part, as a chauvinistic (in the proper sense of the word) endeavor. Thus, the Cathedral of Milan could be disparaged as a work of Germanic barbarism according to the new, and largely Florentine, standards of appreciation at the same time that the almost equally Gothic Duomo of Florence was being acclaimed for its novel interpretation of what was considered a stylistic evolution of the ancient, and correct, manner of building.

That contrasting stylistic metaphors actually could coexist quite happily is amply demonstrated architecturally by many a building project of Michelozzo or even at the reconstituted city of Pienza, where the cathedral blends an exuberant Germanic interior (sanctioned here by its humanist papal patron) behind a sober external veneer of classicizing paraphrases (figs. 3, 4). The simple fact is that the classical orders (and all that they implied proportionally and aesthetically), once reintroduced into the Italian canon, were simply added to the medieval vernacular and only replaced it over time.[19] The rebirth of classicism came more through subversion than by revolution. Even such a scholarly critic as Leon Battista Alberti could delight in the aesthetics of the Florentine Duomo without conceding a compromise in his classical inclinations.[20] Such selective thinking may seem to be rather a muddle in our own more-knowing era, but it was quite in keeping with the periodizing (and nationalistic) notions of fifteenth-century Florence.

Why was it Florence that gave birth to the Renaissance, and why not Rome? At first glance, Rome seems the likeliest place for the restoration of classical ideals initially to appear. It had the glorious memories and the great ruins to inspire a reawakening of the classical tradition. But it was not Rome that was to give first birth to the revival of that European culture. Why not? Actually, it could have happened in Rome—it even may have started back in the thirteenth century with the initiative of the painter and mosaicist Pietro Cavallini—but Cavallini had no followers, at least not local ones; his true successors were the Florentines Cimabue and Giotto di Bondone. What cut short the first Roman renascence? Political and consequent economic fate intervened. The Avignon captivity, which relocated the papacy in southern France for three-quarters of a century, and the subsequent disappearance of the patronage framework necessary for artistic flourishing were the deciding factors in removing the cultural stimulus from Rome. The arts, like most everything else, follow the money, and when it is gone seek another berth. Then, too, the Roman economy was feudal and not entrepreneurial—it was based upon pastoralism and not mercantilism.[21] The leading families of the Roman nobility were *bovattieri*—not the wool or silk merchants or even the bankers of Florence—and cowboys do not, as a rule, make natural patrons of the arts. Tuscany and, most especially, Florence offered an inviting refuge.

Only forty miles separate Florence and Siena, and stylistically the art of the two cities during the trecento is also close. Certainly Giotto and Duccio are different, but both masters were great innovators, following separate but parallel paths. In the next century, however, the distance between the two Tuscan cities widens into a light-years separation. Why this gap? What makes Florence progress and formerly thriving Siena lag in respect to Renaissance innovation? One could suggest some political developments as a cultural catalyst. What transpired in the intellectual and artistic life of republican Florence consequent to the city's seemingly miraculous delivery, first from the threat of the Visconti of Milan at the beginning of the fifteenth century and then from Ladislaus of Naples a few years later, echoes the experience of the Athenians following their repulse of the Persians. In both cases "miraculous victory" was celebrated in an ebullient burst of creative glory. Aristocratic Siena, on the other hand, had allied herself with the "foreign" and autocratic enemy. Thus, there are political and economic reasons to explain the differences, but the real answer lies in the respective attitudes of Siena and Florence toward humanism and the rediscovery of the classical tradition. Differences in the history of physical environments also may help explain their contrasting receptivity toward the antique.

Evolving from the gridiron layout of its Roman foundation, the city plan of Florence may have stimulated the logical thought processes that led its citizens toward "Renaissance" conceptions, while the meandering street pattern of Siena, following as it does the contours of its irregular hilltop location, suggests a more confusing and less structured organization, one more in tune with the mystical thought of the Middle Ages. Florence's Roman foundation may also be contrasted with the Etruscan traditions of

Siena, and it must be remembered that Etruscan culture was motivated by a subjective religiosity, more in keeping with later medieval thinking.

In his delightful and valuable volume *Homeless Paintings of the Renaissance,* Bernard Berenson noted the profound difference in artistic attitude between Florence and Siena as the quattrocento commenced: "The ages of ecstasy were at this time beginning to make way for ages of inquiry. It was an inquiry that dispelled the mirage of the Middle Ages, and nowhere more than in the field of art. . . . But the spirit of inquiry never found a home at Siena."[22] Berenson went on to explain that "ecstasy does not invent and perfect new instruments of expression. It uses what it finds at hand." The tale of the superstitious rejection of antiquity by the Sienese citizenry, who discovered and then destroyed a statue of Aphrodite, although it took place in the mid–fourteenth century, seems to set the mood for the next (chap. 3, this vol.).

Florence, indeed, has been awarded the Renaissance laurel, but has the prize been awarded fairly? Are there other contenders? Skeptics might wonder if the concentration of scholarship devoted to Florentine art and culture has been overweighted, perhaps, due to the accident of location, pleasant situation, and the presence of active "support group" colonies of foreign residents in the last century. Certainly, there has been a broadening of focus during the last several decades. I remember with particular clarity that great presence of Renaissance scholarship, Ulrich Middeldorf, telling me, in an aside, that had he the opportunity to do it all over again, rather than concentrating upon Florence, he might have chosen Milan as his primary locale.[23]

In his 1987 review of the state of research on the art of the Italian Renaissance, William Hood noted that, of late, "even American undergraduates now see, often on their own, that Vasari's Florence-centered view of the Renaissance was not only badly skewed and even wrong but that it imposed on Venetian art a canon that was in many ways not only foreign but even inimical to it."[24] True enough, no doubt, but only up to a certain point. While Hood was quite correct in applauding the recent attention accorded to places other than Florence, I believe that a distinction must be drawn between the stylistic and the chronological. Venice was, for instance, a worthy competitor of Florence in terms of fifteenth-century economy, politics, and culture, but Florence was preeminent in terms of what comprises the Renaissance artistic style. One cannot help but wonder if the search for novel dissertation topics or innovative (and fundably attractive) research projects has led the art historical interests of many away from the overworked city of Florence. If so, this has been, in many ways an enlightening—even healthy—consequence, but it might also be misleading. Florence *was* the birthplace of the Renaissance, and not just on the say-so of Giorgio Vasari and other patriotic propagandists of the city. It was truly in Florence that the Renaissance seed was first sown, and it was there that it first flourished. This was because it was in Florence that the link to the antique past was first actually appreciated and, most important, where it first was utilized. Despite all the many arguments against "the traditional view of Italian Renaissance art as the accommodation of antiquarian taste," it was precisely just that.[25] Proof is found in the writings of the period itself and in how those living at the time regarded themselves and the character of their age. Citations and quotations on the pages that follow should provide an ample demonstration of the "classical" (self-) consciousness of the Renaissance. A passage from Leon Battista Alberti's treatise *On Painting,* which appeared in 1435, should suffice for the moment as an indicator of this antiquizing revival and Florence's preeminent role in the process:

> But after I was brought back here to this city of ours [Florence] . . . I realized that in many, . . . there was talent for every noble thing not to be ranked below any who was ancient and famous in these arts [architecture, sculpture, painting].[26]

George Holmes has pointed out that there were a number of humanist centers in other Italian cities in the early years of the Renaissance, and their scholars were just as significant as those based in Florence.[27] The difference and the historic distinction achieved by Florence is due to what its humanists did with their scholarship. "Although," writes Holmes, "the Florentines were inordinately proud of their scholarship and their distinguishing characteristic, in retrospect, it is not their command of classical learning but the thoughts of contemporary significance which devotion to the classics inspired in them."[28] It was what the classical revival led the Florentines to achieve that gave their city its recognized position of leadership. It was a matter both of recognition and application. The rediscovery of antique texts and cultural principles was but a means to a new and improved end. The Florentines truly grasped the meaning of meliorism—the key characteristic of humanist thought.

That the citizens of Florence believed in their specialness is exceedingly important to their achieving a special cultural distinction. That eminent humanist civic propagandist, Coluccio Salutati, in writing his polemic in favor of Florence (ca. 1400), proclaimed:

> What town, not only in Italy, but in the whole world, has safer walls, more superb palaces, more ornate churches, more handsome buildings . . . has more inexhaustible wealth, more cultivated fields . . . what city, lacking harbor, imports, and exports so much . . . where is there greater trade, a richer variety of goods?[29]

To which, Leonardo Bruni, writing to Salutati in the autumn of 1405 from the papal court in distant and gray Viterbo, could append, "There is no place in the world to compare with the splendor of Florence or the urbanity of the Florentines."[30]

A simulated Latin inscription placed by the painter Ghirlandaio on his fresco *The Angel Appearing to Zacharias* in the Tornabuoni Chapel in the church of Santa Maria Novella graphically demonstrates this sense of Florentine self-worth: "The year 1490 when the most beautiful city renowned for abundance, victories, arts, and noble buildings profoundly enjoyed salubrity and peace."[31] Special note should be taken of its mention of both "arts" and "noble buildings." That they are included among the four testimonials of the city's pride is telling and, of course, a key factor in our discussion.

All this ebullient Florentine civic pride could be proclaimed despite a drastic drop in population (from some 90,000 to 60,000 during the fourteenth century) and the ravages of flood, famine, plague, and banking collapse. In many ways, however, misfortune prepared the city for the Renaissance. Plague-accelerated population reduction freed up property for palace building and invited in new blood from the countryside; economic reversals discouraged venture capitalism and encouraged "nonproductive" investment in the arts and building, those very items included at the end of the early Renaissance in the frescoed inscription in the Tornabuoni Chapel.

Having dealt, in this rather abrupt fashion, with the two easier questions of when and where, and having stated, for the sake of argument, that the Renaissance is best defined as having taken place in Italy between 1400 and 1600, I will now wrestle, in the principal essay chapters of this volume, with the remaining and more thorny problems. Symonds posed the overall issue well:

> How was it then, that at a certain period, about fourteen centuries after Christ, to speak roughly, the intellect of the Western races awoke as it were from slumber and began once more to be active?

> That is a question which we can but imperfectly answer. The mystery of organic life defeats analysis; whether the subject of our inquiry be a germ cell, or a phenomenon so complex as the commencement of a new religion, or the origination of a new disease, or a new phase in civilization, it is alike impossible to do more than to state the conditions under which the fresh growth begins, and to point out what are its manifestations. In doing so, moreover, we must be careful not to be carried away by words of our own making. Renaissance, Reformation, and Revolution are not separate things, capable of being isolated; they are moments in the history of the human race which we find it convenient to name; while history itself is one and continuous, so that our utmost endeavors to regard some portion of it independently of the rest will be defeated.[32]

As warned, these issues cannot be easily separated and, accordingly, must be assailed along a unified front.

CHAPTER 2

Virtual Reality

Native Americans (and Scandinavian organizations, as well) are, of course, quite correct—both politically and historically—that Christopher Columbus did not *discover* America. Nevertheless, this fact remains: Columbus's four voyages, between 1492 and 1504, did open up the American continents, for better or for worse, to massive European intervention. His journeys across the Atlantic actually were part of a sequence of unifying events that form the general theme of this book. What Columbus ventured to do—and what artists and architects such as Brunelleschi, Donatello, Piero della Francesca, and Leonardo da Vinci built, sculpted, and painted—were all parts of the inquisitive and connective environment that encompassed what we call the Renaissance.

The phrase "American discovery" may not have been considered politically correct during the Columbus quincentennial, but, for Europeans in the 1490s, the voyages of Columbus were indeed part of an exciting age of discovery. Great events, such as Christopher Columbus's several expeditions to the Americas, do not simply happen, of course; they are part of the spirit of an age—part of a distinct period style and, in this case, part of the Renaissance style. In actuality, however, this exploratory character had its origins in a cultural reawakening that had begun several centuries before the *Niña, Pinta,* and *Santa Maria* ever set their sails westward into history.

The Renaissance, in the furthering of which Columbus had a significant role, represented an enormous shift in a historical course that had been set with the collapse of the old order of classical antiquity a millennium earlier. That fundamental upheaval had brought with it not only the end of the Roman Empire but also a breakup in contextual thinking and cultural associations. This profound change in European thought patterns was, in part, the product of the spirituality and otherworldly focus of the new religion of Christianity. The cosmopolitan existence of Roman civilization also was shattered by the onslaughts of the barbarian tribes that overran and repopulated much of the Mediterranean-based culture of ancient Europe during the migrations of the fifth to seventh centuries. As a consequence, urban life largely disappeared, communication networks were severed, commercial activity was interrupted, and interrelationships and interdependencies were destroyed. Physical fact produced a vast change in conceptualization. The ancient philosophical thought structures of Plato, Aristotle, and the Stoics and the harmonic logic of mathematicians such as Euclid, Pythagoras, and Claudius Ptolemy were replaced or radically reinterpreted in the early Middle Ages. Instead of understanding the world as the sum of its interdependent parts, like a universal illustration of the golden mean, medieval man saw only individual and largely disconnected units operating under a system of divine guidance to which he was not privy, nor could aspire to be. The teachings of the church directed the attention of the medieval European away from earthly connections to the spiritual kingdom beyond, and the dissolution of the old organized order caused an emphasis upon the particular rather than upon the general or universal. Europe had fragmented socially, and so, in large measure, had the ways Europeans thought and processed ideas.

By the time of the Crusades, however, in the eleventh and twelfth centuries, changes had begun to occur that would pave the way for the fifteenth-century Renaissance and the Age of Discovery. Contact with the more advanced cultures of the Islamic world, the seizure of Constantinople by freebooting crusaders, the growth of trade, the renewal of communication networks, the reestablishment of town life, the rise of a new urban (and increasingly urbane) middle class, the appearance of universities, and the emergence of a more secularized educational curriculum—these were all parts of the evolving environment of the later Middle Ages. The widening vision of the new Europeans and a growing interest in expanding earthly knowledge and profit through trade can be seen in the celebrated travels of Marco Polo and the even earlier attempt, in 1291, of the Vivaldi brothers of Genoa to reach the East by sailing westward into the Atlantic, thereby anticipating their fellow Genovese's first voyage by almost exactly two centuries.[1]

Also indicative of the climate for change in the late Middle Ages was the approach taken by the Italian lay preacher Francis of Assisi. The far-reaching and long-lasting impact of the Franciscan theological agenda upon the course of history and upon the arts is worth considering in some detail at this point. Let us begin, however, some two centuries after the birth of the gentle saint.

Leonardo da Vinci's great mural *The Last Supper* (fig. 5) certainly must be one of the most recognizable images in the world. A once-popular American television game show of the 1980s, *Family Feud,* even ranked it among the five best-known works of art of all time. *The Last Supper* is familiar to all of us, even if we haven't been to Milan to actually stand before it. It is almost a cliché, visually popularized through a wide variety of reproductions—photographic illustrations, slides, framed prints, or in curious renditions and adaptations appearing on wooden wall plaques, scarves, rugs, chinaware plates, black velvet, even as wax tableaux. In fact, the first time that I ever "saw" Leonardo's *The Last Supper,* the composition was presented as a life-size wax tableau set up in a trailer in the streets of Alexandria, Virginia. Visitors were led in by one door, marched down the length of the table past the awe-inspiring images of Christ and his astounded apostles, and out the rear door. The effect was certainly not that intended by Leonardo, but the visual experience was imprinted in the impressionable mind of this eight-year-old viewer. I've seen a number of such wax versions of Leonardo's mural since then, and they are all as artistically lamentable as any such perversion of a work of great art must be. (Marisol's *Last Supper* tableau of 1982 is something else again, although it may well have been influenced by wax museum versions of the type I have seen.)

In any case all these three-dimensional derivatives do help to make a very real point. *The Last Supper,* as painted by Leonardo on the wall of a Milanese monastic dining hall in 1495, does look tangible, so real in fact that wax museum artisans think they can do it justice in sculptural translation. Leonardo's thirteen figures appear fully three-dimensional and completely integrated into the surrounding setting. With *The Last Supper,* Leonardo da Vinci—deliberately, it almost would seem—summed up the spirit of the early Renaissance in Italy and defined the course of the coming High Renaissance. It is a watershed masterpiece.

The Last Supper represented on the great painted crucifix known as *Pisa Cross 15* (fig. 6) makes quite a contrast to Leonardo's realistic rendition, although it, too, was painted by an Italian and depicts the same biblical scene. In style, however, the contrast could hardly be greater. It simply looks far older, less advanced and more primitive, less realistic and far less a part of our world. This particular work was painted in the late twelfth century, some three hundred years before Leonardo's version. Pictorially and spiritually, there are more than just years separating the two versions. In this medieval depiction all is flat and iconic. It was not the unknown Tuscan artist's intent to re-create a real-life drama but, instead, to present a didactic illustration of a biblical event. For him it was the image, the icon, that counted. We are shown the symbol of Christ's bodily sacrifice, and we understand, but the unnatural appearance both of the participants and of their location prevents us from truly *experiencing* the event. Leonardo's great painting displays the modern spirit of the Renaissance; the earlier piece is part of the preceding Middle Ages. Both representations are intrinsically Christian—deeply so—but the approaches to Christianity chosen by the two artists are vastly different. Between the two lies the birth of the Renaissance.

This medieval depiction of the Last Supper forms but a part of a larger work and, once we understand that, its disassociation from reality becomes even more evident. It was one of several scenes of Christ's life and passion flanking the figure of the Lord on a great crucifix from Pisa intended for suspension high above the main altar of a church. This Pisan cross is similar in style and period to another, simpler, painted cross that played a most significant role in the reshaping of Western culture (fig. 7). Happenstance has made this particular cross one of the most important works of art ever created. It was before this very cross in the hill town of Assisi that the young Francis is said to have been praying in the year 1206 when he experienced the miracle that changed his life, and it was St. Francis who, more than anyone else, was responsible for the vast theological changes that made possible the Renaissance and the birth of the modern era.

The instrumental role played by this crucifix is described in St. Bonaventure's fourteenth-century biography of St. Francis:

> For on a certain day, when Francis had gone forth to meditate in the fields, he was walking nigh the church of Saint Damian . . . and, at the prompting of the Spirit, went within to pray. Prostrating himself before the Image of the Crucified [this same cross], he was filled with no small consolation of spirit as he prayed. And, as with eyes full of tears he gazed upon the Lord's Cross, he heard with his bodily ears a Voice proceeding from that Cross, saying thrice, "Francis, go and repair My House, which . . . is falling utterly into ruin." Francis trembled, being alone in the church, and was astonished at the sound of such a wondrous Voice, and, perceiving in his heart the might of the divine speech, was carried out of himself in ecstasy.[2]

The points that should be noted here, in terms of the evolution of the arts, are these: (1) that Francis had had a personal, one-on-one, religious experience and (2) that the vehicle for that supernatural experience was an artwork. These two factors were fundamental to what was to happen to the arts of Italy over the course of the next couple of centuries.

The power of the image to provoke the kind of intense religious experience of the type enjoyed by St. Francis before the crucifix in Assisi was understandable to many of his most devoted followers. In his book *The Mirror of Perfection,* St. Bonaventure records another such art-stimulated miracle:

> St. Francis was then standing before the altar in prayer, and Brother Pacificus waited for him without the choir praying likewise before a crucifix. And when Pacificus began to pray, he was raised up and snatched into Heaven, whether in the body or out of the body God only knoweth.[3]

The anonymously written *Little Flowers of Saint Francis* records yet another of these occurrences:

> It befell on a day when Friar Peter was at prayer and pondering most devoutly on the Passion of Christ, and how that most blessed Mother of Christ and John the Evangelist, the most beloved disciple, and St. Francis, were all painted at the foot of the cross, crucified in sadness of soul with Christ, a desire came upon him to know which of these three had suffered the greatest sorrow in the Passion of Christ. . . . And being thus absorbed in meditation, the Virgin Mary appeared to him, with St. John the Evangelist and St. Francis, clothed in noblest raiment of beatific glory.[4]

The importance attached to a tangible experience of the impossible is also demonstrated by what has become a Christmas commonplace. It was St. Francis who according to legend was the first to conceive the Christmas Crib as a means of stimulating the actuality of spiritual vision. His devotional re-creation of the nativity scene, perhaps initially staffed with actors and then with sculptures, was not intended as some passive commemoration of a onetime event but as a participatory, reoccurring occasion intended to place the worshiper into the constant historical moment of the Savior's birth. As we are instructed in the Franciscan *Meditations on the Life of Christ:*

> You too . . . kneel and adore your Lord God and then his mother, and reverently greet the saintly old Joseph . . . beg his mother to offer to let you hold [the infant Lord] a while. Pick Him up and hold Him in your arms. Gaze on His face with devotion and reverently kiss Him and delight in Him.[5]

Francis and his followers also placed a new emphasis upon the demonstration of one's spiritual faith through doing good works in this life. Salvation thus was increasingly seen as being an act of personal responsibility, and clear connections were made between our earthly voyage and our heavenly destination. Direct and personal involvement was key in this new, activist theology, and it is no wonder that the monks—not only the followers of Francis but those from the other orders as well—now came into the towns from their rural retreats to establish great and complex monastic institutions within the urban setting. The monastic purpose was no longer to be served through abstract prayer and detached meditation but rather through an active application of the Christian ideal as seen in social service, both spiritual and material.

A tangible, liturgical testimony to this new clerical involvement can be found in the change instituted early in the thirteenth century regarding the position of the priest during the saying of the Mass.[6] Formerly, the priest had stood behind the altar and faced his congregation across the table. Now he took up a position in the forefront as their representative before God and faced the altar. This simple alteration of location not only demonstrated a congregational-clerical unity but it had a very significant impact on the art of painting: it allowed for altarpieces. Previously, such painted panels would have concealed the priest; now, once he had joined his parishioners in front of the altar, a visual focus was demanded. An entirely new category of painting was invented that eventually replaced the suspended crucifix and gave to artists a breadth of surface that eventually would encourage narrative and more naturalistic depiction. Painting was brought down to earth, as was religion.

During the earlier Middle Ages, the wooden panels that served as the support for paintings maintained a definite and almost exclusive association with the religious icon in a context that concentrated upon the representation of a spiritual personality and not a narrative composition. After about 1200, this thematic restriction began to be lifted as the contextual surrounding started to envelop the saintly image. The actual panel retained its religious dedication, however, and this prevented its use in a profane context. The depiction of secular and, later, mythological subjects was deflected onto other sorts of pictorial supports—murals, fabrics, illuminations, jewelry. By the year 1400 and the dawning of the Renaissance, the panel had begun to assume a far greater role in the narrative process. This enlarged role for panel painting, joined by the other contributing factors of spatial exploration, technical advances, and societal and theological changes, led to increased pictorial innovation, shifting attention away from the former focus upon image toward the natural and earthly surroundings that served to define the actuality of the composition, be it Christian or, eventually, mythological.[7] The preparatory work for this transformation had been a necessary corollary to the theological interpretations of Francis of Assisi.

St. Francis and the mendicant order of activist friars that he established in the early years of the thirteenth century became a powerful force for theological change within the Church and a motivating element in the late medieval culture that we know as the Gothic.[8] The concept of individual accountability encouraged by the Franciscan reform resonated with the soon-to-be-devised system of double-entry bookkeeping that would revolutionize the accounting procedures of Italian businessmen—debits and credits now seen as having a clear connection and totaled up in heaven as well as in earthly countinghouses.[9]

As Christian worship became increasingly personalized, new attention was paid to the human nature of Christ, the Virgin Mary, and the company of saints who act as archetypes for us. Christ, for the Franciscans and, increasingly, for all of Christendom, was leaving behind his earlier role as the stern adjudicator at an awesome Judgment Day and becoming the compassionate deity who easily remembered his onetime humanity and was mindful of mankind's frailty. His considerate intervention into our daily lives was thus to be expected. The focus placed upon Christ's humanity altered the course of art: *necessity controls content, and content controls form.*

As the medieval European's view of Christ's nature changed, as Christ was perceived as less otherworldly, less distant, less abstract, so changed the manner in which he was to be pictorially presented. As his relationship to us became more tangible and as his humanity was increasingly stressed, the accurate depiction of his physical nature became increasingly emphasized. As Christ went, so did the entire company of heaven and, since religion ruled medieval concerns, so went all aspects of the arts that served religion.

These changes and the many others taking place at the time all pointed toward a greater sense of inquisitiveness and a desire to apprehend our place within the universal structure of the natural order. St. Francis and the Dominican St. Thomas Aquinas, seemingly so different in their approaches to religious truth, were united in a shared belief in personal accountability, the notion of a heavenly inspired meliorism, and the possibility that man could select the correct course to salvation.

After St. Francis miraculously had received the wounds of Christ in his own flesh and especially as his body lay in state after his death, hundreds came to inspect the evidence of the stigmata. As St. Bonaventure noted, "the people flocked together . . . so that they could perceive with their bodily eyes that which might remove every doubt from their reason and add joy to their feelings."[10] The curious faithful came not just to see the wounds on the body of Francis but to see, through the visible stigmata, the injuries inflicted upon the very sacrificial body of Christ—to become, as it were, latter-day St. Thomases—to have any vestige of doubt erased by this tangible proof of Christ's divinity and St. Francis's all-consuming belief.

Following the interment of St. Francis in the great new basilica in Assisi dedicated to his memory, his followers continued to witness the evidence of Christ's atonement for our sins through the attested stigmata depicted on images of the saint. By contemplating paintings of St. Francis, they believed that they could draw nearer to the symbol of the Savior's redemptive sacrifice. As a matter of fact, there was a general tendency to almost equate Francis with Christ. Some saw Francis as the inaugurator of the anticipated Age of the Holy Spirit, promised earlier in the prophecies of Joachim da Fiore.[11] This "confusion" between Christ and St. Francis increased throughout the thirteenth and fourteenth centuries. Bartolommeo da Pisa's *Life of Saint Francis,* written in 1390, really asserted the spiritual fusion of Christ and Francis.[12] In his book, the persons of the saintly man and the God-Made-Man seemed practically to merge. Certainly if this were possible, this sort of spiritual transformation and commingling, one might ask if it were not also possible for any truly devout Christian with sufficient fervor to achieve a similar state of wondrous grace.

The shock of the mid-fourteenth-century plague years drove many into a mysticism in which it was felt that a direct union with Christ almost could be achieved.[13] Such feelings are reflected in the late-fourteenth-century writings of St. Bridget of Sweden and St. Catherine of Siena and in such widely read books as *The Passion of Our Lord Jesus Christ, The Childhood of Jesus,* and *The Meditations on the Life of Christ.*[14] The thrust of all of these works, and a host of others, was to bring us closer and closer to the actual person of Christ through an intensely intimate association with him. His life and passion were treated not only as a heavenly intervention but also as a human tragedy, meant to be experienced again and again. The sympathy and compassion of the worshiper for the physical suffering of the sacrificial Christ were demanded, and this mood made itself felt in the artworks of the age. Such change in spiritual attitude does much to explain why artists strove to make the figures they painted as real as possible and the depicted surroundings as natural as they could.[15]

Paintings, consequently, became valued not just as symbols or as illustrations but as the actual instruments through which we might attain a state of spiritual rapture. The more real they looked, the better they worked and the more real the experience. According to her early biographers, St. Catherine of Siena was one of those who enjoyed several visions in which the heavenly figures who appeared to her were "as she had seen them in the churches."[16]

The early-fourteenth-century mural of the Crucifixion (fig. 8) painted by the great medieval precursor of the Renaissance, Giotto di Bondone, in the Arena Chapel in Padua is a good milestone by which to judge the changing use and appearance of Italian art. In his representation of Christ's sacrifice, Giotto strove to make the figure of Christ look as real as possible, to understand the anatomy of Christ's human form as accurately as possible in order to make us intensely aware of the agony he had endured. The angels are not mute, ethereal witnesses; rather, they wail their grief loudly and actively and, thereby, direct us to do the same. The iconic tradition expressed in the crucifix in Assisi's Church of St. Damian, the cross that had instigated the mission of St. Francis a hundred years earlier, has been replaced by a sincere attempt to transport our imagination to the very moment and place of the Passion. Thanks to Giotto's ability to render nature in a believable fashion, we have made the journey to Golgotha to stand beneath the very cross of our salvation.

Giotto also has taken us well along the road to the Renaissance. Only one hundred years later, Giotto's contribution to personalizing the artistic image was recognized by Leon Battista Alberti, who, after describing how the ancient Greek painter Timantes expressed the emotions of the various participants in the *Immolation of Iphigenia,* immediately began a discussion of Giotto's *Navicella* at St. Peter's:

> They praise the ship painted in Rome by our Tuscan painter Giotto. Eleven disciples, all moved by fear at seeing one of their companions passing over the water. Each one expresses with his face and gesture a clear indication of a disturbed soul in such a way that there are different movements and positions in each one.[17]

Thus, Alberti points to Giotto as the modern psychological equivalent to the legendary Timantes and emphasizes the rebirth of human emotion in art.

Giotto was clearly the precursor, but we really have arrived at the threshold of the new era when we stand within the Florentine church of Santa Maria Novella before Masaccio's magnificent fresco of the Holy Trinity (fig. 9). Here, in the mid-1420s, the youthful father of Renaissance painting presents us with a fully humanized treatment of Christ's body. The very real figures of the Virgin and St. John demand that we witness and testify to the actuality of the Crucifixion and accept the meaning of our Savior's bodily death. Before such a depiction, we might easily feel ourselves in a state of spiritual ecstasy. In the earlier words of St. Bonaventure:

> He who with full face looks to this propitiatory by looking upon Him suspended on the cross in faith, hope, and charity, in devotion, wonder, exultation, appreciation, praise, and jubilation, makes a passover . . . with Him . . . where he may taste the hidden manna and with Christ may rest in the tomb as if outwardly dead, yet knowing, as far as possible in our earthly condition, what was said on the cross to the thief cleaving to Christ: "Today thou shalt be with me in Paradise."[18]

The insistent reality of the salvation promised in Masaccio's *Trinity* is enhanced by the skeletal corpse painted below it and by the fact that the fresco is situated directly opposite a side door to the church through which one passed from its cemetery yard. Clearly, as we move from one space into another, from the outer world of mortality to the inner world of salvation, we are meant to see and experience the very real connection between life, death, and heaven—an instant and connected vision of the Christian mission.

The state of spiritual trance, of religious rapture, described by St. Bonaventure and by many a late medieval or early Renaissance writer was made even more attainable once artists such as Masaccio were able to provide their naturalistically rendered figures with an equally realistic environment. The rationality of the architectural space in which Masaccio placed his great cross of the Trinity tells us that what we experience was and is also a perfectly real event. The inspiration for this new emphasis upon the physical world, this time of space and structure, may be found implied in the new Christianity that St. Francis had initiated two centuries before. In figure 10 we are looking at what probably is the earliest portrayal of St. Francis of Assisi, painted but nine years after the saint's death in 1226. Despite the attempt of the painter, Bonaventura Berlinghieri, to present us with the likeness of the saint, it is no real portrait but rather an emblematic icon of the subject's saintliness. The little scenes that complement and narrate the image celebrate his many charitable works and miracles. One of them represents the famous story of his preaching to the birds. Francis was no madman but talked to his fellow creatures as a testimony to his recognition of the commonality shared by all of God's creation. This ability to see the essential connections within a universal environmental system was one of the elements that typified the newness of Francis's outlook.

Berlinghieri, however, was not able to capture the unity of his subject's vision. Saint and setting are still rendered as separate, distinct, and disjointed elements. This essentially medieval depiction gives us the ingredients necessary to decode the story, but we cannot actually experience it. A hundred years later, however, changes toward that end were quite evident in, for instance, the fresco of St. Francis preaching to the birds (fig. 11) painted within the great basilica of Assisi dedicated to him. It is one of a cycle of paintings glorifying the saint's life, a series often attributed to Giotto di Bondone.[19] The same story of Francis preaching to the birds is presented to us but now painted in a way in which we may truly visualize and experience the miracle. St. Francis and his avian audience are more than an iconographic device. They are joined within a physical environment that, while still suggestive, goes a long way toward making the physical connections necessary to a realistic representation and a psychological understanding. A start at visual unity has been made.

More than a hint of the desire to achieve this sort of comprehensive vision can be found in the objectives of that encyclopedic medieval scholar Roger Bacon—not coincidentally, I believe, a monastic of the Franciscan Order. Bacon (ca. 1260) attempted to coalesce all knowledge into his *Opus majus,* in a grand demonstration of God's intention for universal relationships. Bacon saw geometry as a binding element in this divine ordering, as humanist mathematicians and Renaissance artists would come to do. His plea for just this sort of visually logical rendering by artists is both eloquent and prescient.

> Oh, how the ineffable beauty of the divine wisdom would shine and the infinite benefit would overflow, if these matters relating to geometry, which are contained in Scripture, should be placed

> before our eyes in their physical forms! . . . Surely the mere vision perceptible to our senses would be beautiful, but more beautiful since we should see in our presence the form of our truth, but most beautiful since aroused by the visible instruments we should rejoice in contemplating the spiritual and literal meaning of Scripture because of our knowledge that all things are now complete in the church of God, which the bodies themselves sensible to our eyes would exhibit. Therefore I count nothing more fitting for a man diligent in the study of God's wisdom than the exhibition of geometrical forms of this kind before his eyes.[20]

Roger Bacon's prediction of things to come was, however, not to be realized for more than a century, and certainly not in his native England.

Let us use yet another set of visual comparisons to illustrate the profound change in conceptualization—in thought processing—that took place as the Middle Ages evolved into the Renaissance and the Age of Discovery. Figure 12 represents a detail of a fresco painted in 1352 in the meeting hall of a lay confraternity in Florence.[21] The entire painting depicts the Virgin Mary standing protectively above the citizenry of Florence, her outspread mantle sheltering this schematic representation of the city. Anyone familiar with the monuments of medieval Florence would recognize enough of them here to identify the city with certainty. The towered town hall, the cathedral under construction, the venerable baptistery, the church of Santa Maria Novella—they all are there and quite identifiable as individual structures. But there is no indication of the distances separating them nor of their appropriate relationships to each other. They exist in a patchwork, like earlier medieval thinking, as a compilation of independent and disconnected physical units. The parts may make a sum but not a whole. We are given not a real depiction of Florence but a heterogeneous hodgepodge of emblematic buildings by which we may identify the name of the city.

Compare this iconic medieval view with another topographical rendition (fig. 13), executed a century and a quarter later, some fifteen years before Christopher Columbus began his first voyage of discovery.[22] This artist approached his treatment of the city of Florence with a sense of unifying logic that would have been inconceivable to his predecessor. The composition has benefited from the same rethinking of the world that guided Columbus. The artist, who so accurately rendered this view of his city, has selected a specific perspectival vantage point (on Monte Uliveto overlooking the city and the road to Pisa) and maintained that single viewing position throughout the depiction. He has emphasized this fact by seating, in the right foreground of his panorama, a young draftsman, who is busy drawing this very view. We are invited to identify ourselves with this internal observer and to see as and what he sees. Our artist recognizes himself (and, through him, us) as an integral part of his depicted environment, and that recognition has given to his representation its sense of logical and unifying harmony. His medieval predecessor had illogically shifted his vantage point as he looked at and reassembled each individual building in his emblematic reconstruction of Florence. As he looked about Florence, he did so detached from its actuality; he and what he depicted existed as separate and unrelated entities. The difference in viewing attitude as the Renaissance took root has produced a dramatic shift in the acknowledgment of space, distance, and physical relationships.

This late-fifteenth-century view approaches visual accuracy, as we easily can see if we compare it with a modern-day photograph of the city taken from a similarly sited hillside (fig. 14). In the Renaissance urban portrait, not only is Florence identifiable from its individual buildings and its distinctive skyline, but its streets are navigable and can be followed from one landmark to the other. The draftsman protagonist seated on the slope of Monte Uliveto can descend the hillside, walk along the Via Pisano and through the Pisan gateway into the Santo Spirito quarter of the city, and make his way with confidence past a succession of not only recognizable but also topographically connected landmarks into the very heart of the city. What this anonymous Renaissance artist has done is to show us the whole city constructed from the sum of its clearly interrelated parts.

What lies between these two views of Florence, the first emblematic and the second perfectly experiential, is a new awareness of spatial relationships and the discovery of a method of plotting them. The medieval mind saw this world as a list of unconnected elements, the harmonizing of which was a matter for heavenly concern; the new Renaissance consciousness believed that God had imposed an order upon this world that could and should be understood and, consequently, represented.

Sculptural examples also offer opportunities to evaluate changing visual attitudes. Nicola Pisano's *Nativity* panel from the Pisa Baptistery pulpit of 1260, for all its novelty and overt classicism, remains an assemblage of antique quotations loosely strung together and not a true synthesis of classical past with spiritual present (fig. 15). Nicola has taken, as it were, bits and pieces of antiquity and assembled them into a composition without the contextual references and spatial continuum later available to Renaissance artists that would allow them to create a new totality. The same was true for the somewhat earlier (1234–39) sculptures adorning the Volturno River gateway into Capua, surviving most unfortunately in only fragmentary condition (fig. 16).[23] The patronage of the Holy Roman Emperor Frederick II, who wished to emulate the Augustan imperium, dictated their formal association with antique prototypes, but the classical conceptual spirit is curiously absent. An answer to Bacon's plea for an application of geometrical unity is missing in both attempts. Consequently, there remains a disquieting sense of disharmony.

At this point a comparison between Lorenzo Ghiberti's *Jacob and Esau* panel (fig. 17), from his famous *Gates of Paradise* on the Florentine Baptistery, and Nicola Pisano's reliefs in the Pisa Baptistery is instructive. In the former relief, Ghiberti's story of the aged Isaac and his two sons flows episodically through spatial "time zones" within an encompassing architectural environment whose existence is made believable due to the unifying presence of scientific perspective. What Ghiberti achieved in this sculptural narrative was not unique.

Much the same, but in paint, already had been accomplished by the young Masaccio in the same Brancacci Chapel in which Adam and Eve stride so believably into mortality. There, in other frescoed scenes, Masaccio constructed narrative compositions in which the participants are naturalistically situated within a believable environment shaped through an understanding of both linear and atmospheric perspective. Furthermore, they are given formal definition and connection to one another by the single source of light that appears to come from the actual chapel window and then streams illusionistically on into the fresco itself, bonding the world of viewer and the viewed within a single cohesive environment. The consistent casting of shadows is a fundamental tool in this illusion. What is more, the shadows that are cast within the painted scenes would seem to be directed by the actual light that enters into the chapel from the window above the altar. What is real has joined what seems real in the Brancacci Chapel. Masaccio's expansive *Tribute Money* (fig. 18) is the prime example of this, although such scenes as *Peter Healing by His Shadow* also respond to the same unifying urge.[24] In this latter fresco, a new immediacy is achieved through the rendition of what easily could be a Florentine street illuminated by a fictive light that seemingly is a continuation of the actual. This light at once real and miraculous is the motivating instrument of the spiritual healing power, and its realistic presence is essential in activating the miracles.

Only a few decades earlier such consistency could not have been imagined. Cennino d'Andrea Cennini, the Florentine painter whose *Libro dell'arte* (*The Craftsman's Handbook*) of ca. 1400 brought its author a long-lasting celebrity, also was conscious of the physicality of form revealed through the fictive rendition of light and shade.[25] He describes in detail how an artist should build up painted relief through modeling from lights to darks; he even predicts the methods of Leonardo da Vinci in his use of the term *sfumato.* Yet Cennini remains a part of the Middle Ages in that his chiaroscuro technique operates independently of reality and is not conditioned by the unifying effect of a natural light. Each figure for Cennini remained a separate unit—even in a crowd scene. In the end, Cennini still belongs to the same fragmented world depicted in the 1350s view of Florence.

If Masaccio's *Tribute Money* is examined with Cennini in mind, it is evident that a radical transformation has occurred, resulting in a new ability to suggest episodic events. Not only are the figures integrated into their surroundings through a uniform handling of light and shade, but Masaccio's innovative approach to the human form itself displays his understanding of how cloth and flesh respond—he starts with the imagined nude and dresses (builds) the figure outward. Moreover, so perfect is the harmony of the constructed scene, based as it is upon the application of a coherent system of perspective, that it even allows for a temporal sequencing of events. Masaccio is not limited to depicting a single moment in the sacred narrative. He is able to shift his viewer's attention through a sequence of events as if he were on a visual pilgrimage. Each element in the story occupies its own position in space and is in harmonic association with the total environment of the scene. In this respect, Masaccio's *Tribute Money* is informed by the same unifying Euclidian principles that guided his mentor, Brunelleschi, in his design for the Loggia of the Innocents. Furthermore, in the *Tribute Money,* Masaccio explored another aspect of time. Masaccio's newly acquired ability to treat the spatial and physical environment with consistency has afford him the opportunity of creating a chronological continuum. Through Masaccio's mixture of biblical and contemporary costume, the time frame of the event depicted became blurred and was compacted into a single moment in which the individual elements operate both in the biblical past and in the Florentine present.

It was this sort of connective association that Florence's great humanist statesman Leonardo Bruni had in mind when he wrote in his *Laudatio Florentinae Urbis* of 1403–4.

> For just as harpstrings are attuned to each other so that, when they are twanged, a single harmony arises from all the different tones, . . . just so this farsighted city has so adapted all her parts to each other that from there results a harmony of the total structure of the republic. . . . Nothing in this state is ill-proportioned, nothing improper, nothing incongruous, nothing left vague; everything occupies its proper place which is not only clearly defined but also in the right relation to all others.[26]

In this passage, Bruni, of course, was talking particularly of the institutional organization of the Florentine Republic (or his idealized view of it), but his further description of the "inner order, neatness, and workmanlike construction" of the governmental systems was clearly meant to encompass the visual and spatial as well as the sociopolitical homogeneity of his city.[27]

In his *Laudatio,* Bruni expanded his allegory of Florentine greatness by claiming that city "stands in the center, like a guardian and master. . . . Around the suburbs lies a belt of rural mansions and estates [and] towns surround her on the periphery, each in its place . . . and the whole outermost region is enclosed in a still larger orbit and circle. Between the towns there are castles, and towers reaching to sky." Florence, thus, is to earthly (at least to Tuscan) geography as the sun is to the post-Galilean universe. One also finds in Bruni's interpretation of Florentine centrality a clear sense of sequential topographical linkages—a unified picture of social organization and geographical relationships.[28]

The evolving shift in focus from the specific to the general can be seen in the very way in which painters of altarpieces set about organizing their compositions, in their rejection of the neutral golden backgrounds of the Middle Ages in favor of increasingly naturalistically depicted environments into which they might set their narratives, and in their abandonment of the compartmentalized format of the polyptych in favor of the conceptually unified single-panel composition. A comparison between Giotto's *Stefaneschi Altarpiece* (fig. 19) of the early fourteenth century and a mid-fifteenth-century work such as Domenico Veneziano's *St. Lucy Altarpiece* (fig. 20) is illustrative.

In Giotto's case what is shown remains firmly iconic. What that great artist might have preferred is perhaps another matter, but the design decision for such a work lay in the hands of its patron, in this case Cardinal Stefaneschi, and he chose to stick to the traditional segmented altarpiece. The paired saints on either side of the central panel with the enthroned St.

Peter are quite literally "waiting in the wings," gigantic in size, and standing on a surface differing in both pattern and viewing point from that of the middle panel. Each of these paired saints, furthermore, is separated from his partner by a colonnette. The artificiality of the total image is accentuated by the brilliant gold ground behind the frontally posed figures and by the decorative treatment given the architectural elements. The background is radiant but neutral, and any sense of spatial unity will be left to a heavenly determination. The viewer is denied entry; we are to stand without in awe.

In Domenico's *St. Lucy Altarpiece* the effect is altogether different, far more personal and engaging. St. John the Baptist even catches our eye and, pointing toward the enthroned Mother and Child, ushers us into their holy presence. A trace of the old tripartite division lingers in Domenico's composition but only through the subtle suggestion of the architectural loggia in which the Virgin and Christ Child are placed. The Madonna is flanked by the conventional pairing of saints, but they are not separated by any sort of spatial dividers; instead they stand on common ground before the architecturally framed Madonna. This sort of painting is termed a *Sacra Conversazione* (Holy Conversation) for the simple reason that all of the personages represented occupy the same setting and, thus, are able to converse. St. John's motivating gesture, in fact, would seem to invite our input into the holy discussion.

As John Shearman pointed out more than twenty years ago, the earliest hint of this sort of spatial amalgamation and narrative integration is to be found in Masaccio's now-dismembered *Pisa Polyptych,* which, according to the evidence, was never a multipaneled altarpiece at all.[29] Traces of cast shadows here and there in the surviving parts argue for its reconstruction as a cohesive painting. Undivided compositionally as well as physically, it offers the spatial continuity requisite for the Renaissance's first *sacra conversazione* panel.

This painting and the thought process whereby it achieved its compositional unity also reveal a new appreciation of the totality of the physical world. As Leonardo da Vinci would later proclaim:

> And truly this is a science and the legitimate issue of nature, for painting is born of nature—or, to speak more correctly, we shall call it the grandchild of nature, for all visible things were brought forth by nature, and these her children have given birth to painting. Hence we may justly call it the grandchild of nature and related to God.[30]

Several years ago, in a most perceptive and provocative article, Samuel Edgerton described how the geographic knowledge of a Florentine physician named Paolo dal Pozzo Toscanelli not only spurred on the dreams of Christopher Columbus but encouraged the architectural endeavors of the founding father of the artistic Renaissance, Filippo Brunelleschi.[31] Edgerton showed how Toscanelli's reutilization of the cartographical techniques of the second-century Alexandrian scholar Claudius Ptolemy was an active influence upon Columbus's abilities to navigate confidently into uncharted waters with some notion of just how far he would have to go in the wrong direction to get to the right place. Though he was unaware of the interruption of the Americas, Columbus thought that he could do it. Previously, medieval sailors had been largely restricted to coastal voyages, navigating by maps called "portolan charts" that plotted sequences of landfall and harbors but did little to tell sailors of distances or to provide a visualization of actuality. These medieval sailing charts lacked the necessary grid of longitudes and latitudes to define the geographic relationships in any more than the most approximate way.

"What Toscanelli demonstrated," wrote Edgerton, "was that once the surface of the Earth was conceptually organized into a rectilinear grid, it took on a new sense of conformity. It was no longer to be thought of as a heterogeneous assemblage of frightening unknowns."[32] Edgerton went on to point out that "the ideas that underlay the new cartography were also applicable to the art of Renaissance Florence. Judging by painting, sculpture, and architecture, medieval 'visual space' was usually additive. It was governed by no single, controlling viewpoint. Contemporaneous with Toscanelli's new cartographic thinking, however, there arose in Florence a new concept of 'visual space' as continuous and relative to the fixed eye of the observer." This fundamental change in the way in which the world was conceived and perceived was, according to Edgerton, "to have profound effect upon the way painters and architects composed the spaces and masses that gave Renaissance style to their pictures and buildings."[33]

Certainly the revival of Ptolemaic mapmaking concepts goes a long way in explaining the dramatic change we witnessed earlier in the two representations of the city of Florence. The later view benefited from the same Ptolemaic grid–determined logic as did Columbus's voyage. The ancient geographer, Ptolemy, had recommended that a specific point be selected from which to view the global map before it was transferred onto the flat pages of a navigator's chart. In much the same way, our fifteenth-century view painter had selected his fixed vantage point and erected in his mind's eye a receding gridwork similar to the longitudinal and latitudinal compartments of the Ptolemaic map. In his treatise, Ptolemy had noted that "we are able therefore to know the exact position of any particular place; and the position of the various countries, how they are integrated in regard to one another, how situated in regard to the whole inhabited world."[34] The same impetus to mentally and visually merge parts into a totality also lay behind the abandonment of the medieval polyptych in favor of single-panel compositions. The science of optics is the key to the Ptolemaic map, the painted view of Florence, and the new single-panel altarpiece—all are based upon specific spatial coordinates, an imagined grid network that provides the relationships between objects. All answer a new urge for conceptual and visual coherence.

Paolo Toscanelli, who revived and popularized Ptolemaic cartographical concepts (even teaching Columbus), was also an associate of his fellow Florentine Filippo Brunelleschi. Brunelleschi's architectural designs led the way in shaping the new artistic style of the Renaissance. His very first Renaissance building, the portico in front of Florence's public orphanage, the Hospital of the Innocents, demonstrates this very well (fig. 21). Part of its originality lies in the detail and the conscious reemployment of the architectural language of the ancient Romans in the treatment of capitals, columns, and fluted pilasters. Certainly this recognition and revival of antique forms is essential to the rebirth of the arts that we call the Renaissance. But the newness of Brunelleschi's Hospital of the Innocents goes deeper than this surface allusion to the glorious decorum of the ancients. It lies in how Brunelleschi has assembled the various elements of his design into an interrelated totality, thereby reviving the harmonious architectural orderings of the architects of Greece and Rome as well as applying the revived principles of Ptolemaic geography.

Underlying Brunelleschi's scheme I see a thorough knowledge of Euclidean geometry and the use of the ancient harmony of the golden section and the square-root rectangle, in particular (fig. 22).[35] According to this Euclidean interpretation of Brunelleschi's design, the architect selected as the basic module the height of his chosen column with its capital. Three times the height of this module equaled the height of the planned structure and two times the height of the column the proper place for the top of the entablature. Using this same module, Brunelleschi determined the width of the arcade openings. A square thus was formed within each arcade, and upon this geometrical unit Brunelleschi could construct systems for further refinement and integration. Greek geometry, of the same sort that motivated Ptolemy's mapmaking, provided the solution to the harmonious arrangement of the remaining parts of the elevation. By using the diagonal of his basic arcade square, Brunelleschi created a root-two rectangle that fixed the height of the arch. The diagonal of this root-two rectangle determined a root-three rectangle, and a logical progression ensued. Each of the units of progressive measurement established the placement of the various architectural details up the facade. In this fashion, the location of architraves, cornices, entablatures and other moldings, frieze, and windows were all worked out within a common system that provided a harmonious bond for the entire arrangement.

Each bay formed a separate vertical unit, visually emphasized by the pilasters that had been intended for but never installed in the second story. The bays themselves were held together horizontally by the interlocking rhythm of double golden sections. These Euclidean golden sections are based upon the fact that a smaller segment is constructed so as to relate to a greater segment as the greater relates to the whole. This principle can be applied to a unit of linear measure or to an area, thereby providing a scheme of interrelated harmonies and proportional balances. These factors give to Brunelleschi's facade at the Hospital of the Innocents its sense of measured and understandable balance. That harmony would have been visually even more intelligible had the story above the portico been articulated with the pilasters envisaged by Brunelleschi (fig. 23).[36]

Euclid's geometry has the further advantage of being based upon an idealized scheme of human proportions through which we can connect with Brunelleschi's building. The golden mean is itself not just some abstract calculation or pleasing balancing act, but is, in fact, derived from the proportions of the idealized man. The distance from the top of the head to the navel is to the distance from the navel to the soles of the feet as the latter measurement is to total height of a man. In this manner the ancients, who utilized this principle of the golden mean to guide their architectural designs, instilled their own presence into the buildings they constructed. The Florentine Brunelleschi, by reviving this Euclidean scheme, has done the same thing at the Innocenti and has given us a microcosmic insight into the macrocosmic universal. In fact, far from rejecting the divine by once again assigning an anthropomorphic proportional system to architectural design, he actually has accorded God an even more persuasive role in the creative process: if man had been created in the image of God, then he must also acknowledge the presence of the Deity in all those things created in concordance with the human measure.

Brunelleschi had provided his generation—painters, builders, and sculptors—with essential mathematical tools by which discrete elements could be united within an encompassing field of vision. The ability to situate the observer within a fictive space was given further realization when an atmospheric (often termed *aerial*) rendition of distance was united with the illusionary capabilities of linear perspective. This second step in the creation of the visual impression was later succinctly described by Leonardo da Vinci:

> There is another kind of perspective which I call Aerial Perspective, because by the atmosphere we are able to distinguish the variations in distance of different buildings, which appear placed on a single line . . . while you wish to represent them in a picture as more remote one than another and to give the effect of a somewhat greater atmosphere. You know that in an atmosphere of equal density the remotest objects seen through it, as mountains, in consequence of the greater quantity of atmosphere between your eye and them—appear blue and almost the same hue as the atmosphere itself when the sun is in the East. . . . And by this rule the buildings . . . will plainly be distinguished as to which are the most remote and which larger than the others.[37]

The optical understanding that this entailed reveals the ability of the artists who created the new style of the Renaissance to think and see beyond the visual confines that the medieval approach had dictated. While the perspective grid was a formula invented by the Renaissance, precedents for atmospheric recession abounded in ancient Roman paintings. Most of these examples, however, would not have been accessible to the quattrocento experimenters. Nor would they actually have been needed. The shift in thinking that was taking place as the late Middle Ages unfolded into the Renaissance would have been sufficient to open the eyes of Masaccio (and Donatello, whose *schiacciato* sculptural reliefs achieved the same pictorial effects) to a more cohesive and consistent way of seeing.

The snow-covered mountains newly revealed in the background of Masaccio's *St. Peter Distributing the Communal Goods and the Punishment of Ananias* during the recent restoration of the Brancacci Chapel come to mind at this point and deserve some thought. Remarkable as they are, are they just the product of the naturalistic vision of the quattrocento, or do they convey a deeper meaning? Certainly snowfalls are not altogether unusual in Tuscany, but snow-covered peaks are not what one thinks of when remembering the countryside about Florence. Could they have been inspired by another concern, one dictated by an allusion to the importance of Florence itself? In the *Laudatio,* Bruni, emphasizing the breadth of his classical erudition, had used Homeric imagery as a metaphor to justify Florentine territorial domination.

> And as Homer writes of the snow . . . on the mountains and hills . . . in like fashion handsome buildings cover the entire region outside the city [of Florence] and all the mountains, the hills, and the plains, so that they seem more to have fallen from heaven than to have been constructed by the hands of men.[38]

Within the context of Masaccio's demonstration of St. Peter's authority, is there a visual echo of Bruni's civic parable? At a time when the *catasto* (Florence's universal property tax, introduced in 1427) was being put into place, these whitened hillsides may have been intended as a reminder that all had a duty to the city and that the city had the authority to compel obedience in the fulfillment of its divinely ordained destiny.[39] From an accurately portrayed winter view, to an allusion to Homeric snowfields, to an allegory of Florentine expansionism, to a reminder of the shared responsibilities of its citizenry—this progression is suggested in this re-creation of the socially significant passages of St. Peter's Gospel. Certainly the new visual techniques given birth by the Renaissance were making possible new and more complex pictorial contexts.

It actually was a technological trick imported from across the Alps that liberated the Italians from the medieval and Byzantine visual confines of radiant but space-denying golden backgrounds. The oil-glazed grounds of the paintings left behind in Florence by Rogier van der Weyden on his Jubilee Year pilgrimage to Rome in 1450—his *Medici Madonna,* now in Frankfurt, and his *Pietà,* in the Uffizi Gallery—must have captivated their Italian audiences. The same would have been the case for the altarpieces sent home by Florentine banking-house representatives stationed in the Low Countries. The great adoration panel of Hugo van der Goes commissioned for his home church by Giovanni Portinari is such a painting. Although lacking the accomplishments of the Italian refinements in scientific perspective, such examples illustrated what could be accomplished in atmospheric recession through the transparencies of oil glazing. It took a while for the locals to embrace the technical aspects; in fact, it was Leonardo who was one of the first to utilize the procedure to produce his celebrated hazy sfumato backgrounds. The result put to final rest the residue of medieval iconic passivity.

Basing his interpretation upon distinctions in thought processes drawn by Plato in his *Politics,* Robert Zwijnenberg has summed up what we might take to be the fundamental difference between the medieval and the Renaissance representational mind-set: "A true philosopher," writes Zwijnenberg, "has a synoptic view, 'can view things in their connection,' has the point of view of an eagle. Ultimately, the philosopher has access to the Good and the Beautiful, to the transcendent world of ideas. The opposite of a philosopher is the doxophilist, someone 'who views many beautiful things but does not see the beautiful itself.' . . . The doxophilist has a micrologic view, paying meticulous attention to the individual . . . and to the infinite variety of nature without noticing their connections in a rational, ordered totality. The micrologic view," Zwijnenberg continues, "is dynamic, but also is limited and fragmentary. This distinction between a synoptic view and a micrologic view is a distinction not between two ways of seeing the external world, but between two ways of thinking about it."[40] In short, we again are reminded that the medieval vision focused upon the trees while the Renaissance mind could now comprehend the broader forest vista.

CHAPTER 3

Means to the End

At this juncture, I should note that I do not subscribe to Voltaire's caustic description of the Middle Ages as a period of "barbarous rust," nor do I fully agree with John Addington Symonds's overly polemical defense of the Renaissance against the medievalist attacks of John Ruskin.[1] Time and study have blunted the sharp edges of such distinctions and allowed both periods to be viewed with less passion and more evenhandedness. As long ago as 1927, Charles Homer Haskins reminded his readers: "Both continuity and change are characteristic of the Middle Ages, as indeed of all great epochs of history. This conception runs counter to ideas widely prevalent not only among the unlearned but among many who ought to know better. To these the Middle Ages are synonymous with all that is uniform, static, and unprogressive."[2]

Yet one might ask, just what did distinguish the renascence of the twelfth century (really 1050–1250), in which many changes did occur, from what we today call the "real" Renaissance? Again, if one refers to Haskins:

> The [twelfth] century begins with the flourishing age of the cathedral schools and closes with the earliest universities already well established. . . . It starts with only the bare outlines of the seven liberal arts and ends in possession of the Roman and canon law, the new Aristotle, the new Euclid and Ptolemy, and the Greek and Arabic physicians, thus making possible a new philosophy and a new science. It sees a revival of the Latin classics, of Latin prose, and of Latin verse.[3]

Haskins's recitation of twelfth-century accomplishments goes on and on, an extraordinary compendium of achievements, "a mass of new history, poetry, and correspondence; the philosophy, mathematics, and astronomy unknown to the earlier medieval tradition and recovered from the Greeks and Arabs in the course of the twelfth century."[4] Yet, despite all its novelties, this splendid Romanesque renascence remains medieval. Where Haskins is in error was in not accepting the traditional period distinctions: modern-day opponents of periodization did not invent their particular wheel. According to Haskins, "The fourteenth century grows out of the thirteenth as the thirteenth grows out of the twelfth, so that there is no real break between the mediaeval renaissance and the Quattrocento."[5] This early attempt at deperiodization might seem acceptable to some, but it defies the general view of history and (this is critical) that of those living in the quattrocento.

Despite all the rediscoveries credited by Haskins to the twelfth century, its scholars were "prohibited" from integrating and applying their new knowledge. The information they retrieved was simply stored in separate files. The contrary is the case with the quattrocento, and I would agree with Lynn Thorndike that "the Middle Ages loved variety; the Renaissance, uniformity."[6] Thus, it is not that the Middle Ages lacked the capability for innovation but that the medieval mind, focused so intently upon the spiritually eternal, did not see fit to demand conceptual cohesion and universal linkages for the earthly realm.

Yet the atmosphere of Europe was being changed as the Middle Ages unfolded; the theological shift toward demonstrable faith, as championed by St. Francis of Assisi, was one definite indicator of this shift in direction. And so were all the developments noted by Haskins. Another sign of what was to come can be found in the way in which the visual arts and those who produced them were regarded. Increasingly, works of art came to be appreciated not for their iconic value alone but for the creativity expressed in their production. Petrarch, for instance, took particular pride in owning paintings by both Simone Martini (a posthumous portrait of the poet's beloved Laura) and Giotto. Concerning his *Madonna* by Giotto, Petrarch remarked that "the ignorant do not understand the beauty of this panel, but the masters of art are stupefied by its beauty."[7] Even in France, a dawning appreciation of the artist was evident. When Queen Jeanne d'Evreaux prepared her will she identified her precious little book of hours (now in New York's Cloisters Museum) as being "by Master Jean Pucelle," obviously attaching much importance not just to the prayers in the volume but to the painter who illuminated them.[8] In her mind, his artistic presence evidently enhanced the spiritual value of the book, and the fact that the queen had sought out the best painter to embellish her prayer book attested to her own piety and devotion. It should also be noted that Pucelle was no scriptorium illuminator but a professionally active lay artist. Art was his livelihood. These circumstances clearly pointed to changes in medieval attitudes and practices.

As the Middle Ages reached maturity, the medieval cloister and its monastic artisans were replaced by urban workshops and a rising class of professional artists. In similar fashion, theologians and prelates began to be replaced by humanist philosophers and merchant-bankers as the advisers and patrons of the arts. Both the character of the artist and that of his supporters and clientele changed as the Middle Ages evolved into a definable Renaissance. Devotional panels were still very much the staple of artistic production, but those who laid out the programs for these paintings were often laypersons and humanists rather than the clerics who had previously monopolized the task, and these new advisers had different perspectives and intentions. The principles of humanism now joined those of theology in determining the standards, sources, and objectives of artistic production.

The term *humanism,* coming from the Latin word *humanismus,* is really less than two hundred years old and should not be equated with the word *humanista,* used in the Renaissance to denote the study of classical literature, philosophy, and culture.[9] The early-nineteenth-century German scholar who came up with the discipline-based term *humanism* was inspired by the use of *humanista* during the Renaissance, a word that described an academic curriculum of study in the liberal arts distinct from the other curricula of *legista, jurista,* and *canonista. Humanista,* in turn, had its own origins in the program of literary studies followed in antiquity (and revived toward the end of the fourteenth century) known as the *studia humanitatis.* Not only do we today have a general confusion between the use of the words *humanism* and *humanities,* but there persists a tendency to interchange the word *humanitarian* with *humanist.* Suffice it to say that, despite the common mortal root, they are not the same, although one might hope that humanists are humanitarians while recognizing that humanitarians certainly need not be humanists.

Even more confusing is the term *secular humanism,* which might have been decried as loudly by the original humanists of Renaissance Italy as by the antihumanist fundamentalists of today's religious right. In point of fact, what really distinguished the Renaissance humanist from the world of medieval scholasticism—far more than an allegiance to purified Latin or Greek and an appreciation of ancient literature or even the concentration upon the liberal arts—was a newfound belief in the concept of progress.[10] This awareness of man's power of self-determination and his ability to improve himself was the new and key ingredient in Renaissance humanism. It was just this sort of complementary mixture of anthropomorphism and meliorism that had dominated the culture of archaic and classical Greece and that had enabled the ancient Athenians to attain their golden age. A similar and conscious concept of a human-centered evolution was fundamental to the birth of the Florentine Renaissance.

A passage from the eccentric architectural treatise of Antonio Filarete written around 1460 reveals just how clearly the "new" man of the Renaissance saw the break with the traditional medieval manner of thinking:

> I advise everyone to abandon the modern [Gothic] style and not be advised by those masters who use this crude system. May he who invented it be cursed! I believe that none other than barbarians brought it into Italy.[11]

Filarete was thinking architecturally here, but what he advised could be applied more broadly. As Filarete continues, his comments help to explain the new classicizing atmosphere of the Renaissance and point to the author's ability to see the linkages between the various branches of cultural expression.

> I shall give this illustration to show the relation of ancient to modern architecture. It is the same as in literature: that is, as the relation of the speech of Cicero or Virgil to that used thirty or forty years ago. Today writing in imitation of the classical past is the best usage, contrary to the practice in the past. After several centuries, prose today is enhanced by ornamentation [rhetorical devices?]. This has been accomplished only through following the ancient style of Cicero and of other worthy men. The same occurred in architecture. The man who follows the ancient practice in architecture does exactly the same thing as a man of letters who strives to reproduce the classical style of Cicero and Virgil.[12]

Today, one might argue that Filarete's alignment of the acceptance of classical modes of expression into literature and the arts is chronologically in error. In truth, the recognition of ancient rhetoric by Italian writers came decades earlier than the incorporation of ancient aesthetics into the visual arts. The point, however, is that Filarete wished to see the correlation and, in fact, insisted upon it. The very fact that he saw a simultaneous recognition of the "imitation of the classical past" in both literature and the arts is a product of his desire to harmonize the cultural qualities of what he definitely saw as a new stylistic age.

As the last remnant of the old Roman Empire (what we call the Byzantine) began its final struggle, a trickle of scholarly refugees began to arrive in Florence. Florence welcomed them and, through its newly founded (1321) university, popularly known as the *studio,* offered them haven.[13] Perhaps the studio's very lack of a long tradition allowed it to be open to new ideas. In any case, the Florentine faculty embraced the émigrés, and the whole city profited by the presence of, first, Manuel Chrysoloras, and, then, his eventual successor, Janos Argyropoulos, both of whom occupied chairs of distinction at the studio. Such scholars from the East had a special cachet in Florence, seeming, as they did, with their antiquizing appearances and manners, to bridge the gap between past and present—to step across the Middle Ages, as it were, and to offer Florence a connection with its severed origin in Roman antiquity.[14]

Manuel Chrysoloras had come to Italy in 1394 as the emissary of Byzantine emperor Manuel II to seek aid against the Turks. The Florentine chancellor, Coluccio Salutati, invited him to take up a professorship at the University of Florence, where he taught from 1397 to 1400. In those three brief years he trained some of the most decisive humanists of the next generation: Leonardo Bruni, Pietro Vergerio, Palla Strozzi, Niccolò Niccoli, Poggio Bracciolini, and Guarino da Verona. Of this encounter with Byzantine-styled instruction and with its messenger, Guarino could later comment:

> Indeed, after for a long time the study of the greatest arts lay sick and abandoned in the dirt, it was certainly Chrysoloras of Byzantium who brought across the sea that discipline to Italy, under whose guidance for the first time our men, ignorant of the entire training and art of eloquence, once they knew Greek letters, dedicated themselves with passion to its study.[15]

Chrysoloras was the perfect match since he had studied not only ancient Greek but some Latin under the tutelage of a convert from Roman Catholicism. Thus the shock of the new was moderated and eased through his instruction, since he championed the cause of eloquence and refinement, as reflected in the works of Cicero. His pedagogy, furthermore, delivered lessons in more than flowing speech; it also taught the

Ciceronian ideal of a "good man speaking well." The emphasis was placed on moral elevation and total personal development through humanist education. This was quite in keeping with current patriotic Florentine objectives in the face of Milanese political pressures. Against the brute force of Milan, the Florentines opposed nationalistically grounded idealism. It was a case of propaganda against power. Guarino lauded his mentor for

> how much he had of liberality, constancy, faith, integrity, religion, modesty, holiness, greatness of soul, and knowledge of all the arts and of the greatest matters, [and] how much cause for praise [he] sowed for himself on account of the integrity of his life; the sanctity of his character; the brilliance of his learning; his zeal for divine matters and vast experience of human affair; and his prudence.[16]

Education in the Middle Ages had compartmentalized the various aspects of knowledge; Greek-influenced education reforms initiated in Florence by Manuel Chrysoloras and his Cicero-inspired students treated the branches of learning as being mutually complementary and forming parts of a whole. The holistic Byzantine approach to education that Chrysoloras brought to his pupils in the Florentine studio can be thought of as a sphere within a theological (spiritual) core, itself surrounded by rings of secular knowledge and distinct from the Western medieval conception of learning as a series of separate and generally unrelated compartments.[17] One can, therefore, speak of this Byzantine educational (and now Florentine and Renaissance) focus as being based upon the complete *body* (a symbolic anthropomorphic metaphor) of knowledge.

This imported scheme for an interconnected education found its best expression in the attempt to devise terminologies that could be used interchangeably between the disciplines—the new "disciplines without walls." Both Michael Baxandall and Christine Smith have commented on Leonardo Bruni's use of common terms in his *De Interpretatione recta* through which he could parallel the copying of an artist and the translating work of a scholar.[18] If such shared terms could connect artist and scholar, then similar connections in value and in status might also be found.

Smith, furthermore, perceptively noted that the spread of this Byzantine-engendered decompartmentalization of terminologies abetted the growth of conversational interchange among scholars and the spread of informal colloquiums.[19] This, of course, was part of the general process of

Renaissance unification that has emerged as the major theme of this book. Cosimo de' Medici's later Platonic Academy was one of the outcomes. The origin of this development lay in the ancient symposium and the dialectic method of Socrates; it was a form of conversation, albeit rather controlled (and controlling), and a form that continues to survive in our own age of ever-decreasing conversation and intellectuality within the debate societies of the modern university.[20]

Intimately connected with this Byzantine (and, ultimately, antique) construction of the humanist basis for Renaissance thought and action was the conception of the *uomo universale,* an obvious product of the interaction between (and cross-fertilization of) the previously compartmentalized branches of learning. Lorenzo Valla, in his *De Voluptate* (*On Pleasure*) of 1431, praised an individual of this new sort as being the complete embodiment of consistency in speech, gesture, clothes, food, house, and gardens, all of which united in a display of ordered beauty.[21] An analogy could also be drawn with the changing techniques of painting, between the line-for-line stroke of the brush applied by the tempera panel painter and the broad-brush and oil paint–laden sweep of a Titian.

The early years of the quattrocento had been enamored with literary style, with the carefully selected word and well-turned phrase and, most especially, with variety of expression learned from the rediscovered rhetoric of Aristotle and Cicero. Later in the century the emphasis switched away from form to substance, from pluralism to unity, from how things were argued to what was concluded. With this change in emphasis came a renewed interest in metaphysical philosophy and the scholasticism of Aquinas and, ultimately, Neoplatonism. Variety in expression and in art was sacrificed to the perfected objective. Recognition of beauty, thus, no longer lay in the interpretation of the beholder but was a fixed quality inherent within a certain ideal. The abundantly varied architectural phrasings of Michelozzo, mixing motifs copied from antiquity with medieval holdovers, were replaced with the attempted archaeological purity of Alberti.[22] In short, the variety of Aristotle was vanquished by the idealism of Plato. Donatello was Aristotelian; Michelangelo was a Neoplatonist.

Under Chrysoloras's instruction, *varietas* was regarded as a virtue. This had to do with the rhetorical style he made popular. According to Smith, "variety," in this early Renaissance Florentine society, expressed "the values of a culture that believed that art should give pleasure to its audience and that the absence of *varietas* was a fault. It was essentially a rhetorical culture."[23] One can see such monuments of early Renaissance architecture as the Florentine Duomo, Alberti's Santa Maria Novella, and perhaps even Bernardo Rossellino's Pienza as being expressive of this quality. "But," Smith goes on to say, "it was to give way to a very different culture in which beauty would be measured not by the pleasure it gives, the form it has, or the task it fulfills, but by consonance with an idea."[24] Smith sees this development as indicative of the "shift in focus of Florentine Humanism from rhetoric to metaphysical philosophy, especially Platonism."[25]

It was Chrysoloras's successor at the studio, Argyropoulos, who really introduced the Florentine humanists to Platonism (and its Neoplatonic variant) as a philosophical entity divorced from its veneer of medieval Christianity.[26] It was not just in its content that the studio instruction of Argyropoulos was new but in its structure; he taught both Aristotle and Plato, and he taught them in their entirety.[27] Thus his teachings embraced a unity of philosophical thought, presenting both the physical and metaphysical branches of ancient speculation and avoiding the selectivity and segmentation of the medieval approach.[28]

Florentine Neoplatonism was first clearly enunciated in the lectures of Argyropoulos-trained Cristoforo Landino, then driven to the forefront by Marsilio Ficino. By the end of the 1460s, the Neoplatonists, led by Ficino, were busily demonstrating the compatibility of ancient philosophy with the tenets of Christianity, confidently reintegrating it, as it were, into the mainstream of the Western tradition. Cosimo de' Medici, by the way, saw no inconsistency in encouraging the foundation of an academy of philosophy at the same time he sponsored the great Dominican monastery of San Marco [29] He seems to have enjoyed the hospitality of both establishments.

The fusion of Christian theology and ancient philosophy was coming into being by the mid–fifteenth century when humanist scholar Lorenzo da Pisa used his *Dialogues of Humility* to create a disputation between those advocating the teachings of the church fathers and the exponents of the newly redeemed ancient philosophers. Lorenzo's cleric proclaims:

> O would that that pure and sincere wisdom of the ancient Fathers had flourished, a flower yet fresh and giving off the scent of eternal life! O would that through this great reference the mouths barking out shameless things should come to their senses and become greatly ashamed to cry out I know not what fables and lies of the pagans!

To which, his opponent, the actual Leonardo Dati, replies:

> Clearly your method of speaking is of long standing: nor is this method uncultivated or alien to the wise. But these times have changed along with many other things your type of teaching, and they have given us new and not unpleasant laws of wisdom.[30]

This philosophical discussion is carried forward in the same Lorenzo's *De amore* in which it is argued that all things have an "appetite" toward their natural good, peace, beauty, and, ultimately, their unity.[31] Through all of this argumentation can be found an ever-tighter interweaving of Christian theology and Platonic harmony. Spiritual and philosophical love in *De amore* become inextricable. This fusion of thought was well expressed by Marsilio Ficino, who, in writing to a colleague in 1457, spoke of following "in the footsteps of Socrates and Christ by philosophizing in action as well as in disputation."[32]

This sort of union between traditional theology and rediscovered philosophy was also on the mind of Cristoforo Landino, who, in delivering the funeral oration for Donato Acciaiuoli in 1478, praised the deceased for having investigated "not only those things which the Platonists and Aristotelians said about God, but also the things from Christian theology."[33] In his commentary on the *Nicomachean Ethics,* written at the behest of Cosimo de' Medici (ca. 1463–64), Acciaiuoli, in fact, had utilized all the arguments of Aristotle to advance a theological proof of the immortality of the soul and its eventual unity with the Deity.[34]

Landino, himself, in his interests and his knowledge, epitomized the intellectual unity of the age. He lectured to students on both the ancient and the modern poets, emphasizing and explaining both Virgil and Petrarch; he wrote with authority in ancient Latin as well as in modern Italian; and he published both on moral philosophy and on the niceties of grammatical usage.[35]

An illustration of the new sense of Renaissance harmony and unity can be found in Marsilio Ficino's view of the role of the modern philosopher.[36] He did not regard philosophy as an academic pursuit but as a civic virtue and a beneficial necessity for everyone (at least for those of a certain social station). An example of Ficino's attitude can be seen in his friendship with the cloth merchant Tommaso Benci, who actually translated into Italian Ficino's own Latin translation from the Greek of the *Pimander* of Hermes Trismegistus.[37] Benci did this so that other merchants, without a knowledge of Latin, could share in the philosophical wisdom found in the manuscript. Ficino and his friends did not discriminate between the professions of philosopher and businessman (certainly an enlightened view that could be emulated today).

The intellectual relationship between Ficino and Benci was in marked contrast to the medieval norm, with its clear distinctions and division of labor between the clerics, who attended to matters spiritual and scholarly, and the merchants and craftsmen, who concerned themselves with secular affairs.[38] This compartmentalization began breaking down through the growth of confraternities in the years leading up to the Renaissance, as secular members increasingly addressed theological issues. That set the merger in motion. The humanist-trained or -influenced Florentine merchant increasingly read, owned, and even debated spiritual texts—a further indication of the unifying tendencies of the new age and a step toward a greater synthesis of knowledge and its broader dissemination.

In the sphere of intellectual productivity and educational activity, the trecento had been dominated by individuals; the quattrocento began to forge schools of thought and to create academies of learning. Again, the emphasis is upon wholes rather than parts. Despite the new age's seeming glorification of the individual, there was an overriding shift in focus toward broader and more sweeping academic activity. Interestingly, Italian intellectual life, especially that which took place within the universities, had traditionally concentrated less upon theology and more upon the law. This civil inheritance from ancient Rome stimulated a general interest in the broader aspects of secular learning; such studies were in the forefront in medieval Padua and nurtured the eventual Renaissance in Florence.

From the first years of the fifteenth century, even back to the time of Petrarch and Boccaccio, antiquarian bibliophiles and their wealthy patrons were scouring all the monasteries of Europe in an effort to recover the lost literary heritage of Italy.[39] Ofttimes, they utilized as their agents the widely dispersed representatives of the great Florentine commercial houses, and there was money to be made in the search. Despite the fact that he served for a half century in the Vatican curia, Poggio Bracciolini kept up an active sideline business ferreting out and copying lost manuscripts by ancient authors. For a time, in the days of Poggio and his associates, Niccoli and Aurispa, the ancient texts—in their entirety or in scraps—were indiscriminately collected, just as the relics of multitudinous saints had been amassed in former years. Later on, there came attempts at critical cataloging and qualitative appraisal. In a way the earlier methodology of book collecting was still systematically medieval; the next stage in which the ancient materials were incorporated into the corpus of learning was more Renaissance in its unifying objectives.

Humanist scholars often were led from their acquisitive fascination for the texts of the ancients to an interest in the marbles of the classical masters. As one might suppose, there already were hints in the fourteenth century of what was to come in the next.[40] Petrarch's friend and literary executor, Lombardo della Seta of Padua, purchased an ancient statue unearthed beneath one of the Brunelleschi family houses in Florence. Another of Petrarch's associates, Giovanni Dondi dell'Orologio (d. 1384), actually traveled to Rome, where he measured and took detailed notes on the ancient remains and monuments in the city. Dondi thus initiated the archaeological inquiry into the city's antiquities, perhaps inspiring, three decades later, the investigations of Filippo Brunelleschi and Donatello that proved so essential to the initiation of the Renaissance movement. Dondi also had in his possession one of the few extant copies of the architectural treatise of Vitruvius and displayed a passion for ancient Roman coinage as well.[41] Both Lombardo della Seta and Giovanni Dondi were worthy predecessors of the antiquarians of the fifteenth century.

Interest in the physical remains of antiquity soon proved infectious. Poggio once wittily described himself as being "headstrong" because of his love of the ancient portrait heads with which "I want to decorate my 'Academy' in the Val d'Arno," where he had a villa.[42] His associate, supporter, and correspondent Niccolò Niccoli "patronized painters, sculptors, and architects as well as men of letters, and he had a thorough knowledge of their crafts."[43] Vespasiano da Bisticci's late-fifteenth-century biography of Niccolò records that "he had a wide judgment, not only in letters, but also in painting and in sculpture, and he had in his house a number of medals, in bronze, silver, and gold; also many antique figures in copper, and heads in marble."[44] His personal collecting interests were felt by his commune for "through Niccolò Florence acquired many fine works of sculpture."[45] This interest in the art of the ancient world led him, in turn, to expand his interests beyond the purely antiquarian and to appreciate the art of those who, in his own day, had revived the human-based precepts of the visual arts. Accordingly, he "especially favoured Pippo di Ser Brunellesco, Donatello, Luca della Robbia, Lorenzo di Bartoluccio [Ghiberti] and was on intimate terms with them."[46] These were the very masters who were at the forefront of the Renaissance advance in the visual arts. Niccolò's fascination with learning for its own sake led him into encyclopedic investigations that set the stage for the exploratory efforts of the next generation. He "had a great knowledge of all parts of the world, so that if anyone who had been in any particular region, and asked him about it, Niccolò would know it better than the man who had been there, and he gave many instances of this."[47] It was but a step from this armchair scholarship to the sort of scientific inquiry that both Leonardo da Vinci and Christopher Columbus were to represent at the end of the century.

In the period of transition from medieval to Renaissance, even normally committed humanists could occasionally doubt their purposes and vacillate. Poggio wrote to his friend Niccolò Niccoli in 1421:

> The sacred books which I have read and which I am reading every day have cooled off my former interest in the Humanities, to which as you know I have been devoted since childhood. For the sources of these studies are vain and partly false and all worthless. But the source of sacred eloquence is truth and, when that is lost, we can hold nothing to its true course, we can accomplish nothing.[48]

The Middle Ages were hardly over when Poggio did his backsliding, and this spate of pious contrition seems to have been but momentary (and may even have been a contrived affectation). His hunt for the documents fundamental to humanist learning continued, and such expressions of temporary remorse and intellectual doubt did not recur.

Much the same sort of conceptual dichotomy can be found if we compare Donatello's classically nude (really naked) *David* (fig. 24) with his ascetically rendered *St. John the Baptist* in Venice (fig. 25) or with his more famous *Mary Magdalene* in Florence (fig. 26). Conservation procedures have revealed the date 1435 on the base of the *St. John,* thus placing it and (more than likely) the *Mary Magdalene,* with which it shares so many stylistic features, into the same decade as the *David.* Thus, the question of an old-age style for Donatello is thrown into doubt, and we are confronted by two conflicting interpretations of Donatello—the traditional one of the classically minded sculptor who, with advancing years, embraces his religion with ever-intensifying fervor and the other, based upon the unsettling evidence of the new dating, of a complex personality capable of simultaneously pursuing divergent approaches in his art (and, perhaps, his faith). The deperiodizationist can take considerable comfort in this. However, John Pope-Hennessy has noted: "As on all expeditions, detours were made and false trails were explored, but the objective remained unchanged and the course from first to last was guided by the pole star of the antique."[49]

With the arts based more and more upon the lessons of *il modo antico* (to quote from Filarete's description of the Rucellai Palace in Florence) and with the practitioners of the arts aspiring, more and more, to an increasingly elevated social status, well-placed patrons began to savor connoisseurship of the arts just as they relished the manuscripts of the past. The appreciation of "progressive" artistic styles, like the sponsorship of book searches and manuscript copying, became a point of pride and prestige for prince, prelate, and merchant-prince alike.[50] The collector of ancient texts demonstrated his erudition and took pride in the authors he had assembled; in like fashion, the patron of the arts could display his visual acumen and his selectivity in his choice of artists. He clearly began to prefer works that were no longer anonymously pious but were autograph. Who had done the painting, chiseled the sculpture, or designed the building increasingly became as important as the work itself.

It also happened that humanists, upon occasion, could be artists. Such was the case with Leon Battista Alberti, who not only was one of the most accomplished of the new breed of literati but also was a theoretician and practitioner of the arts of painting, sculpture, and (most especially) architecture. Scholars such as these, either of the hands-on or eyes-on variety, were familiar with the community of artists and, due to their social position, often with princes and popes, who sought their advice in matters not only literary but also artistic. These humanist cognoscenti encouraged artistic awareness and sensibility among potential patrons, first for antiquities and then for contemporary arts conditioned by the antique model. That a number of the artists were now distinctly middle class in their backgrounds (Brunelleschi and Leonardo both had lawyer fathers; Michelangelo's was a civil servant), not common artisan-craftsmen, did nothing to discourage the new affinity.

Just as the humanist scholars had begun to reestablish a bond with the ancient literary tradition, so did the artists and their patrons attempt to revive the connection with the classical past. In the formative stages of the revival, however, the artists and architects of the early Renaissance revived the visual articulation not so much of the pagan world as of early Christian antiquity. Thus a true understanding of the ancient heritage did not come all at once; it came in stages in the arts as it did in philosophy and the other branches of the new humanism.

The architectural style developed by Filippo Brunelleschi demonstrates the process of gradual acceptance and assimilation. Despite his quotations from ancient Roman architectural detailing and his application of Euclidean geometry in such projects as the Hospital of the Innocents, it must be admitted that Filippo Brunelleschi constructed no literal copy of Roman architecture but rather translated Roman concepts into the present-day idiom, rendering Latin into vernacular Italian as it were. The interiors of Brunelleschi's churches and chapels—the Old Sacristy, San Lorenzo, the Pazzi Chapel—recall Constantinian era Christian basilicas such as Santa Maria Maggiore, St. Paul's without the Walls, and St. Peter's rather than any classical temple type.[51] For his general inspiration, Brunelleschi also drew upon Florentine buildings of hallowed yet medieval origin—SS. Apostoli, San Miniato ai Monte, the Baptistery—perhaps even mistaking their age for something far older, looking for local early Christian connections to the late antique. In any case, the Florentine Romanesque sources that he chose represented for him an even earlier fusion of the ancient and the Christian. By proceeding back to antiquity via a conscious return to its early Christian origins, it was as if Renaissance Christianity recognized its Roman roots and redeemed its classical context. The early Christian amalgam of antiquity and faith also provided a model for the new synthesis.

This reforming interest in early Christian design was perhaps linked to the revivified, post-schism papacy. In rejecting the imported transalpine contemporary Gothic style, this reactionary revolution also asserted a native Italian heritage that had Roman roots. Brunelleschi's new manner of building could be interpreted as being assertively patriotic—a bold declaration of Florentine independence in the face of Milanese or Neapolitan adversaries. Whatever the motivation, such buildings as the loggia of the Hospital of the Innocents and the church of San Lorenzo did provide a historical avenue to an eventual acceptance of a more purely ancient Roman aesthetic.

For the most part, and especially in the earlier phases of his career, Brunelleschi's Romanisms are more suggestive than actual.[52] Those earlier designs, from the portico of the Hospital of the Innocents to the Pazzi Chapel at Santa Croce, also are conceived in a two-dimensional fashion. The underlying precepts upon which they were designed were based upon the principles of plane geometry. It is in Brunelleschi's last projects, at Santa Maria degli Angeli and Santo Spirito (as originally planned but not so much as actually constructed) that we glimpse his dawning comprehension of the true power of Roman spatial manipulation, as demonstrated in such monuments as the Pantheon or in the ruins of the so-called Minerva Medica. The third dimension is taken into account in these buildings, and the space between the walls is activated. In them, the concepts of solid geometry are asserted. This more literal and antiquarian aspect of the revival finally was established in the next generation of Renaissance buildings designed by Leon Battista Alberti—the Tempio Malatestiano, with its archaeologically interpreted facade and the intended dome at the crossing and, most especially, in the manipulated interior spaces of San Sebastiano and San Andrea (all three, of course, found not in Florence but in Rimini and Mantua). As the humanist philosophers shifted their emphasis from Aristotle to Plato, the builders progressed from the planar to the spatial. Lying behind this evolution was the overt desire to peel back the medieval curtain to reveal and give new life to the glorious heritage of the peninsula's ancient past.

Actually, just when the ancient world ended and the Middle Ages began was not agreed upon, with Flavio Biondo perhaps coming the closest to the present-day historical conception.[53] Yet, in general, the ability to differentiate stylistically and chronologically remained rather unrefined. Thus, the notion of there having been an emphatic cultural break with antiquity had not yet taken root, and the concept of historical periods still awaited formulation. For most who lived at the start of the Renaissance, ancient and medieval were part of a single Italian episode (into which Germanic Gothic had ungraciously intruded). While this might seem to have made a "rebirth" impossible, it actually allowed it to happen. Trepidation over a pagan versus Christian conflict could be avoided and attention directed at a simple restoration of "better" practices formally current among the ancient Romans.

That the Renaissance humanist had a narrow view of history and failed to understand the nature of the previous medieval period is beside the point (or perhaps it *is* the point). Filarete and his contemporaries seem to have had a self-serving and telescoped view of the Middle Ages; for them the "perversions" of the Migration period loomed large. The interlaced zoomorphic bestiaries, gargoyles, and fanciful drolleries of the earlier age rather than the gracefully swaying virgins of the immediate past lingered in their minds. A letter written by the humanist poet and diplomat Aeneas Silvius Piccolomini (the future Pope Pius II) in 1449 makes that point.

> From the tenth or eleventh to about the fourteenth century there was no one who could speak correctly and clearly in Italy. The art of this period illustrated the drop in culture because if you inspected the tombs and paintings which are about two or three hundred years old you would find only the shapes of beasts and monsters and not of men. . . . We derive the image of ourselves from statuary which lends all the more force to Virgil's statement, "I admit they will fashion living faces from marble." Painting in antiquity has received great praise from celebrated authors who thought ancient

> painting as beautiful or more so than statuary. In our age painting and sculpting have revived! Eloquence too has been restored and is especially strong in Italy.[54]

Since the naturalistic and reasoned approach found in ancient art seemed to offer the best way to re-create the concept of an ordered world, it was felt desirable to restore respectability to that art. An examination of antique survivals promised a key to understanding the secret laws of existence. Had the ancients, they wondered, once possessed the rules to the universal system? Had they only missed the celestial goal because they did not know the code of Christianity? This was quite plausible. The notion of divine truths having been concealed within the writings of pagan authors was neatly expressed by Cristoforo Landino in his *Disputationes Camadulensis* of 1472, when he spoke of Virgil as someone who "hid that most profound knowledge, by which he described in a divine way the highest good of man and expressed in a wonderful way the path by which we set out toward it."[55]

The Middle Ages, in contrast, either had seen the concepts of antiquity as things separate and distinct, unrelated to their own Christian concerns, or else had retained those pagan elements deemed worthy of salvation through a sort of baptismal transformation in their semiotics.[56] The Renaissance united pagan knowledge with Christian revelation just as surely as the Ptolemaic grid united the geography of the globe.

Ancient culture in the Renaissance was interpreted as offering a possible means to the desired end; an appreciation and emulation of it was one way of gaining valuable knowledge. This contrasted with medieval custom, which had separated the visual from the theoretical. In reviving and reconstructing antiquity, those creating the Renaissance recognized the truth in Aristotle's statement that "without sense-impressions no one could learn or understand anything, and in scientific thinking one must with one's thought contemplate images."[57]

The apparent Renaissance adoration of ancient and, therefore, pagan art, so mistakenly decried by the English critic John Ruskin more than a century ago, was not embraced for its own sake. It, instead, was based upon a belief in the perfectibility of man and an eventual union with the Godhead through knowledge and the imitation of the logically organized nature that he had created.

A new sort of secular symbolism frequently came to be mixed with traditional religious didacticism.[58] While much of this fusion was probably not consciously overt or even recognized as being new, it nevertheless was there. The worshiper who entered the Lama Family Chapel in the Florentine church of Santa Maria Novella in 1475 to kneel in prayer before Sandro Botticelli's magnificent painting *The Adoration of the Magi* (fig. 27) not only followed the wise lead of the three kings but also would have discerned in their faces the clearly recognizable features of the leaders of the Medici family.[59] Florentines believed that the commune enjoyed the special protection of the Madonna, and the Medici, in the role of the Magi and their entourage, were now presented as the wise men in whom the citizenry entrusted its management. Botticelli's painting remains a religious document, but it has added an overlay of secular symbolism and political persuasion. Its propaganda is both theological and civil.

Already, in the late Middle Ages, several factors had come together to produce a more compassionate and humanized view of Christianity. St. Francis and the mendicant orders were particularly significant, and their influence continued to grow as the period we call the Renaissance took form.

Although St. Francis's emphasis upon justification of one's faith through active engagement in good works helped to stimulate the birth of the Renaissance spirit, one aspect of Franciscan morality had to be rejected, or at least reinterpreted—the commitment to poverty. It was difficult to reconcile the economic changes with the Christian warning that "it is easier for a camel to go through the eye of a needle, than for a rich man to enter into the kingdom of God" (Matthew 19:24). It was a warning repeated in the teachings of St. Francis. For those living in the Middle Ages, the ultimate virtue lay in a retreat from worldliness; the ascetic life of the monk was the true ideal, a life in which the disconnected soul might contemplate the eternal and unknowable glory of Salvation. How could one now reconcile the Franciscan stress upon virtuous poverty with the growing emphasis upon mercantile property? Actually, this detached view of earthly existence could be shown as inconsistent, if applied universally, with the Franciscan idea of living an engaged life in imitation of Christ. Taking a Franciscan lead and the advice of the Ciceronian approaches of the first generation of humanist practitioners, the Renaissance rejected this otherworldly ideal and replaced it with a new ethical standard that applauded connection and interaction with the ongoing affairs of this life. Renaissance humanists defended the idea of "virtuous wealth." More is better than less became an accepted virtue in the Renaissance.[60] This concept would seem to be in total contradiction with the Franciscan doctrine of poverty. St. Francis, certainly, would have seen it that way. Renaissance logic, however, was able to turn the precepts of the saint inside out by pointing out that in order to demonstrate one's faith through good works it was necessary to have the means whereby the good works could be produced. Christian charity had to have a sound financial foundation: in order to share with one's fellow man, it was necessary to have something to share.

By the fifteenth century, the concepts of worldly withdrawal and the virtuous rejection of wealth were in retreat, replaced by an attitude that saw the ability to accumulate wealth as proof of God's favor. The traditional medieval notion that the acquisition of wealth ran against the Christian grain was amended and then overturned by the increasingly conspicuous consumption of the Renaissance. Yet this was not just a "greed is good" philosophical defense of avarice (certainly a concept more in tune with the 1980s than the 1380s or 1480s) but rather a way of both enjoying comfort and doing good for one's fellow citizens, encouraged by the reinterpreted example of the holy friar. The theological defense of the accumulation of wealth was also supported by the humanists who cited Aristotle's conception of money as the natural consequence of the translation of labor and profit.[61]

Florentine statesmen and humanists such as Leonardo Bruni, Matteo Palmieri, and Poggio Bracciolini encouraged a judicious display of wealth through such overt expenditures as the construction of patrician palaces and public patronage. To be "magnificent" in decorous display became the new standard of the Renaissance. The arts were one way to demonstrate both wealth and virtue. Of course, such humanist architects as Alberti concurred with this position. In one of the essays included in his *Intercoenales* (*Dinner Pieces*) of ca. 1440, Alberti has his grandfather, Benedetto, say: "Now, wealth in human life is like a game with a ball. For it is not holding the ball in your hands a long time, but throwing it with skill and returning it accurately, that helps you win the victory. Just so, I judge that it is not the possession but the use of wealth that contributes to happiness."[62]

The Florentine merchant-banker Giovanni Rucellai saw just this sort of meritorious virtue in the expenditure of large sums of money upon public and personal projects. His memoirs record the expenses he made to complete the facade of the church of Santa Maria Novella, to embellish his parish church of San Pancrazio, and to unify his several family dwellings behind a single palatial facade.[63] This latter endeavor, which created one of Florence's most noble secular structures, the Palazzo Rucellai, was undertaken, in his own words, "for both the glory of God and for his city."[64] His building investments, which included a new facade for the church of Santa

Maria Novella and refurbishing the local parish of San Pancrazio, also testified to his wealth and social position—a tangible demonstration of his pious virtue. The *al modo antico* style of each of these projects also signified his modernity and humanist pretensions. In the case of the Rucellai Palace (fig. 28), the blending of the eight original housing units on the site into a single residence concealed behind a harmonious exterior seems a metaphor for the Florentine experience. Such a veneering of classical regularity over the hidden clutter of separate medieval constructions offers an architectural simile for what was transpiring in Florentine culture during the same period, as medieval tradition was subsumed beneath the new humanist agenda. The wealthy Florentine banker who built this palace, Giovanni Rucellai, seemed determined to leave a tangible record of his presence, and his considerable expenditures to that end might be seen as expressive of the new aggrandizing and solidifying ambitions of the Renaissance age.

The architect likely responsible for the design and construction of the Rucellai Palace, Bernardo Rossellino, was closely allied with Leon Battista Alberti; and one of his own architectural projects provides us with yet another metaphor for the Renaissance. His Tempio Malatestiano in Rimini began life as the medieval church of San Francesco, then was altered and became, for all practical purposes, a shrine to Rimini's prince, Sigismondo Malatesta. To accomplish this end, Alberti encased the old church within new walls based upon overtly classical motifs, thereby once again offering up a visual demonstration of how medieval Christianity was given an overlay of ancient semiotics resulting in a Renaissance bonding of the two cultural mainstreams of the European tradition. The triumphal arch motif of the unfinished facade presents itself as both a symbol of Christian victory and a reminder of the immortal fame of its patron.

The medieval philosopher and intellectual speculator had been monastic in his attitude; his Renaissance successor was aggressive and involved in the affairs of worldly life, actively applying his rediscoveries of ancient thought to contemporary issues. If the Middle Ages had its renascences, they were stillborn; the Italian Renaissance issued forth, like Athena Parthenos, fully vibrant and culturally militant. Hans Baron and others have pointed to the different treatments of Cicero by medieval and Renaissance writers as illustrating the fundamental changes between the passive Middle Ages and the active quattrocento.[65] Petrarch had condemned Cicero for not having kept to his retirement "and there hadst meditated upon eternal life and not upon this trifling existence here below." In contrast, Leonardo Bruni's biography of Cicero demonstrated that the

Roman's success and fame was not in spite of his civic engagement but was precisely because of it; Bruni saw Cicero's life as a fusion between his literary accomplishments and his active career as a statesman.[66] The basic tenet of medieval Christendom was "don't"; that of the Renaissance was "do." The Middle Ages thought heaven imposed limitations; the Renaissance saw an infinity of possibilities.

By and large, Renaissance man no longer was inclined to think of himself, in Romanesque fashion, as a damned and miserable sinner, buffeted by fate and at the mercy of his own base instincts. Instead, he began to believe in a salvation to which he might aspire through his own efforts as well as through the continuing intercession of the Blessed Virgin and through the grace of God. This interpretation, of course, interlocked with the melioristic goals of humanism.

As he grew increasingly confident in his ability to exercise personal control over his own fate, Renaissance man began to see himself and his role in the divine scheme of things in a different way. He began, for instance, to place a more literal interpretation on the biblical passage that proclaims:

> So God created man in His own image,
> In the image of God created He him. (Genesis 1:27)

The Renaissance philosopher Marsilio Ficino added the logical corollary:

> Let him revere himself as an image of the Divine God. . . . Let him love God with all his heart, so as to transform himself into Him, who through singular love wonderfully transformed himself into Man.[67]

In much the same vein did Michelangelo approach his task of sculpting as he peeled away the stony (and earthly or fleshy) husk to reveal the godly conception within. Consequently, man appears in Renaissance art and thought as the microcosm of the macrocosm.[68] The tremendous consequences of such a pretentious view are obvious. If God reigns as the ultimate Reason and Order of the Universe, then man must represent a similar force in this world. Man, thus, becomes the central theme and predominate preoccupation of the Renaissance, *but* with the explicit (as well as implicit) understanding that through an understanding of man and the world over which he presides, a better knowledge of God and his plan for our salvation might be attained.

Man, thus, has as his duty the discovery of the eternal laws of harmony and reason that govern the universe. By discovering these laws and applying them within the context of a rational life, man might attain a surer footing along the path to salvation. The microcosm of man in the world ought to duplicate the macrocosm revolving about the Deity.

This, of course, was related to the concept of *concinnitas,* or congruity, which was the leitmotif of Alberti's writings. Alberti firmly believed that, in order to achieve harmony, all the parts—even if disparate or in evident conflict—must be brought into an accord. This eventual state of fusion and totality was as necessary in the arts as it was in statecraft. Accordingly, there was no place in nature for even a dispute between, say, pagan antiquity and Christian modernity: thus, the effective unity of the Renaissance spirit.[69]

Sometimes the harmonious objectives of the Renaissance led to the unexpected. Alberti's facade for the Florentine church of Santa Maria Novella, for instance, stands apart from his overtly classicizing designs for San Francesco/Tempio Malatestiano in Rimini and San Sebastiano and San Andrea in Mantua. In fact, it seems much more in keeping with the Romanesque exteriors of San Miniato ai Monte and the Florentine Baptistery. This is not due to any latent "medievalism" upon Alberti's part but rather to his desire to harmonize his design with the lower portion of the facade previously initiated by the Gothic builders who had kept to the striated marbling of the Florentine building tradition. Alberti simply went back to sources that embraced this decorative element but seemed closer to his classical ideal—the Romanesque examples of San Miniato and the Baptistery. Such an approach is in marked contrast to the medieval patterns of building in which designs and techniques were modified during the course of construction in accordance with technical improvements since to do otherwise would be to dedicate something less than the best to God. The change in style from a four- to three-part elevation along the nave of Notre Dame in Paris is but one obvious example of that approach. For Alberti and the new Renaissance aesthetic, the harmony of unity took precedence.

In its pursuit of earthly order, harmony, and congruity, the Renaissance period witnessed a revival of ancient mathematics and geometry.[70] As part of his Neoplatonic philosophical doctrine, the great Florentine thinker of the late fifteenth century, Giovanni Pico della Mirandola, insisted that the universe was structured in accordance with mathematical principles as a reflection of the rational and perceivable order of God. "Through numbers," Pico claimed, "is to be had the way to the investigation and understanding of all that is knowable."[71] His mentor and colleague, Marsilio Ficino, asserted that, along its Neoplatonic progression toward perfection, the soul had to pass through the sequential levels of moral, natural, and, finally, mathematical philosophy.[72]

This is well demonstrated in Leonardo da Vinci's famous *Vitruvian Man* (fig. 29). The description inspiring Leonardo's drawing came from a passage in the treatise of the ancient Roman architectural writer Vitruvius and demonstrates that a well-proportioned human being fits neatly into the two most perfect geometric forms, the circle and the square.[73] Leonardo meant to present more than a beautiful lesson in the dynamism of natural geometry, however. His message was philosophical and theological—almost mystical. It is at the core of the nature of the Renaissance and central to the meaning of the period. Leonardo's drawing demonstrates to us that man is (or has been placed) at the center of a logical and orderly system. A harmonious relationship exists between man and the world about him just as there does between God and the universe he created and governs. Man is not meant to conform to nature so much as nature is to conform to man, for man is the central microcosm, the earthly module.

One could even take Leonardo's demonstration as a visual paradigm for the centrality of Florence as given in the passage from Bruni's *Laudatio* cited in the previous chapter. The glorious role assigned to ourselves found clear expression in Pico della Mirandola's celebrated *Oration on the Dignity of Man:*

> At last it seems to me I have come to understand why man is the most fortunate of creatures and consequently worthy of all admiration and what precisely is that rank which is his lot in the universal chain of Being—a rank to be envied not only by brutes but even by the stars and by minds beyond this world. It is a matter past faith and a wondrous one. Why should it not be? For it is on this very account that man is rightly called and judged a great miracle and a wonderful creature indeed.[74]

This belief in man's worldly centrality even found an echo in distant England in the words spoken in 1602 by William Shakespeare's Hamlet (2.2).

> What a piece of work is a man!
> How noble in reason!
> How infinite in faculty!
> In form, in moving, how express and admirable!

In action how like an angel!
In apprehension how like a god!
The beauty of the world!
The paragon of animals!

But Leonardo da Vinci's drawing is more than a visualization of the ancient text of Vitruvius. In that treatise, Vitruvius describes how the human body defines both the dimensions of a square and the circumference of a circle. One could easily imagine the two figures taking their places within two separate geometrical forms, and that is how the Vitruvian lesson was often depicted. But Leonardo has chosen to do it otherwise by putting his figure (really, I believe, his self-portrait) into motion, an exercise (both literally and figuratively) as it were, combining action with the two perfect geometric designs.[75] And he even goes beyond this by neither placing circle in square nor square in circle but by intersecting them in dynamic fashion. In Leonardo's interpretation of these geometrical icons of universal order, the perfect shapes of square and circle lie not within one another but are situated in more active interpenetration with the base of the circle resting upon the interior base of the square and with its upper curvature arching above it. This results in an energetic relationship between the two forms that binds them together in an inseparable construction. Thus, both the physical counterpart of God's symbolic perfection and the two flawless symbols of his universal order are shown in complementary activity. Leonardo's *Vitruvian Man* reveals himself as the generative force of nature stretching his limbs in centerpiece gesture to demonstrate the fusion of forces by which order is brought out of disorder—once again a positive illustration of the Renaissance's urge to unify.

Actually the meaning of this force-filled diagram has a greater significance than this. In the iconography of the day, the square was generally taken as symbolic of the earth while the circle was representative of the eternity of heaven. Thus, the Vitruvian man of Leonardo's conception, as the earthly replica of the divinity, takes on the role of the medium by which heaven and earth are inseparably conjoined. Man is consequently both of this earth and of heaven, the instigator of the fusion and the unifier of the universe.[76] The active centrality of Leonardo's human progenitor is made clear by the fact that the radial point of the heavenly circle is found in the figure's navel and that of the square in his genitalia, thus affirming the nourishing source of man's connection with the universal infinite and his own procreative role in establishing the boundaries of the earthly realm in the center of which he has been placed by the Deity.

The world, with man as its focal point, thus became of immense importance in solving the riddle of existence. This world was like a builder's wooden model designed to earthly scale in accordance with the actual universal plans of the Divine Architect. If Renaissance thinkers and artists seem to concentrate their attentions upon the measure of man, it is because man was felt to hold the key to the final comprehension of the Infinite. One of the most influential thinkers of the period, Luca Pacioli, said that all the ratios and proportions "by which God reveals the innermost secrets of nature" were to be found in the human body itself.[77] This reinterpretation of man's role in the universal design is not alien to the doctrine of Christianity, but it did introduce several concepts that certainly were foreign to traditional medieval thinking.

Since man had been created as the microcosm of God, it stands to reason that man, like God, possesses the power to create. Like God, he, too, may draw order out of disorder, and, just as God subdued the chaos of the universe, it is possible for man to tame the wildness of this world. Just this sort of an interpretation of the human condition can be found in the words of Pico della Mirandola, who imagined that God took

> man as a creature of indeterminate nature and, assigning him a place in the middle of the world, addressed him thus: "Neither a fixed abode nor a form that is thine alone nor any function have peculiar to thyself have we given thee, Adam, to the end that according to thy longing and according to thy judgment thou mayest have and possess what abode, what form, and what functions thou thyself shalt desire. . . . We have set thee at the world's center that thou mayest from thence more easily observe whatever is in the world. We have made thee neither of heaven nor of earth, neither mortal nor immortal, so that with freedom of choice and with honor, as though the maker and molder of thyself, thou mayest fashion thyself in whatever shape thou shalt prefer. Thou shalt have the power to degenerate into the lower forms of life, which are brutish. Thou shalt have the power, out of thy soul's judgment, to be reborn into the higher forms which are divine. . . ." On man when he came into life the Father conferred the seeds of all kinds and the germs of every way of life. Whatever seeds each man cultivates will grow to maturity and bear in him their own fruit.

> . . . And if, happy in the lot of no created thing, he withdraws into the center of his own unity, his spirit, made one with God . . . shall surpass them all.[78]

A heaven on earth is thus at least conceivable. It is due to imaginings such as this that the exuberant confidence and exhilarating self-assuredness of the Renaissance were born. Innocent perhaps; maybe even naive; but, nevertheless, how marvelously grandiose and glorious in audacity!

A similar reasoning altered the course of artistic expression. Man in general is empowered to create order out of disorder in this world. The artist has this as his specific goal in the images or structures that he creates. The artist who forms something out of nothing actually is a pretty good example of the divinely created microcosm.[79]

Cennino Cennini, operating at the end of the Florentine Middle Ages, saw the art of painting as deserving "to be enthroned next to theory, and to be crowned with poetry."[80] The justification in this elevation of the visual arts, wrote Cennini, "lies in this: that the poet, with his theory, though he have but one, it makes him worthy, is free to compose and bind together, or not, as he pleases, according to his inclination. In the same way, the painter is given freedom to compose a figure, standing, seated, half-man, half-horse, as he pleases, according to his imagination."[81] By the end of the trecento, the painter's craft had been elevated to an art and, at least in the view of one of its practitioners, had achieved a parallel position to those more traditionally valued cognitive pursuits.

Only a single generation later, the writings of the humanist Leon Battista Alberti included not only classically inspired dramas, moral discourses, and other scholarly endeavors but also treatises devoted to painting, sculpture, and architecture. Cennini's little volume was a practical how-to manual of advice and recipes for the would-be painter. Alberti's publications were intellectually grounded essays intended not only for artists but for art lovers and patrons. Alberti's orientation brought the visual arts into the company of all creative activity.[82] His approach toward artistic expression and appreciation was universal in nature, aimed at uniting the former artistic crafts with the intellectual disciplines.

In fact, erudition was seen by Alberti as an essential element in the makeup of a successful artist, as is made clear in the following iconographical discourse.

> I should like to see those three sisters to whom Hesiod gave the names Aglaia, Euphrosyne, and Thalia, who were painted laughing and taking each other by the hand, with their clothes girdled and very clean. This symbolizes liberality, since one of these sisters gives, the other receives, the third returns the benefit; these degrees ought to be in all perfect liberality. How much praise similar inventions give to the artist should be clear.[83]

That Alberti's description of the three Graces is based upon a passage in *De beneficis* (1.3.2–7) by the Roman author Seneca is also interesting and a demonstration of the humanist's own erudition. That it may have been the inspiration for Botticelli's dancing trio in the *Primavera* is a point of additional interest.[84] So, too, is what Alberti immediately does with this iconographic information.

> Therefore, I advise that each painter should make himself familiar with poets, rhetoricians, and others equally well learned in letters. They will give new inventions or at least aid in beautifully composing the *istoria* through which the painter will surely acquire much praise and renown in his painting.[85]

Thus, Alberti's ideal artist was no longer to be a simple craftsman who executed work according to instruction or tradition but rather an innovator who looks to classical sources for his inspiration in similar fashion to the poets with whom he now was to associate. In short, this new Renaissance artist needed the knowledge of the scholar: most especially, Alberti added, "it would please me that the painter . . . should be a good man and versed in literature. . . . I like a painter to be as learned as he can be in all the liberal arts, but primarily I desire him to know geometry."[86] Alberti's efforts to intellectualize the visual arts and to adorn them with the fabric of classical learning were made clear in his further comments.

> I like the saying of Pamphilus, an ancient, most noble painter, with whom the noble youths began to learn of painting. He held that no painter could paint well if he did not know a great deal of geometry. . . . So I maintain that a painter has to undertake geometry. And for their mutual delight he will make himself one with poets and orators, for they have many graces in common with the painter and are plenteous in knowledge of many things.[87]

Three-quarters of a century later, Leonardo da Vinci stated firmly that "painting is poetry which is seen and not heard, and poetry is a painting which is heard but not seen" but noted that "whatever is painted must pass by the eye, which is the nobler sense, and whatever is poetry must pass through a less noble sense, namely, the ear, to the understanding."[88] For Cennini, the artist had come to occupy a position comparable to that held by the poet; Alberti offered him a joint appointment; Leonardo, by implication, accorded him the front bench—*ut pictura poesis.*

CHAPTER 4

Manifest Miracle

During the Middle Ages, theologians such as St. Thomas Aquinas had maintained that the creative power was reserved to God and that man, his flawed creation, could but hope to copy and emulate.[1] The shift in religious emphasis that was initiated by St. Francis and that contributed to the inauguration of the Renaissance acknowledged God's omnipotence but, at the same time, pointed out that not only had mankind been created by God, but Scripture also specifically stated that God had shaped man in God's own image. Thus, man, like his maker, was felt to have been endowed with a unique potential for creativity. This earthly manifestation of mankind's special position was best illustrated and paralleled through artistic creativity. In fact, the production of art actually was seen to mimic the creative energy of God. By first determining and then applying the divinely established laws that governed the universe, art could be perfected in accordance with the celestial attributes of order, harmony, and clarity. Art could become the earthly approximation of God's own infinitely divine and supremely rational and beautiful Creation. Art thereby achieved a twofold imitative power: on the one hand, it reproduced the earthly environment, while, on the other, it replicated the divine act whereby that environment had been created.

As a consequence of this theological reinterpretation, the Renaissance artist was accorded a far more important status in society than that to which his craftsman predecessor in the Middle Ages could ever have aspired. It, therefore, was only natural that this emerging awareness of the artist's mimetic and melioristic task, as the earthly equivalent of the Creator, would dictate a change in the very nature and practice of artistic production. In an earlier age, one in which a clear notion of progress was impossible, the craft guild concept was fully sufficient to assure the maintenance of professional standards. A refined replication of the master's product was the desired end for the artist-in-waiting. Just as monks in their medieval scriptoria strove to duplicate words and images, so too did painters, sculptors, and architects. Changes in production methods and artistic styles did occur in the Middle Ages, but they were incremental and never a priority. Along with the new notion of a mandated anthropomorphic advance came a belief that each succeeding generation of artists *must* not only maintain the quality of that of the previous but that it had an obligation to improve constantly and to advance toward a definable perfection.

Thus the arts emerged from the stigma of an association with the purely mechanical crafts to assume a more elevated position alongside (and often in advance of) the liberal arts and sciences.[2] It was only to be expected that, with time, the artistic disciplines would outgrow the constrained learning framework of the craft guilds and move toward the motivational environment of the art academy. The training program that the young Michelangelo Buonarotti enjoyed was part of this innovation in artistic education. He began as a traditional apprentice to the painter Ghirlandaio and then entered the academy newly established by Lorenzo de' Medici in his private sculpture garden on the Piazza di San Marco in Florence. Here were gathered antique fragments intended to serve as archetypes for the young talents being trained in the sculptor's discipline by the garden's curator Bertoldo di Giovanni, himself a student of the legendary Donatello.

The separation of the practice of the fine arts from that of the crafts also was typified by the inauguration early in the fifteenth century in Florence of the St. Luke confraternity of painters. This society gradually replaced the guild of doctors and pharmacists as the primary painters' organization. But, of course, the entry of painters into that elite professional guild had signaled the rising importance of the visual arts, as practitioners of the arts advanced in status and self-esteem from craftsmen, to artisans, and finally into the ranks of professionals, from blue- to white-collar workers as it were.[3] It took a bit longer for stonemasons, woodworkers, and builders to separate from their own guilds and to establish the distinct professions of sculpture and architecture demanding coequal status with the painters.

In keeping with his changing status, the very character of the artist and his training changed as the new age evolved. The apprentice/master system of training held fast throughout the quattrocento, to be sure, but a new ingredient was added. The inquisitiveness of the age led its artists along a pathway of continuous learning and experimentation. No longer was proof of competency and admission to the guild sufficient for success; the better artists—those who enjoyed the favor of the best patrons and who could look forward to fame within their communities (an equivalent to "national treasure" status of the sort enjoyed by Brunelleschi or Leonardo or Michelangelo)—were not content to just simply be granted the status of a maestro.

The result of all this effort at realignment meant that the artist in the Renaissance began to be seen and, perhaps even more important, began to see himself differently. One of the great personalities of the period declared that "any master painter who sees his work adored will feel himself considered another god."[4] This self-serving sentiment was echoed a half century later by Leonardo da Vinci, who wrote that "the painter's mind transmutes into a resemblance of the divine mind. With free power it reasons concerning the generation of the diverse natures of the various animals, plants, fruits, landscapes, fields."[5] With this change in professional attitude came the recognition that what the artist produced was something greater than a mere commodity but more akin to the eternal forces of beauty created by the Deity. This ennobling conceit, while socially elevating, gave to the arts a new mission and imposed certain creative duties.

And by what means was the Renaissance artist to set out on his creative mission? By following the universal rules of creation, of course. It was understood that divine laws must govern art just as they were now seen to govern all of God's creation. In the Middle Ages, such divine laws seemed beyond human knowing. Those living in the new age believed otherwise. The confidence with which the Renaissance spirit was associated encouraged a conviction that God had intended for these generative laws to be discovered. This newly imposed inquisitive responsibility led Renaissance artists to calculate rules for proportion and perspective. These guides to rational rendition helped to transform the art of the Renaissance into a more ordered, more perfect, and more divine practice.

The artist in this new age was required to be more than a copyist, as discussed earlier; he was to actively search out the rules of nature that governed his creative duties. "For my part," Alberti proclaimed, "I believe that every art and discipline contains by nature certain principles and procedures, and whoever applies himself to recognizing and learning them may perfectly accomplish whatever he sets out to do."[6] The same investigative impulses encouraged scholars, such as the Florentine Paolo Toscanelli, to search out Ptolemaic mapmaking logic and to see in it further guidelines for the establishment of rules of proportional relationships and scientific perspective. These mental structures helped to transform the art of the Renaissance into a more ordered, more perfect, more divine thing just as surely as they encouraged Columbus to unify our understanding of the world. The encompassing requirements of humanist scholarship demanded a global knowledge of place and time.

Quite naturally, Renaissance artists discovered a new respect for the art of ancient Greece and Rome that had been shaped by anthropomorphic and naturalistic goals similar to those they were now revealing and embracing. Antique art, they recognized, also had centered upon man as the earthly manifestation of the divine.

During the Middle Ages, the physical and, of course, pagan heritage of ancient Rome had been preserved only insofar as it could be made to relate to Christian doctrine and objectives. Mythological heroes such as Hercules and Perseus were absorbed into the biblical personalities of Samson and St. George. Antique ruins and sculptures were looked upon with a superstitious mistrust, and a whole world of knowledge was either condemned or radically transformed. The following tale, recounted by the quattrocento sculptor Lorenzo Ghiberti, illustrates the situation only a generation before his own time.

> One ancient statue was found . . . in the city of Siena, for which a great festival was held. The experts considered it a marvelous work, and on the base was written the name of the master, . . . whose name was Lysippus. . . . Everyone admiring praised it; to each of the great painters that were in Siena at that time it appeared to be of the greatest perfection. With much honor they set it on their fountain as a thing of great eminence. . . . In that place it reigned for a short time. All the country [having] met with much adversity in a war with the Florentines, the flower of their citizenry assembled in council. One citizen arose and spoke in this vein of the statue: "Signori, citizens, consider that since we found this statue we have always been overtaken by misfortune. Consider how idolatry is forbidden by our faith. We must believe that God sent us all our adversities because of our errors. And see the result, since we have honored this statue, always have we gone from bad to worse. I am sure that as long as we have it in our territory we shall always come out

> badly. I am one of those who would advise taking it down, destroying it entirely, and smashing it and sending the pieces to be buried in the land of the Florentines." All in accord affirmed the opinion of their citizen, and so they put into action the plan and it was buried in our land.[7]

By the time the next century had gotten under way, the intellectual context had changed. A new belief in a rational and knowable environment, defined and limited through exploration and the utilization of both deductive and inductive reasoning, resulted in a reconstituted theological and philosophical structure in which superstition and magic were not seen as appropriate constituents.[8] An acceptance of magic requires an admission that our world can be neither understood nor controlled. In the new economic and social condition of the later Middle Ages in Italy, secular and religious thinking was forced to reject this premise in favor of a more practical association with existence.

Once shorn of their religious associations and powers, the old gods and goddesses of antiquity could be used conveniently as allegorical devices or even depicted wittily in a wide variety of literary and artistic contexts. They could be melded into the controlling Christian continuum, used as grotesque decorations or pornographic principals, or even stood upon the table in the guise of clever little inkpots. Eventually a countertransformation occurred, and the saints of Christianity took on the physical attributes of pagan deities. Even the Virgin Mary, in the hands of the Mannerist painter Parmigianino, could convey a seductiveness worthy of Venus, and the rumored past of the Mary Magdalene could now be given full visual expression through the brushwork of Titian.

Ghiberti's sad tale of what befell Siena's Lysippian treasure in the trecento is countered by the archaeological respect accorded antiquities in the more enlightened environment of the quattrocento. An extract from a letter written in 1466 by a rather obscure humanist named Antonio Ivano da Sarzana offers a dramatic foil to the earlier antiquarian misadventure. While passing through Volterra, Antonio Ivano was shown some obviously Etruscan tombs and their sepulchral contents.

> One of these was marble, with carved lids depicting various reclining figures and the ancient clothing of the bodies. The tombs [cinerary urns] were very short and narrow, from which we easily concluded that, like urns, they preserved ashes not bodies. There were also several partly broken clay vases preserved in the same cave.

> The many different types of these quite delighted me. On the cover of the marble tomb, however, was carved the figure of a venerable matron wearing a bracelet and arm bands painted in light gold. On the front of another tomb a horseman was painted in a red color in the old style. Two foot soldiers were seen accompanying him. One went before carrying a sling on his shoulder. The other followed carrying a shield.[9]

Although this may well be the earliest surviving written description of an Etruscan relief, from the matter-of-fact way in which the writer offered his descriptions of these Etruscan sculptures, one might conclude that such sights were no novelty to him.[10] His appreciation is quite objective and without any sign of a "magical" association. While, a century earlier, the Sienese had superstitiously smashed their find, Antonio Ivano was able to assure us that the contents of these tombs were being "preserved by the diligence of the abbot of San Giusto." The conservator of these pagan relics was a priest!

Antiquity offered needed exemplars for Renaissance civic leaders. Whereas, in the Middle Ages, the moralizing allegories of Ambrogio Lorenzetti in the Sala della Pace of the Palazzo Pubblico instructed Sienese counselors in righteous action, their successors two centuries later (and after the conservative Sienese no longer could either ignore or resist the impetus of the Renaissance aesthetic) drew their inspiration from the mythical and historical legends and pagan heroes painted by Domenico Beccafumi across the vaults of the nearby Sala del Consistoro.

As early as 1416, the papal secretary, Cencio da Rustici, who had accompanied Poggio Bracciolini to St. Gall where they had resurrected a manuscript of Vitruvius, was fulminating against not only those who had corrupted the writings of the ancients but also those who had despoiled antiquity's physical monuments, including sculptures of pagan deities. Not even the popes escaped this humanist's wrath.[11]

It is, of course, true that the brutalization of antique monuments did not stop with the end of the trecento. A discursive letter written in 1411 by the emigrant Greek scholar Manuel Chrysoloras to his emperor noted that, in visiting the holy shrines of Rome, pilgrims still deliberately despoiled the city's ruins that they associated with ancient persecution: "They trample them underfoot, strike them with their fists, break off pieces, spit on them . . . and throwing them to the ground, smash them."[12]

But, gradually, the superstitious mistrust of ancient sculptures began to disappear, and a statue of Venus similar to that demolished by the Sienese in the mid–thirteenth century was being appreciatively preserved one hundred years later.[13] In many ways Niccolò Niccoli, for instance, was more the antiquarian than the pure humanist for he was active in collecting material memorials of the ancients as well as emulating their rhetorical forms. For this he was roundly chastised by fellow scholar Guarino Guarini of Verona.[14] Yet there is abundant evidence for a renewed interest in the remains of classical Italy and for a desire to record and preserve its sculptural monuments.

The same was not yet the case with architecture; rather, its conservation was erratic. That Rome was still being despoiled throughout the quattrocento is well documented.[15] In one of his letters, Poggio Bracciolini remarked on a "temple which they are tearing down to get lime."[16] This was in 1427. Fortunately, within three decades the situation was beginning to change, although respect for the visible presence of the antique past was certainly not universal during the Renaissance's first century. The dawning interest in architectural preservation is nicely seen in the actions taken by Pope Pius II Piccolomini (the humanist Aeneas Silvius Piccolomini). Admittedly, he did transport marble from the Colosseum to rebuild the steps leading up to St. Peter's and went on to despoil the Portico of Octavia for columns to be used in the construction of the new Benediction Loggia that he ordered built across the front of the old atrium entrance to the same basilica.[17] But, on the positive side, he also issued a Papal Bull on 28 April 1462 prohibiting the destruction of antiquities in Rome and the adjoining district of the Campagna.[18] According to this bull (perhaps the first official document in the annals of the historic preservation movement), the citizenry was enjoined, upon pain of excommunication, from burning ancient marbles for lime or otherwise tampering with the ruins of the region. That the same document accorded the pope the privilege of violating his own injunction is interesting and demonstrates two aspects of the early Renaissance's attitude toward its antique heritage. It prohibited the unrestricted dismantling of Roman ruins by the lower classes but allowed the utilization of the surviving remnants of Roman glory in new campaigns of officially sponsored construction. In this quattrocento version of "adaptive reuse," the Christian context was given a veneer of classical grandeur while the pagan past was "pardoned" through its enlistment into the ranks of the faithful. This curious merging of the remains of pagan antiquity into the fabric of a reconstituted Christian Rome was typical of the age's attitude toward the past and provides yet another metaphor for the unification theme that I have found to be the dominant characteristic of the Renaissance.

Some three decades earlier, Pope Eugenius IV had established a precedent for Pius's formal decree by instructing the civic authorities of Rome to safeguard its ancient monuments, especially the Colosseum, which was then serving as a ready quarry for building stone. Pope Eugenius warned that "to demolish the monuments of the city is to diminish the excellence of the city and the whole world."[19] This conservationist caution was given a more formalized character in the *Roma instaurata* (*Rome Restored*), which the humanist Flavio Biondo addressed to Eugenius. Curiously, ten years after Flavio Biondo's treatise appeared in 1446, Pope Pius, while yet a cardinal, critiqued its title by complaining, "Even if all the forces of Europe were to unite, they could not restore Rome to its early form, for towns also have their end; the fallen ones cannot rise any more than the old can grow young."[20]

Perhaps the future Sienese-born pope was expressing a momentary fatalism inherited from some ancient Etruscan forebear or was simply imitating the cyclical view of history found in the writings of Augustan-age Roman philosophers.[21] In any case, the concept of rebirth was very much on the more confident mind of the new Pope Pius II only a few years later. It formed a conscious part of his plans for the refurbishing of the Vatican and was very much evident when he set about reforming his own rustic birthplace, renamed Pienza in his honor.[22] Pius must have recollected his earlier comments concerning the futility of attempting a Roman restoration when he visited his hometown in February 1459. There he found both the companions of his youth and the community "bowed down with old age" but, instead of accepting the inevitable—that towns like people "also have their end"—he determined upon a truly Renaissance course of action that led to an extensive reconstruction of the town, incorporating much of the classicizing vision he must have held for papal Rome.[23] Pienza exists as a very model of the integrating spirit of Pope Pius's generation, which adapted the vocabulary of ancient art and architecture to new, postmedieval circumstances.

The design of the piazza at the heart of the reborn Pienza is expressive of the connective spirit of the new age. The buildings adjacent to this square reveal it as a meeting place of the regional styles in contemporary architecture: the Florentine grand manner is present in the facades of both the Cathedral and the Piccolomini family palace (fig. 30); the tastes of

Rome can be seen in the Bishop's Palace (fig. 31) and in the towering belvedere loggia of the Ammannati Palace (fig. 32); the local Sienese style is conveyed in the town hall with its bell tower (fig. 33) and, generally, in most of the buildings throughout the town. The great cathedral itself brings together seemingly discordant architectural features, its facade clearly responding to the new classicizing aims of the Renaissance, while its interior transports to Tuscany from across the Alps a version of a Gothic hallchurch (this latter element was so designed at the express command of Pope Pius, who admired similar constructions when he lived in Germanic regions). All of these diverse styles are tied together, prevented from pulling apart in their separate aesthetic directions, by the unifying pattern of the gridded pavement of the square upon which they front. The geometry of the grid establishes the order and the common ground at Pienza. The individual parts of this architectural tableau remain distinct, but they are conjoined within a new framework of Renaissance consistency much as the science of perspective had created its new pictorial harmony or Ptolemaic cartography would establish new geographic relationships by which the world could be explored.

The Renaissance had done what amounted to an about-face in attitude and accepted the art of antiquity for its own sake as something to be appreciated because it was beautiful and also for what it could show current artists about the laws of re-creation and artistic perfection. "Grace and beauty of things," Alberti said, "should be intensely sought for. It seems to me that there is no more certain and fitting way for one who wishes to pursue this than to take them from nature, keeping in mind in what way nature, marvelous artificer of things, has composed the planes in beautiful bodies. In imitating these it is well both to take great care and to think deeply about them."[24] Investigation, for Alberti, was the artist's necessary and God-directed task: "Since nature has here carried the measurements to a mean, there is not a little utility in recognizing them. Serious painters," he said, "will take this task on themselves from nature," adding that "they will put as much study and work into remembering what they take from nature as they do in discovering it."[25] Alberti thereby condemned both the pattern-book formula of the medieval artist and the fantasy drolleries of the earlier age. It was only natural that inquiry would become the fundamental task for the artist as it had been for the humanist scholar. Part of this change in attitude may be seen as early as the late fourteenth century among certain progressive scholars. The statement of Petrarch's friend, the

Florentine statesman and humanist Coluccio Salutati, says much concerning the changing perceptions.

> I think . . . the feelings about the Roman's religious images were no different from what we, in the full rectitude of our faith, feel about the painted or carved memorials of our saints and martyrs. For we perceive these not as saints and as gods but rather as images of God and of the Saints. It may indeed be that the ignorant vulgar think more and otherwise of them than they should. But since one enters into understanding and knowledge of spiritual things through the medium of sensible things, if pagan people made an image of Fortune with a cornucopia and a rudder—as distributing wealth and controlling human affairs—they did not deviate very much from the truth. So too, when our own artists represent Fortune as a queen turning with her hands a revolving wheel very fast, so long as we apprehend that picture as something made by a man's hand, not something itself divine but a similitude of divine providence, direction, and order—and representing indeed not its essential character but rather the winding and turning of mundane affairs—who can reasonably complain.[26]

Salutati still could not accept antiquity quite on its own terms, but he and his generation had made a start. This growing respect for the past was clearly embraced and furthered by the enlightened few of the next generation. The story of Brunelleschi and his friend Donatello wandering among the ruins of ancient Rome demonstrates this well. So too does another story of Brunelleschi's and Donatello's awe for antiquity. According to Vasari, one morning shortly after he had returned to Florence from his first sojourn in Rome (ca. 1407), Filippo Brunelleschi

> was on the piazza of S. Maria del Fiore with Donatello and other artists discussing antique sculptures, and Donatello was relating how, when he returned from Rome, he had made a journey to Orvieto, to see the far-famed marble facade of the Duomo, the work of various masters [principally Lorenzo Maitani, ca. 1320], and considered a notable thing at the time, and how, in passing afterwards through Cortona, he had entered the Pieve, and seen a remarkable ancient marble sarcophagus, with a bas-relief, a rare thing then, for the multitude of things discovered in our day had not then been dug out. Donato went on to say how excellently the master had

> done his work, describing the perfection and beauty with which he had completed it, and so enflamed Filippo with an ardent desire to see it that, just as he was, in his mantle, hood, and sabots, he left them without saying a word of where he was going, and proceeded to Cortona, led by his love and affection for art. He saw the sarcophagus, admired it, and made a drawing of it, with which he returned to Florence without Donatello or anyone else being aware that he had left the city. . . . On his return he showed his carefully executed drawing, and Donatello greatly marvelled at this proof of Filippo's love for his art.[27]

This event took place only a half century after the superstitious reaction of the Sienese caused the destruction of their antiquity, and it illustrates both an awakened respect for the artistic glories of ancient Italy and a newfound desire to reintegrate the pagan past with the Christian present; motifs, in particular the mourning figures from the lid, from this sarcophagus are found on a number of Renaissance sculptures, including the Crucifixion panel of Ghiberti's first set of doors.[28] Apparently Brunelleschi's drawing, or copies of it, even passed through the hands of his rival.

Another telling example of the reuse of an antique composition concerns what was probably a relief on a Roman sarcophagus (fig. 34), described in book 2 of Alberti's *On Painting:*

> An *istoria* is praised in Rome in which Meleager, a dead man, weighs down those who carry him. In every one of his members he appears completely dead—everything hangs, hands, fingers, and head; everything falls heavily.[29]

It is likely that this Meleager relief, which so attracted Alberti through its evocative display of morbidity, also inspired the sculpted panel of the *Entombment* on the tabernacle that Donatello executed while in Rome in 1430 through 1433 (fig. 35). This same ancient relief, or something akin to it, also inspired Andrea Mantegna's engraving *The Entombment* of the 1460s (fig. 36). One or more of these compositions, in turn, was the source for Raphael's first major masterpiece, *The Baglioni Altarpiece,* which he painted in 1507 for a church in Perugia (fig. 37). Raphael certainly took to heart Alberti's advice that "anyone who tries to express a dead body—which is certainly most difficult—will be a good painter, if he knows how to make each member of a body flaccid."[30] Alberti recognized the natural obstacles to such a rendition through his study of the Meleager relief, and his challenge was just the sort of thing that Raphael needed to answer. *The Baglioni Altarpiece* brought him the desired recognition and certainly paved the way for his successful entry into Rome and access to the papal apartments of Pope Julius II.

Only a single generation after Salutati had pointed to a new awareness of the past, the Florentine scholar Matteo Palmieri could set down a progress report of notable change in his *Vita Civile:*

> Where was the painter's art till Giotto tardily restored it? A caricature of the art of human delineation! Sculpture and architecture, for long years sunk to the merest travesty of art, are only today in process of rescue from obscurity; only now are they being brought to a new pitch of perfection by men of genius and erudition. Of letters and liberal studies at large it were best to be silent altogether. For these, the real guides to distinction in all the arts, the solid foundation of all civilization, have been lost to mankind for 800 years and more. It is in our own day that men dare boast that they see the dawn of better things. For example, we owe it to our Leonardo Bruni that Latin, so long a bye-word for its uncouthness, has begun to shine forth in its ancient purity, its beauty, its majestic rhythm. Now, indeed, may every thoughtful spirit thank God that it has been permitted to him to be born in this new age, so full of hope and promise, which already rejoices in a greater array of noblygifted souls than the world has seen in the thousand years that have preceded it.[31]

Was Palmieri's pride in the wisdom of his day pure vanity? Today, no reasonable person would deny to the Carolingian ninth century, the French twelfth century, or the Italian age of Dante and Petrarch the glory of their enlightenments. That is not the point. As faulty as their historical perspective might have been, Palmieri and his fellow humanists believed the entire medieval period to have been a Dark Age of near barbarianism. They saw themselves, on the other hand, as belonging to a more enlightened and encompassing era, a time of reawakening.

One must remember that the word *Renaissance* is more than just a period designator; it, like the Italian word from which it comes, means "rebirth." The Renaissance signified the rebirth of the cultural standards that had governed antiquity (chap. 1, this vol.). This newfound rapport with the Greco-Roman heritage is what really motivated the Renaissance, and it is what distinguishes the Italian Renaissance from that of northern Europe, at least until the sixteenth century. The Middle Ages had found its authority solely in Scripture; the Renaissance, in its quest to get at the logic of God's truth, turned to the ancients for additional assistance.

The active regeneration of the culture of antiquity became a fundamental underlying factor in the arts of Italy during the fifteenth and sixteenth centuries. The Italian of the Renaissance believed that he was witness to a long-overdue rebirth of the ancient glory of his peninsula, and that belief was what truly set him apart from the rest of his fellow Europeans. Stimulated by a reawakened confidence in his illustrious heritage, he strove to erect new monuments of human creativity upon the noble structure of the antiquity from which he had been rudely separated by almost a thousand years of barbarian-initiated Middle Ages.

Since the naturalistic and reasoned approach found in ancient art seemed to offer the best way out of this unfortunate medieval situation as well as the best way to re-create the concept of an ordered world, it was felt desirable to restore respectability to ancient art. An examination of antique survivals promised a key to understanding the secret laws of our existence.[32] Had the ancients discovered the universal rules, and had they only missed the celestial goal because they did not possess the necessary code of Christianity? This was quite possible. Ancient art, thus, provided a possible means to the desired end, and an appreciation and emulation of it was a way of gaining knowledge valuable to our salvation. Humanist scholarship attempted to rediscover the totality of literature, philosophy, and history in an integration of the pagan past with the Christian present. The apparent Renaissance adoration of ancient art was not for antiquity's sake alone but was based upon a belief in the perfectibility of man—the melioristic element at the core of the Greco-Roman experience and an integral part of the expanding humanistic interpretation of life. It promised an eventual union with the Godhead through knowledge and the imitation of the nature which he had created.

The concept of a Renaissance, it again must be emphasized, was not an idea thought up at some later time and imposed upon the period (as was the notion of Romanesque or Gothic). The word *Renaissance* itself was invented and used as a term of pride in the very period (albeit not until late in the period).[33] That point is quite important, for it indicates not only an unprecedented historical consciousness but also an enormous feeling of pride and sense of duty. The great Lorenzo de' Medici, who presided over some of Florence's most brilliant years, used as his personal motto the French phrase "Le temps revient"—the times revived—by which was signified the rebirth of his own city in a new golden age.[34] Clearly, Lorenzo regarded his Florence as Augustus his Rome or Pericles his Athens. Already, returning from Rome in the first Jubilee Year of 1300, Giovanni Villani had determined to chronicle the history of his native Florence as "the daughter and creature of Rome."[35] A century later, Leonardo Bruni praised his city as "the new Athens on the Arno."[36] The conceptual lineage was both noble and prophetic. Lorenzo's personal insignia, the laurel leaf, also was emblematic of rebirth since the laurel was reputed to revivify itself even when severely pruned or desiccated. Both motto and emblem signified for Lorenzo the Renaissance spirit he so skillfully championed. Renaissance men, such as Lorenzo the Magnificent, truly believed that they were living in a special time of rebirth—an age in which culture and civilization finally were being reborn after long centuries of aimless cultural confusion and stagnation.[37]

Despite the best efforts of the bibliophile investigators it was apparent that much of the literary accomplishments of the ancients could not be retrieved. What was being brought into the light by the literary condottieri obviously constituted no more than the mouthwatering leavings of a largely destroyed heritage. It seemed as if every new fragment of Pliny or Horace or Lucian that was redeemed hinted at far more, of which no trace could be found. What were the eager antiquarian scholars to do when now confronted by this lacuna? In order to fill in the gaps, they reconstructed and even simulated. And so, in 1426, Alberti forged his play, the *Philodoxeus,* which, attributed to an unknown ancient writer named Lepidus, demonstrated the actual author's linguistic and scholarly abilities and solidified his prominent position within the classical tradition.[38] At the same time, the future Pope Pius II, Aeneas Silvius Piccolomini, and other like-minded humanists did their best to purify their Latin and to imitate in their writings the very best stylistic nuances of Cicero. In complementary fashion, artists such as Botticelli or Michelangelo set about reconstructing lost masterpieces known through description or existing in fragmentary form.

To the constant frustration of classicists and curators, the Renaissance discoverers of antiquities insisted on "restoring" almost every piece of ancient sculpture they unearthed, and such restorations were often flights of fancy rather than attempts at accurate reconstructions.[39] Archaeological veracity, in the modern sense, was not on their minds. The modern approach to classical remnants is passively archaeological; that taken by

Renaissance antiquarians was actively re-creative and dedicated to incorporating the past into the present. The case of the falsely restored arm of the *Laocoön* is but one obvious case in point.[40] But beyond the unscientific approach that produced such restorations, it is important also to note that those who performed them thought it imperative to give completeness to the fragments of the past. To be properly resurrected, antiquity had to be reconstructed. In this fashion, the remains of ancient Rome were fused with modern interpretations to produce a new aesthetic totality quite symbolic of the era—a renaissance that in many ways was a metamorphosis.

The regenerative impulse became very much a part of the Renaissance spirit whether literary or visual. Botticelli, for instance, attempted to duplicate a celebrated but lost painting by the Hellenistic artist Apelles, as described by Lucian (and echoed in perhaps more accessible form in Alberti's treatise *On Painting*), when he painted his *Calumny* (fig. 38).[41] His purpose may have been a posthumous defense of the reforming monk Savonarola, but his vehicle was a classically inspired allegory. The setting in which Botticelli has chosen to re-create the ancient tale of Apelles' *Calumny* resembles an ornately outfitted Roman civic structure derived, perhaps, from a version by Donatello shown on that sculptor's pulpit reliefs in San Lorenzo; however, more than likely, the painter drew upon his own recollection of the massively vaulted Basilica Nova (fig. 39). He certainly would have toured this great ruin during his Roman residence of 1481–82 as part of the team decorating the newly completed Sistine Chapel. It might seem inappropriate that Botticelli chose an ancient law court as the location for this miscarriage of justice, but it is even more ironic that, in his day, the Constantinian basilica was thought to have been the Emperor Vespasian's Temple of Peace.[42] Thus, the perjurious events represented by Botticelli transpire in normally tranquil, harmonious, and just surroundings now rudely perverted by the vengeful whisperings of calumny.

Earlier, and in a more totally humanist vein, Botticelli probably had used an ancient Homeric hymn as the inspiration for his great *Arrival of Venus* (fig. 40).

> Of august gold-wreathed and beautiful Aphrodite I shall sing, to whose domain
> belong the battlements of all sea-loved Cyprus where, blown by the moist breath
> of Zephyros, she was carried over the waves of the resounding sea in soft foam.

> The gold-filleted Horae happily welcomed her and clothed her with heavenly raiment.[43]

This hymn was included in the volume of the *Iliad* and *Odyssey* published in Florence in 1488 by the Greek refugee Demetrios Chalcondyles. In all likelihood it already was being circulated in manuscript form among members of the humanist circle who gave the necessary thematic instructions to Botticelli when he painted the picture a few years earlier.

More, however, than a reclaimed Homeric hymn was probably in the mind of the Medici family member who commissioned the painting from Botticelli. He and the erudite scholars who undoubtedly advised him also would have recalled Pliny the Elder's mention of the lost painting *Venus Rising from the Sea* by the same celebrated artist, Apelles, who had painted the *Calumny* in his own defense.[44] According to Pliny, Alexander the Great, noting that Apelles had fallen in love with his own mistress, Pankaspe, while he was painting her, presented the girl to the artist in a gesture of extreme magnanimity. "There are those," continued the ancient author, "who believe that she was the model from whom the *Aphrodite Anadyomene* [*Venus Rising from the Sea*] was painted."[45] Pliny went on to record that this painting, like the *Calumny,* was later in its history "dedicated by Augustus in the shrine of his father Caesar." Pliny also stated that "the lower part of it was damaged, and it was impossible to find anyone who could restore it; thus the injury itself contributed to the fame of the artist. This picture decayed from age and rottenness, and Nero, in his principiate, substituted for it another painting by the hand of Dorotheus."[46] Thus, in a sense, what even the mighty Romans could not restore, their worthy successors, the Florentines, through Botticelli, could re-create. Pliny, at another point, makes mention of a second painting of Aphrodite, "superior even to his earlier one," begun by Apelles but left unfinished.[47] Once again, Botticelli might be seen as completing the task of his ancient predecessor, even excelling him. Pertinent to this interpretation of Botticelli as a born-again Apelles is the fact that that very claim was made for the artist in a poem entitled "On Giving Praise to the History of Florence," written in 1488 by Ugolino Verino.[48]

Such a deliberately re-creative act as Botticelli apparently performed with his *Arrival of Venus* would help explain the curious linearity and flatness of the painting, which seems so out of keeping with not only the direction of Renaissance painting but also with Botticelli's own manner. Was the two-dimensional emphasis of this composition a calculated device intended to simulate a more archaic approach? In his effort to replicate the ancient painting, and in the absence of any existing works by Apelles, Botticelli may well have studied available Greek vases or, like the scholar Antonio Ivano, even have visited Etruscan necropoli. I have long been struck by the stylistic similarities between Botticelli's *Arrival of Venus* and the lyrical frescoes in Tarquinia's *Tomb of the Triclinium.*

While, in his own day, Botticelli might have been seen as a revivified Apelles, his *Arrival of Venus* also testified to the special nature of Florence's chief citizen. Although the painting apparently was executed for another member of the Medici family, it likely was intended to celebrate and flatter Lorenzo the Magnificent. Tradition associates the image of Venus in Botticelli's painting with the lovely Simonetta Cattaneo Vespucci, with whom it is thought both Lorenzo and his younger brother, Giuliano, were, at least, much enamored. Simonetta was, not coincidentally, born in the Tuscan seaside town of Portovenere (the port of Venus). Thus, in Botticelli's interpretation, Pankaspe (the ancient prototype for Simonetta), the mistress of Alexander the Great (the Laurentian predecessor), becomes the lovely model for the lost *Aphrodite Anadyomene* of the legendary Apelles (reborn through the talent of Botticelli) whose painting ends up in Rome, installed by the Emperor Augustus in the temple dedicated to Florence's supposed founder Julius Caesar. Can it be only an accident that when Lorenzo went to Rome in 1471 as part of a Florentine delegation, the newly elected Pope Sixtus IV presented the de facto ruler of Florence with an ancient sculpture of Augustus?[49] In the case of Botticelli's *Arrival of Venus,* the suggested reference to Lorenzo would have been just the sort of thing the Florentines would have appreciated. Thus, by overt implication, in this painting, Lorenzo becomes the new Alexander the Great with an implied link to both Augustus, the first Roman emperor, and even to Florence's supposed founder, Caesar himself. Lorenzo, accordingly, is not only magnificent but, as was Alexander in the story, magnanimous, as well. Ultimately, these allusions (or illusions) flatter not only the Medici and Botticelli but all of Florence, the home of worthy successors to the greatest figures of antiquity, both in governance and in the arts.

The interpretation I have offered of Botticelli's *Venus* is primarily secular, but certainly, despite its surface paganism, the painting could also be read on a spiritual level.[50] Allusions to the Virgin Mary and the advent of Christ can be discerned in both its content and composition. Such a fusion of seemingly divergent interpretations is, in fact, just what one should expect from an era that promoted a total cultural synthesis. An attempt to reconcile pagan antiquity with the Christian faith also is demonstrated in the life of Niccolò Niccoli. The scion of a well-to-do Florentine wool merchant, Niccolò, as we have seen, was given classical tutelage under the Greek émigré scholar and Florentine University professor Manuel Chrysoloras and then proceeded to fritter away his inheritance in antiquarian pursuits. Never a productive scholar in terms of his publications, Niccolò left behind letters and an enormous reputation for classical erudition. In his life-style, he attempted to imitate some ancient Roman patrician, but when he died, it was in the arms of Mother Church.[51]

When Niccolò's contemporary Leonardo Bruni, a far greater scholar and productive individual, translated Plato's *Phaedo* (ca. 1405) and *Gorgias* (ca. 1411) he gave them papal dedications, justifying these actions by pointing out that Plato's philosophical positions differed little from those of Christianity.[52] A similar amalgamation of Christian and pagan symbols defines the iconography of Bruni's own tomb in the Franciscan Church of Santa Croce in Florence. In his design for this monument, which set the standard for many a later Renaissance tomb, Bernardo Rossellino fused Christian and classical into a truly Renaissance funereal statement. The effigy of the Florentine chancellor depicts him crowned with the poet's laurel and dressed in a scholar's robes. Bruni holds a volume of his own writings (and not the Bible!) across his chest, but the book lies face down. Its author, having completed his secular labors, has turned his thoughts to heavenly contemplation. The triumphal arch framework of the monument, filled with classically inspired decorative motifs, attests to Bruni's role in the antique revival but also gives pride of place to a sculpted image of the Madonna and Child in the lunette above the recumbent statesman. This great tomb is both a triumphant testimony to Bruni's renown and a reminder of the gates of heaven through which the deceased will pass on his way to salvation. Classical learning has been no hindrance to the Renaissance scholar; rather it has encouraged Bruni in his quest for religious redemption. Earthly fame has joined with the promise of spiritual immortality in perfect complementary fashion. Bruni's monument, like his life, is a superb demonstration of the humanist ideals of the Italian Renaissance.

Those challenging this new humanist viewpoint were few and far between, or at least they do not seem to have been very vocal in their objections. The anticlassical harangues of the Venetian Dominican monk Giovanni Dominici, who attacked the new philosophic synthesizing, were but the exception.[53] The spirit of synthesis held the high ground as Federico da Montefeltro, both leader of papal armies and patron of humanist learning at his ducal court in Urbino, furnished two chapels in his palace, one dedicated to the Holy Ghost and the other devoted to a mythological grouping of Apollo, the Muses, and Pallas Athena.[54] By that time (in the 1470s) such an incongruous dedication seemed neither inconsistent nor blasphemous. On the contrary, it symbolized the desired synthesis of Christian and ancient concepts. Just such a harmonizing was visually demonstrated on the ceiling of the Sistine Chapel that Michelangelo later painted for Pope Julius II. There, eternal truth is promulgated to mankind through the combined predictions of both biblical prophets and pagan sibyls, the words of one reinforcing the voice of the other to produce a unified chorus of divinely inspired learning. And at almost the same instant, not far away, in the Stanza della Segnatura, Christian theologians joined with secular philosophers to create an intellectual advisory board for their papal patron. That summation of knowledge was given its fictive form by Raphael of Urbino, whose father had served as court painter to Federico da Montefeltro and who had helped in decorating the pantheon chapels of Urbino's encyclopedic ruler.

The notion of intellectual unity is, perhaps, best manifested during the fifteenth century in the person of the first humanist pontiff, Tommaso Parentucelli, who became Pope Nicholas V in 1448. Trained at Bologna, Parentucelli was introduced to the Florentine humanism of Poggio Bracciolini and Leonardo Bruni when he served as Cardinal Albergatti's secretary while the curia was in exile in Florence (1434–43) during the pontificate of Eugenius IV. Once elected to the papal throne, Nicholas attempted to merge the ideals of humanist scholarship and the classical revival with his belief in a new and vigorous papacy. His grand architectural plans for a physically revamped Rome (never realized) were symbolic of this effort.[55] Rebuilt churches, refortified walls, renovated aqueducts, grand squares and thoroughfares, an enlarged Vatican Palace, and, above all, an ennobled St. Peter's were to become the physical testimony to his intellectually harmonious and politically triumphant papacy—a true Roman Renaissance. His unfulfilled dream was renewed a papacy later by his protégé, Pius II. But, once again, little materialized in Rome, and that pope's efforts at Renaissance reconstruction were diverted, in glorious but more modest fashion, to his birthplace town of Pienza. It took the High Renaissance hubris of Pope Julius II to begin to effect the Roman renewal.

The Renaissance desire to combine the virtues of antiquity with the precepts of Christianity is made quite clear in a letter written by Pius II Piccolomini in 1460 to Sultan Mahomet II of Turkey.[56] The humanist pope, in his letter, attempted to convert the sultan to Christianity and, in so doing, alluded to the Turk's considerable learning in the classics. Pope

Pius said that the sultan already possessed the virtues of a classical philosopher; all that he needed, according to Pius, was to accept baptism in order to receive the theological virtues of faith, hope, and charity. The result would be the perfect man. Congruity was the aim, and as Alberti noted, "The business and office of congruity is to put together members differing from each other . . . in such manner . . . as to form a beautiful whole."[57]

Renaissance scholars and artists aimed at a total and all-encompassing understanding of this world and man's place within it. We find, therefore, that the architecture of the Renaissance is simplified, ordered and based upon the proportions of the human microcosm. Michelangelo, for one, was convinced of this when he wrote that "surely the architectural members derive from human members. Whoever has not been nor is not a good master of the figure and likewise of anatomy cannot understand anything of it [architecture]."[58] Brunelleschi's Hospital of the Innocents demonstrates this with profound clarity (chap. 2, this vol.). So too did the classicizing facades of Giovanni Rucellai's Florentine palace and that of Pope Pius II' Piccolomini family palace at Pienza, both of ca. 1460. Their almost identical articulation systems of three tiers of classical pilasters probably were derived from the articulated walls of the ancient Roman country villa of Muro di Santo Stefano near Lake Bracciano just north of Rome (as well as from more obvious examples such as the Colosseum).[59] We also find that the sculpture of the Renaissance aims at producing a physical harmony in the human figure based upon an understanding of the underlying systems of perfect proportions and observation contained in ancient sculpture. We find that the paintings of the Renaissance are constructed within a system of disciplined and rational spatial relationships attained through an understanding of certain basic visual laws such as those of perspective. Just as the world was held to be controlled by a set of universal and identifiable natural laws, so too were the arts held to be governed by certain constant rules of construction and representation. In the Middle Ages, theories about art had sprung out of practice; in the Renaissance, the practice of art evolved from theory, theory grounded in the centrality of man as the earthly module of God.

Brunelleschi's well-ordered front for the Hospital of the Innocents tells us this; so too does the interior of his splendid church of San Lorenzo. Here all is based upon a grid of relationships the result of which is a balanced and steady progress through a building that clearly reflects a divine plan for orderly and reasoned adoration. Clearly, Filippo Brunelleschi designed his buildings in a homogeneous fashion in accordance with carefully conceived systems of proportional relationships. Our visual understanding of their proportional integrity is supported by the claims of his biographer, Antonio Manetti, who wrote his *Life of Brunelleschi* in the 1480s. In his discussion of Brunelleschi's famous sojourn in Rome after his 1401 failure to win the competition for sculpting the Baptistery Doors, Manetti said that "he observed the method and symmetry of the ancients' way of building. He seemed," said Manetti, "to recognize very clearly a certain arrangement of members and structure just as if God had enlightened him about great matters. Since this appeared very different from the method in use at the time, it impressed him greatly. . . . He decided to rediscover the fine and highly skilled method of building and harmonious proportions of the ancients and how they might, without defects, be employed with convenience and economy."[60] Manetti went on to say that Brunelleschi, together with his companion, probable apprentice, and future founder of the Renaissance style of sculpture, Donatello, "when possible . . . estimated the heights from base to base for the height and similarly the entablatures and roofs from the foundations. They drew the elevations on strips of parchment graphs with numbers and symbols which Filippo alone understood." How very like the Ptolemaic grid system this all sounds, and how clearly it relates to Brunelleschi's later designs for the Hospital of the Innocents and for San Lorenzo. The first Ptolemaic treatise had been brought to Florence shortly before 1400 by refugee Greek scholars fleeing the advances of the Turks upon Constantinople.[61] Brunelleschi most likely would already have been an initiate in the new ways of thinking, even before his contact with the Ptolemaic cartographic concepts of Toscanelli. It is just that sort of a logical grid that serves to situate the Rucellai and Piccolomini palaces within a reborn scheme for classical definition.

What Brunelleschi discovered on his Roman study trip and later put into practice became codified as a basic tenet of the Renaissance, so much so that a hundred and fifty years later, Giorgio Vasari would state unequivocally that "rule in architecture is the measurement of antiques, following the plans of ancient buildings in making modern ones. Order is the differentiation of one kind from another so that every body shall have its characteristic parts, and that the Doric, Ionic, Corinthian, and Tuscan shall no longer be mingled indiscriminately."[62] Manetti also described how Brunelleschi devised and demonstrated the rules necessary in convincingly rendering a third dimension on a two-dimensional surface. Once Brunelleschi had invented perspective representation, situating objects within a visually rational spatial context, the system was rather quickly embraced by his contemporaries including Paolo Uccello, who devoted himself, to the detriment of domestic tranquility, to an exploration of perspective and foreshortening.[63]

I called attention earlier to the grid-pattern thought process through which the Renaissance artist of the 1470s had rendered his lifelike view of Florence (chap. 2). This, of course, is what artists call perspective, and it was Brunelleschi who invented it or, at least, who first recognized its artistic application. Edgerton claims that Brunelleschi may have been inspired by conversations he had with Toscanelli in the mid-1420s.[64] Another possible inspiration might have come via another of the noted Florentine humanists, Niccolò Niccoli. Niccolò was a book-hunting friend of Poggio Bracciolini, and it was Poggio who discovered a lost manuscript of Vitruvius in the monastery of St. Gall in 1418. Vitruvius's text describes a Greek system of perspective, and it is conceivable that Brunelleschi, encouraged by Niccolò, had set about reconstructing that ancient technique.[65] In so doing, and with only the enigmatic Vitruvius as a guide, he could have come up with a systematic spatial procedure that went far beyond anything possessed by the ancients. Once again, the process of melioristic rediscovery and revival seems evident.

But I am not so certain of this hypothesis, for it would place Brunelleschi's experiments in perspective into the 1420s. For several reasons I believe that Brunelleschi had hit upon his scheme of scientific perspective a decade earlier, perhaps as a way of preparing architectural renditions without going to the expense of constructing a three-dimensional model.[66] In any case, Brunelleschi prepared two demonstration panels of his schemes for rendering the impression of a third dimension on the two-dimensional surface. These have disappeared but are lavishly described in Antonio Manetti's fifteenth-century biography of the architect.[67] Here we need only note that the system that Brunelleschi propounded, and Alberti later disseminated, was based upon the projection of a grid scheme that would establish clear spatial relationships and re-create the semblance of reality.[68]

We do not know for certain what occasioned Brunelleschi's invention of perspective or what he really thought of his accomplishment, but we do know Alberti's view. Alberti, although an advocate of the antique revival, was delighted to point out the originality of the perspective scheme of his fellow Florentine, noting, with understatement, that "one scarcely sees a single antique *istoria* aptly composed."[69] And Alberti did more than just describe and codify the Brunelleschian system; he improved upon it and did so with great pride. Taking Brunelleschi's two celebrated demonstration panels as his guide, Alberti constructed his own improved painted illusions in the early 1430s. He described them as "these miracles of painting which many of my friends have seen done by me recently in Rome."[70] More about these visual experiments is to be found in an anonymous *Life* of Alberti, which describes his creation of "unheard-of works from this art of painting and unbelievable to those who saw them. These works he displayed in a small closed box through a tiny hole. You saw there high mountains, vast landscapes, the broad moving sea and at the same time such a long vista of distant regions that the sense of the beholder failed."[71] Clearly, for Alberti and the new avant-garde, the sort of gold gilt grounds favored by Cennino Cennini and the older generation were passé.

But why go to all this calculated trouble? The ancients had never made the leap from the science of Ptolemy to the practicality of navigation or to consistent modes of artistic spatial representation. There are many reasons, however, why this should have been accomplished in the world of the Florentine Renaissance. One of the incentives was theological. A more accurate rendition of the world supported the new theology earlier articulated by St. Francis and now espoused in such popular religious tracts as Thomas à Kempis's *Imitation of Christ* or St. Bridget's *Book of Heavenly Revelations.* The shift in emphasis found in these late medieval writings demanded a literal and individual identification with the spiritual experience. A more realistically rendered imagery was a by-product of this change in religious focus. The Renaissance invention of a system of perspective, whereby artists could depict space in a naturalistic fashion, greatly assisted in religious communication.

Bruce Cole has pointed out the utility of Renaissance perspective. "I think that it is a mistake," writes Cole, "to consider one-point perspective as some isolated and self-sufficient force in Florentine art. Rather it should be seen for what it was to the artists of the early fifteenth century—not as a toy or a scientific discovery but as an aid in the convincing representation of form in space and a device that allowed the many supernatural events of the Christian drama to be portrayed in a highly realistic fashion."[72] Cole concludes that the Florentine painters of the early Renaissance "knew that one-point perspective could also be effectively utilized to place irrational and mysterious stories in convincing settings." Cole's point about making the miracle manifest is a good one. The spatial thrust of Florentine artists from the thirteenth century onward was not simply a spontaneous urge, nor was it merely due to a desire to represent the world with greater optical accuracy. Neither was it the result of pure scientific inquiry. There was another and more fundamental reason why first Florentine and then, eventually, all European artists moved in this direction. The primary motivating factor was to achieve a greater spiritual efficacy in answer to contemporary changes in theological emphasis. At least, that is how it started out.

As an example of the use of perspective as a spiritual stimulation let us look at two examples of central Italian painting, one of the fourteenth century and the other from a century later. The first example is the glorious early-fourteenth-century altarpiece by the Sienese painter Simone Martini (fig. 41), familiar to all from its frequent use as a Christmas card illustration. This justly famous panel depicts the Annunciation of the Angel to the Virgin Mary. Despite its sensuously sinuous beauty, it is conceptually similar to the depiction of medieval Florence (chap. 2, this vol.). We see an iconic message, but we are forced to remain outside the scene; there are no spatial relationships that allow us to enter and actively witness and participate. In spite of its heavenly radiance, the typically medieval gold background compels us to keep our distance.

How different is the *Annunciation* (fig. 42) executed by the Umbrian painter, Piero della Francesca, some hundred and twenty years later and after the system of perspective had entered the vocabulary of Renaissance artists. Here the event takes place in a cloister yard setting that invites our entry. Suddenly, as if by a miracle, we are able to leave our present surroundings and stand beneath the splendid arcades of Piero's imagined architecture and witness for ourselves the very start of our salvation. Piero has created a space that duplicates reality, so much so that we are persuaded into believing in what we see as history and the impossible mystery of the Immaculate Conception as witnessed fact. Piero has done this by setting up a spatial grid, as a modern reconstructive scheme of the painting illustrates (fig. 43). We can literally plot out the space and reckon the distances, just as Columbus felt confident he could do as he set sail from Palos, Spain, on that August day in 1492. Piero's painting has transformed a two-dimensional actuality into a virtual three-dimensional illusion. In the same way, navigators no longer felt bound to the two dimensions of landfall sailing but could now predictably set forth into a third-dimensional distance, confident of where they were going even without seeing the way stations along their course. Piero della Francesca, coincidentally, was buried on the very same day on which Christopher Columbus set foot upon the shores of his New World.

CHAPTER 5

Space Transcended

The *Annunciation* by Piero della Francesca discussed in the previous chapter is sited within the re-created environment of a monastic cloister yard. In actuality, such architectural locations were the settings for a whole category of Renaissance paintings whose effect was rather special and very spatial.[1] The idea of the monastic cloister was itself of peculiar significance in Christian religious life. In the dark days of the early church, in the days of Roman persecution, the Christian author Tertullian wrote of the prisons in which his colleagues awaited their martyrdoms: "The prison now offers to the Christian what the desert once gave to the prophets. . . . Let us drop the name 'prison' and call it a place of seclusion. Though the body is confined, though the flesh is detained, there is nothing that is not open to the spirit."[2] Even with the acceptance of Christianity, this idea persisted and was carried over into the institutionalized concept of the monastic cloister. The ideal of the imprisoned spirit of the devout Christian awaiting its release and eventual union with the Deity became a popular piece of medieval symbolism, used particularly in reference to the monastic situation.

Although many supported this interpretation of the cloistered environment as being symbolic of the earthly prison, others, including Saint Benedict, preferred to see the cloister as representing not incarceration but a spiritual paradise, a prologue to the Heavenly Communism awaiting us in the Hereafter.[3] The former interpretation, as seen in Carthusian and Cistercian monastic communities, led to strictures against any sort of decoration, while the latter one favored visual stimuli and richly decorated cloister yards. By the end of the Middle Ages, a fusion of the two opposing positions had taken place, with the balance tilted in favor of the paradise view.

One of the most attractive cloister yards erected during the early years of the Renaissance is located at the Franciscan basilica of Santa Croce in Florence. Here, between the years 1446 and 1453, a new cloister was laid out to replace a fire-wasted predecessor (fig. 44). Known today as the Spinelli Cloister (from the name of its patron, the papal banker Tommaso Spinelli), it offers a splendid example of the application of the classicizing principles of post-Brunelleschian architecture within a monastic context. The spaciousness of the layout, the rhythmic beauty of the arcading, the careful use of mathematical ratios in determining the individual elements, and the overall proportions of the architectural units created a high point in the rational architecture of the early Renaissance. Although the identity of its architect is undocumented, the design is now most often associated with Bernardo Rossellino.[4]

When I first saw it, freshly restored after the flood of 1966, the cloister yard seemed a gleaming, sunlit architectural jewel. The architectural members, the columns, moldings, and capitals in the beautiful grey-green Tuscan limestone called *pietra serena* stood out against the white plastered walls. The crisp, graphic detailing of the cloister yard made me think of an illustration of a geometrical diagram, a visualization of some Euclidean axiom. Restored, the Spinelli Cloister at Santa Croce appears as an architectural blueprint in gray and white—the magnificent yet coldly rational logic that some take for the Renaissance spirit. But was it always so? Were those white walls always so devoid of decoration? Were the Franciscan monks who once walked beneath the vaulted ceiling of its ambulatory as severely rational in spirit as the setting today would have us believe? Not so. Something seems to be missing. Those austere walls seem to cry out for some sign to identify this structure as a Christian cloister and not a center of secular philosophy (fig. 45). This, after all, is not an ancient Athenian stoa, and we look for some sign of its Christian function.

There is evidence that, at one time, such a Christian program of decoration did exist along the now barren walls of the Spinelli Cloister. Giorgio Vasari, in fact, provides us with information about the original appearance of the cloister. In his biography of the mid-fifteenth-century painter Andrea del Castagno, Vasari describes a celebrated painting by that artist in this very cloister: "The work which excited the greatest admiration . . . was a Christ at the column in the new cloister of that convent, at the end opposite the door, where he introduced a loggia with columns in perspective, the crossing of the vaults diminishing and the walls with their oval compartments depicted with such art and so much study that it is clear that he was as completely master of the difficulties of perspective as of design."[5] Castagno's mural has disappeared, but Vasari's description of it allows us to mentally reconstruct its situation and its visual impact. Opposite the entrance and seen through the Renaissance door frame of the entry portal, Castagno's mural would have looked as if it were an extension of the actual arcaded walkway. Vasari describes the artist's expertise in rendering "a loggia with columns in perspective, the crossing of the vaults diminishing." Thanks to Castagno's skill with perspective depiction, the visitor would have been led visually right down the walkway from the entry, not to turn the corner at its physical end but to continue his steps, illusionistically, on and into the re-created biblical space where he would have found himself standing before the figure of the persecuted Christ tied at the column. There, Vasari continues, "the attitudes of those who are scourging the Christ are free and bold, displaying hatred and fury in their faces, while the Christ is all patience and humility. In the attitude of His body bound to the column with the ropes, Castagno seems to have attempted to show the suffering of the flesh, and the divinity hidden in the body preserving a certain splendor of nobility which moves Pilate, who is seated among his counselors, to seek some means of setting Him free."

Through the use of painted illusionism, a secret that Renaissance artists such as Andrea del Castagno now possessed, Franciscan monk and layperson alike could feel himself spiritually transported back through time and across space to stand at the very side of Christ. Once there, he could witness his suffering, and visually hear (and feel) the blows struck by his tormentors. As Thomas à Kempis had recommended in his immensely popular *Imitation of Christ,* he could find, through this painted vehicle, "wings like to a dove, that [he might] fly into the bosom of my Saviour and to the place of His blessed wound, and rest . . . there."[6]

Did this sort of thing really happen? Did people really experience this sort of spiritual transportation when confronted with the new realism of Renaissance religious paintings? It did indeed happen, and some of the especially blessed did not even need a realistically rendered image of the sort created by Andrea del Castagno to motivate them.

The celebrated late-fourteenth-century Franciscan mystic Bridget of Sweden frequently had visions of religious ecstasy that she graphically described in her widely read *Book of Heavenly Revelations.* On one occasion, or so she wrote, she was visited by the Virgin Mary, who vividly gave her the details of the Passion and Crucifixion of Christ.

> He was taken to the pillar of torment, and he took off his vestment Himself, and He laid His hands upon the pillar Himself, and His enemies bound them fast without mercy. . . . Then all of my Son's friends fled from Him, and His enemies surrounded Him and tore His body that was so pure and without blemish, and without infection or sin. . . . And what was still more dreadful to see was that when the scourges were withdrawn His flesh was torn like the earth by a plough. And as my Son was now standing there, bleeding and wounded all over . . . there was one who took courage and asked: "Will you kill Him, though He is not yet judged?"[7]

Not all of the faithful, of course, were the visionary self-starters that St. Bridget was. They needed assistance in achieving their own enraptured moments of requisite religious anguish. Armed, however, with the realistic narratives of a St. Bridget, they were well prepared for the journey. The final impetus came once they stood face-to-face with a vividly rendered painting. Could the realistic environment pictorially created by Andrea del Castagno in the Spinelli Cloister have done this? The answer is yes and is attested to in Vasari's further description of the effect the mural must have had upon those who saw and "used" it: "This picture," wrote Vasari, "is so fine that if it had not been scratched and damaged . . . by children and other simple persons, who have scratched all the heads and arms and almost every other part of the Jews, as if to avenge the sufferings of the Savior upon them, it would certainly be the most beautiful of Castagno's works."[8]

Obviously, Castagno's celebrated painting depicting Christ at the Column did more than provoke a passive contemplation in those who stood before it. The seeds of the painting's own destruction were planted by its very ability to visually convince. Castagno depicted no mere iconic image of an event but attempted an actual re-creation of it, so realistically and forcefully presented in figural treatment and spatial illusion that it compelled those who saw it to actually attack Christ's fictive abusers in defense of the Savior. Although the records are silent on the subject, other such illusionistic scenes may have been represented or intended for other locations along the loggia walls of the Spinelli Cloister.

An examination of documents and descriptions pertaining to Florence's other monasteries shows that, within their cloistered confines, many vividly transporting paintings were executed during the early years of the Renaissance. Most of them, unfortunately, have not survived, the majority perishing for perhaps the same reason as did Andrea del

Castagno's fresco in the Spinelli Cloister. Some few do remain, however, to illustrate a once important use of the spiritual power of visual persuasion. One of the best preserved examples is found in the delightful little Cloister of the Oranges (Chiostro degli Aranci) at the city's Benedictine Abbey (fig. 46).[9] Although the Cloister of the Oranges is located right in the heart of Florence's historic district, only a short walk from the Piazza della Signoria, and the area today is thronged with tourists, and the streets round about are jammed with traffic, the cloister remains secluded and quiet. Architecturally, the Cloister of the Oranges is one of the most interesting in Florence, for it occupies a stylistically transitional position between the old Gothic manner of the Middle Ages and the new classicism of the emerging Renaissance. The Cloister of the Oranges was constructed in the 1430s by a team of stonemasons that included the young Bernardo Rossellino, the architect-sculptor later likely responsible for the Spinelli Cloister (as well as for Pope Pius's project in Pienza and perhaps the Rucellai Palace).

When I first visited the Cloister of the Oranges, it also had just been restored subsequent to the great Florentine Flood of 1966. Freshly whitewashed, the walls behind the arcades gleamed as cleanly as those of the Spinelli Cloister (fig. 47). What I did not realize at that time was that a cycle of ten murals originally had decorated the walls of its upper loggia and temporarily had been removed for cleaning and restoration. Once back in place, their colors and details sharpened, they transformed the entire appearance of the cloister (fig. 48). No longer did the light bounce back from the plastered walls, confining the viewer spiritually within the constricted space of the cloister yard. Now, instead, the eye was allowed to travel past the loggia arcade, through the actual surface of the corresponding wall, and into the painted scenes depicting the life and miracles of St. Benedict, the man who saw the monastic cloister as a premonition of paradise (fig. 49). This series of illusionary murals was painted by an emigrant Portuguese artist known locally as Giovanni da Consalvo right after the construction of the Cloister of the Oranges was completed. He is documented as being at work on them between 1436 and 1439.

Giovanni was no major master but was a competent craftsman working at the very beginning of the Renaissance in a new style recently established by such masters of pictorial veracity as Masaccio and Paolo Uccello. Yet he has grasped the essential importance of achieving the illusion of reality in his work, such as in his depiction of St. Benedict at table with his monks (fig. 50). Giovanni has made a major effort to situate us within the depicted room so that we might truly witness the miracle St. Benedict is about to perform. The artist has tried to eliminate the notion that what we are looking at is a painting and even that the wall on which he executed it exists. To achieve the illusion of reality, he has separated each scene by simulated pilasters that duplicate the actual architectural strips articulating the real facade of the loggia and has used the actual corbels of the vaults as three-dimensional capitals for his painted pilasters. Giovanni means for us to confuse the factual and the fictive. He intends for us to ignore the wall surface, treating each archway as an opening through which we may view and enter the saintly scenes. Thus, we escape the monastic prison and have a glimpse of a saint bound for paradise.[10]

Giovanni da Consalvo, who painted the stories of St. Benedict at the Benedictine Abbey of Florence, was close in his style to that of another, far greater master of the early Florentine Renaissance, the Dominican monk Fra Angelico. Angelico was responsible for the murals painted between 1435 and 1445 in the newly erected cloister of San Marco.[11] An example of his work, a stark representation of the crucified Christ adored by Saint Dominic, immediately confronts today's visitor at the end of the loggia walkway directly opposite the entrance to the cloister (fig. 51). The position is identical to that once occupied at the Spinelli Cloister at Santa Croce by Andrea del Castagno's *Flagellation.*

The exquisite terror and glory in the *Crucifixion* that Fra Angelico has painted opposite the cloister entrance pulls us along the walkway, urging us to fall to our knees and embrace the cross of our salvation in the company of the order's founder, St. Dominic. Dominic seems to command us, in the words of St. Catherine of Siena: "Graft your heart and your affection into the tree of the most holy Cross with Christ crucified, and make in His wounds your habitation."[12] The glorification of Christ's Passion and of the blood shed in atonement for our sins is a dominant theme in the Dominican canon of the period. Fra Angelico gives us reminders of this theme every which way we might turn in the monastery. For a monk, the image of the Lord in one of his roles of *salvator mundi* was present constantly. Even in a sparsely furnished cell, the image was there at the foot of the bed, the last thing you saw when you closed your eyes and the first that you beheld on waking. Nowhere is such a program of spiritual stimulation so completely preserved as at San Marco. The appeal of Thomas à Kempis: "Yes"—"Do thou pluck me away, and deliver me"—has been heard.[13]

Imagine what must it have been like to open your eyes to Angelico's blinding vision of the Transfiguration (fig. 52) and to recall Thomas à Kempis's words: "O Everlasting Light, surpassing all created luminaries, dart Thou the beams of Thy brightness from above, which may penetrate all the most inward parts of my heart."[14] From the bed in yet another monastic cell at San Marco, its Dominican occupant could contemplate a frescoed vision of Christ administering the mass to his apostles. His role as Christ's priestly successor was given dramatic emphasis by the fact that the fictive communion took place in a room that duplicated his own; the actual window of his cell was matched by those within the fresco, and through each of the windows—both actual and illusionary—he could see identical views of a tiled dormitory roof and windows (fig. 53). Place, time, and belief fused as the biblical story was given corporeal reality in this Florentine monastery. Angelico's artistry had provided proof positive of the miracle of Transubstantiation.

Fra Angelico's most famous mural at San Marco, the *Annunciation,* is familiar to all from its frequent reproduction (fig. 54)—in fact, too familiar. Do we really see and understand it today—see it as the good monk meant for it to be seen? Iconographically, the setting of the enclosed garden points to the purity of the Virgin and also alludes to the sheltered nature of the earthly paradise that was the Dominican monastery. This is all clear enough; so is the fact that Fra Angelico's efforts in carefully depicting the spatial depth of the painting and in echoing the actual architectural vocabulary of the monastic buildings at San Marco was intended to relocate us spiritually within the composition. However, another important aspect about how we were intended to relate to the painting needs to be mentioned. Fra Angelico's *Annunciation* was not meant to be seen from the raking angle of the dormitory corridor but was to be appreciated from head on and from a lower point of view. This is only possible from a position on the stairway leading up to the dormitory floor. As you climb the stairs from the cloister yard, head down and watching the risers, you reach a landing and then have to turn sharply to the right to begin the next ascent. You pause, lift your eyes, and there it is—the *Annunciation*—framed in the doorway above, announcing the entry to the monastic dormitory (fig. 55). This direct and absolute confrontation with God's physical entry into our lives was made by the monks of San Marco day in and day out—an unavoidable proclamation of God's love, and a challenge for us to reciprocate.

It should be apparent that the mural *The Last Supper,* painted by Andrea del Castagno in 1447 in the dining hall of the Convent of Saint Apollonia, is more than just a record of a far distant sacramental event (fig. 56). As the Florentine nuns broke their bread in their refectory, they did so in the company of Christ and his Apostles—the only males in attendance. That is why the setting is so realistically rendered, why the depicted space *must* look as if it were an extension of the actual room. That impression is created once again at the Augustinian monastery of Florence's Church of the Ognissanti. This *Last Supper,* painted by Domenico Ghirlandaio thirty years later, appears to be set even more definitely into an extension of the physical room (fig. 57). The wall of the actual refectory seems to give way, and an extra illusionary bay added by the artist extends the architecture of the hall. There is now space for a head table, that presided over by Christ himself, which translates our earthly meal into a spiritual banquet—a kind of continuous Mass. Without question, the Gospel verses of St. Matthew (26:26–29) would have come to mind.

> And as they were eating, Jesus took bread, and blessed it, and broke it, and gave it to the disciples, and said "Take eat; this is my body." And He took the cup and gave thanks, and gave it to them, saying, "Drink ye all of it, for this is My blood of the new testament, which is shed for many for the remission of sins. But I say unto you, I will not drink henceforth of this fruit of the vine, until that day when I drink it new with you in my Father's kingdom."

Symbolically, illusionistically, through their newly acquired representational skills, Renaissance artists and their audiences were able to actually visualize that promised day in the earthly paradise that was the monastery—or wherever else the experience dictated.

This leads us logically back to that Milanese monastery where Leonardo da Vinci painted his own *Last Supper* (chap. 2). We come back with a better understanding of why it simply *must* look as it does. We come back with a knowledge that it cannot be appreciated today in the same way that it originally was by those who once *used* it as an element of their religious lives. Leonardo's *Last Supper* was not intended as decoration and was not valued solely because it was beautiful. The monk who sat at table in the refectory of Santa Maria delle Grazie in Renaissance Milan some five centuries ago looked down to the end wall of the dining room and saw his vision, his physical and spiritual world, expanded. He saw the wall of his temporal (and temporary) prison collapse and felt himself lifted in spirit to the celestial paradise that was the destination he sought. He thus appreciated Leonardo's *Last Supper* not only as a work of supreme aesthetic beauty but also because of its theological utility. Leonardo has made the spiritual space in his *Last Supper* work as a painting, but, most important, he has made it work as an instrument of faith.

The cultural pilgrim to Leonardo's *Last Supper* either overlooks or pays but scant notice to the *Crucifixion* fresco (fig. 58) at the other end of the refectory, painted contemporaneously by a local Milanese painter named Giovanni Donato Montofano (ca. 1440–1510). Artistically, this work suffers by comparison with Leonardo's masterpiece, and it is not surprising that it is ignored by the modern-day visitor. Yet, iconographically, it plays a most significant role. The juxtaposition of these two Passion Week events within a monastic dining hall was not coincidental. Each time the monks sat at table they did so between reminders of Christ's ultimate sacrifice for sinful humanity and his institution of the sacrament commemorating that atonement. Not only were the body and blood shared once more in the Holy Mass but, by analogy, each time the monastic diners broke bread and sipped wine. In this way, the monks were vividly reminded that their Lord had given his life for their sins and that they, as his followers, replicated the roles of the original group of apostles. Situated at table between these two great spiritual ports of call, the monks were spiritual voyagers in a ship of faith. The representational logic of Leonardo's re-creative abilities gave them a solid sense of direction in the spiritual space of their Christianity.

By now, the conceptual links between Columbus's voyage of discovery and the spatial logic of Renaissance art as seen in Leonardo's *Last Supper* are clear.[15] Both were part of a new quest for harmony and a new ability to see a totality of parts—what I am calling the Renaissance's "urge to unify."[16] This desire to consolidate, to see the forest rather than the individual trees, had diverse ramifications.

Seemingly insignificant yet symptomatic of the changes taking place was the way people began to identify themselves.[17] In seventh-century B.C. Italy, the Etruscans had introduced the idea of familial designations (clan or gens). That nomenclature was continued by the Romans, but patronymic usage was revived with the coming of the barbarian invasions that initiated the Middle Ages. It was not until the Middle Ages were waning that family names began to reappear, eventually to become an increasingly universal norm during the Renaissance. In the Renaissance, we may speak of Paolo dal Pozzo Toscanelli rather than simply Paolo dal Pozzo, of Lorenzo de' Medici and not just Lorenzo di Piero di Cosimo, and of Michelangelo Buonarroti and not Michelangelo di Lodovico. In the latter case, and in many others, the definitive surname reflects the given name of the earliest remembered ancestor. Michelangelo's great-grandfather was named Buonarroti. This simple way of precisely identifying oneself through a name that acknowledged a family tie beyond the purely linear points to the general interest in universality that I see as a distinguishing feature of the new age. With the establishment of expanded commercial connections, it also may have been necessary because it allowed for a more precise way of fixing accountability. On the other hand, because it renewed a classical practice, it also may have been a conscious part of the antique revival that was fundamental to the nature of the Italian Renaissance.

This new trend in inclusive family nomenclature ties in to the initiation in Florence of a system of universal property taxation, the *catasto.* The 1427 tax united the heads of household in the city and its dependencies into a broader family of communal economic responsibility, helping to make a civic whole out of the independent many.[18] This system of generating income for the state at the same time that it promoted unity also aided in the establishment of a sense of individual identity. It required that stock be taken of one's physical worth, one's relations and one's dependents, one's assets and one's debts—an individual's personal and earthly totality. Over time, this process of taxation produced a psychological awareness of individuality and position within and as part of a social system. The catasto also reflected the Renaissance's attention to historical accuracy and demanded on the part of both those who recorded the information and those who appraised it an understanding of personal, generational, and fiscal continuity, as property was acquired, improved upon (ideally), and disposed of (through sale or bequest). Each catasto period, therefore, was related to that preceding it. Seemingly mundane, the Florentine catasto signified a recognition of the concept of continuity and a sense for the flow of time.

Examples of the Renaissance desire to tell time can be found throughout Leonardo Bruni's writings. His famous *History of the Florentine People* is particularly illustrative of the new and markedly Florentine view of a sequential sense of history.[19] Inspired by his reading of Livy and Cicero, Bruni constructed a flowing historical narrative. This approach was in contrast to the episodic and essentially medieval chronicle of the type presented in the previous century by Giovanni Villani.[20] The classically indebted Bruni, furthermore, saw the linkages between events in the past and those of his own day; in other words, Bruni tried to grasp the totality of history and understand its lessons.

These Renaissance efforts at clarity and accountability were echoed by changes in how time was being recorded. The general use of dating, other than in official documents, only came into common practice well into the fifteenth century. Dating, once it became customary, signaled a desire to fix one's position in time relative to transpiring events in much the same way that the use of a grid in mapmaking did geographically or perspective illusionism did for depicted space. Perhaps the rediscovery and appreciation of antiquity had led to a true historical consciousness, which, in turn, had engendered an effort to logically understand and preserve the present as part of a recognized continuum.

Chronological thinking and conceptualizing historical episodes into a coherent order were among the more significant accomplishments of the Italian Renaissance.[21] Renaissance scholars refused to be baffled by the past and were determined that events in the past could be sorted out and understood. The humanists actually invented historiography and provided a method by which the past could be viewed with objectivity and be understood from a position within the historical framework.[22] The periodization of history, of arranging the past into a sequence of units defined by events and concepts, is very much akin to the spatial grids employed by the new wave of both geographers and painters. Each system provides a strategy for bringing our physical or intellectual environment under control—a way of managing our microcosm.

Leonardo da Vinci gave appropriate visual form to the earthly microcosm in his drawing *The Vitruvian Man.* Centralization of motivational force as well as unity of purpose were dominant themes in this rendition. Can it then be mere happenstance that Italian architects in the early decades of the cinquecento were fascinated with the central plan? When drawing their designs, they displayed a centrifugal concentration interpreting the expanding area, in the words of James Ackerman, "as a scene such as one would view when standing in the center of space."[23] Ackerman continues with the conjecture that "the centrifugal character all comes from a tendency of these architects to visualize themselves in the center of a given space, looking outward . . . making it possible to view the whole environment from a single point." This is not far removed from what Columbus accomplished; his voyage of discovery was made possible through a new capability for reckoning with certitude one's immediate position in respect to the totality of the heavens. Ackerman has pointed to the organic nature of Italian building practices in the sixteenth century in which each successive architect in a long-enduring project such as that for rebuilding the Basilica of St. Peter's did not consider himself bound to the intentions of his predecessor but "took what was there as an inspiration for new ideas, and this habit of working with and in the building itself brought the efforts of many generations to a cohesive conclusion." This Italian architectural approach might be contrasted with that customary in France where, according to Ackerman, "each successive portion of the structure is methodically isolated from its predecessor."

Other cultural events could be cited to bolster the argument concerning the unification theme that I take to be the hallmark of the Renaissance. It extended even into the area of personal interrelationships. From Alberti's *On the Family* to Castiglione's *Book of the Courtier,* the Renaissance gave rise to a host of treatises on decorum, what might be termed books of ethical conduct or social interaction. In this phenomenon, we again find a unifying and harmonious objective, for they all deal with how one is to behave within a broader social structure.[24]

A similar sequence of occurrences transformed the music of Renaissance Europe. The Gregorian chant of the medieval church was yielding to more complex polyphonic melodies. In music, as in the rest of European culture, there was a new urge to experiment and explore. Modal polyphony advanced as the Renaissance progressed toward a more perfectly unified tonal harmony and overlapping repetition found, for example, in the motets of the celebrated Guillaume Dufay.[25] By the middle of the sixteenth century, polyphony had yielded to homophonic structure in which several musical lines were controlled by vertically constructed harmonies producing sequential chords with a primary concordance of voices.

Visually, the new harmonics of the Renaissance are witnessed in Luca della Robbia's lovely marble choir loft for the Cathedral of Florence. Positioned originally above the sacristy door beneath Brunelleschi's great cupola, it occupied a space between earth and heaven; it was in spiritual ascent. This spatial position was emphasized through the figured panels with their melodic assemblage of music-making children and youths, in spirit both Christian and classical. Della Robbia's choir is of this earth but partakes of the supernatural; his choirboys are truly in concert, at one instant acolyte and ephebe. One might imagine their natures harmonizing in the motet *Nuper rosarum flores,* composed by Dufay for the 1436 dedication of the great dome rising above them.

In much the same fashion, we can consider the scientific reasonings of Nicholas Copernicus as a necessary part of the overall spirit of the Renaissance. When Columbus was making his first voyage of discovery, Copernicus was in his second year at the University of Krakow, where he was studying a Ptolemaic-like curriculum of mathematics, optics, and perspective—just the thing for the Renaissance explorer and essential for someone who would lay out new rules for spatial navigation and plot out a universally harmonious map of planetary relationships. It is, also, not too much of a stretch to see Johann Gutenberg's invention of movable-type printing around 1450—perhaps the single greatest invention since the wheel—as a product of his ability to see separate letters locked into place to form words, sentences, and printed books, just as objects could now be represented in harmonious relationships in paintings, or distant locations visualized as part of a united worldview.[26]

The panoramic view of Florence shown in figure 13 (chap. 2) was, of course, a product of both the new and more spacious thinking and the technological inventiveness of the age. A woodblock print, it likely was published in the 1470s by Francesco Rosselli and is known as the "della Catena" or chain view due to its chain-form border.[27] It was, perhaps, the first occasion in which the relatively new reproductive technique of printmaking was used in such a topographically secular fashion. With numerous copies of Rosselli's view in circulation, those living in the farthest points of Europe could "visit" Florence and admire its features. It was great propaganda for Florence and, consequently, for the nominal head of the Florentine state, Lorenzo de' Medici. Within a couple of decades, this view of Florence was joined by similar graphic depictions of other cultural centers—Rome, Venice—and as the multiple views circulated, they served to visually connect the new European within a common geographical system—a worldview reminder of the Renaissance urge to unify.

Topographical knowledge was not the only visual information being disseminated through the medium of the print at the end of the fifteenth century. Artists were now able to share their accomplishments without the necessity of actually having to go on site. When the young Albrecht Dürer became fascinated with what he had heard of the new art of the Italian Renaissance, he could seek immediate inspiration from Andrea Mantegna's engraving *The Battle of Sea Gods* or Antonio Pollaiuolo's *Battle of the Nudes.* The former he reproduced in a drawing of 1494, and the latter provided anatomical and composing material for a number of his endeavors. Both prints helped to turn the young German's eyes southward toward the Italian Renaissance. Conversely, when Raphael sought exotic details to convey the impression of foreignness in his numerous paintings of the Holy Family, he frequently employed the Germanic village types found in the prints of Dürer. The printed image, like movable type, permitted replication and consequent distribution, which served to transmit regional styles and to unite artistic expression. Boundaries of nation and of national style were breached.

Renaissance printmaking also has allowed us to have some glimmer of the mutilated and then destroyed image *Christ at the Column* by Andrea del Castagno discussed earlier. Although now vanished, a possible derivative of this masterpiece of spatial integration has endured in an engraving executed about 1463–64, sometimes attributed to a Florentine artisan named Baccio Baldini.[28]

Previous mention of a new worldview—one might say "new world order"—brings me to another point having to do with the ability of artists to see beyond the immediate foreground and into distant space. I had previously used Piero della Francesca as one of my perspective models. I return to him to look at what he rendered in the background of that pair of celebrated portraits of the Duke and Duchess of Urbino (fig. 59). In both portraits a great space unfolds, and on the reverse of each of the panels, behind allegorical scenes of triumphs, are even greater spatial recessions (fig. 60). If a recent reconstruction of the way in which these panels were conceived is correct, then the offered vistas were even more expansive, for the spatial segments may have formed a continuous sweep.[29] What a wondrous and evocative opening-up of space!

The ability to see and appreciate nature as a broad and cohesive expanse rather than as a series of parcels was a major step in the formation of the new vision of the Renaissance and, in this case, proved to be one of the factors that helped to integrate the northern and southern aspects of the movement. Giovanni di Cosimo de' Medici willfully chose a rocky and precipitous site beset with all sorts of building problems for his villa at Fiesole, above Florence. He selected the location because it afforded him the most spacious vista—and against the advice of his father, who told his son that the lower and more accessible site at Cafaggiolo was to be preferred because "from there everything I can see is ours, which is not the case at Fiesole."[30] The new generation could see beyond the confines of the immediate concerns of the family and appreciate how that family (and its possessions) fit into the broader scheme of things.

In the expansive spatial reach of Piero della Francesa and the expanding vision of Giovanni de' Medici, one is reminded of the words of their contemporary, the great humanist Pope Pius II, as he described the view (fig. 61) from the palace he erected in his birthplace town of Pienza between 1459 and 1464.

> The view from the upper floor of the palace extends to the west beyond Montalcino and Siena to the Pistoian Alps. As you look to the north diverse hills and the lovely green of forests are spread

> before you for a distance of five miles. If you strain your eyes you can see as far as the Apennines. . . . The view from the three porticoes to the south is bounded . . . by towering and wooded Mt. Amiata. You look down on the valley of the Orcia and green meadows and hills covered with grass in season and fruited fields and vineyards, towns and citadels and precipitous cliffs.[31]

Pope Pius's palace, from which he could glory in his vista views, was articulated by a gridlike facade of vertical pilasters and horizontal entablatures, and it was further tied in a truly three-dimensional fashion to its architectural setting by similar visual webbings across the front of the adjoining cathedral and the paving pattern of the central piazza (fig. 62). This Ptolemaic-style grid may be more than simply an accident or even, as I suggested earlier, a conscious revival of ancient architectural schemes. The humanist pope, through his Florentine architect, Bernardo Rossellino, may have deliberately been suggesting, in architectural metaphor, a world of orderly and integrated relationships implied in the cartographic formula of Ptolemy and ensured by the controlling harmony of the Church.

Pope Pius's word-picture description of the view from his Pienza loggia is no oddity. Such natural encounters dot the pages of his memoirs. Just such a landscape vignette enlivens the narrative of a visit he made to Rocca di Papa and Monte Cavo in the lake country south of Rome, where he "sat there with the cardinals for some time gazing at the seashore and surveying all the coast belonging to the Church" and gazing upon the nearby lakes where "you could form a true idea of their size and shape and of the intervening space, which being at that season covered with leafy forests and green grass presented a variety of gay colors."[32] Pius's eyes had been opened to the beauty of nature, but it was a nature given even greater import by the presence of "the foundations of the ancient walls" and the antique allusions thus conjured up.

Pope Pius's several extensive descriptive passages remind us of the first evidence of such an expansive appreciation of a unified nature found in the fourteenth-century humanist poet Petrarch's tale of his ascent of Mont Ventoux—not undertaken, by the way, as an act of religious pilgrimage but simply to satisfy his curiosity. It may well be that Petrarch was not the first medieval mountain climber, but he was the first such adventurer to leave a lasting impression of his ascent, giving precedent for the wondrously naturalistic descriptions that enliven the memoirs of Pope Pius a century later.

Two seemingly inconsequential events that took place in conjunction with the rebuilding of Pienza may be seen as metaphors for the unifying mood of the Italian Renaissance. One involved the pope's purchase of a clock to be installed in the bell tower of the new town hall of Pienza and the other his commissioning of a painted *mappamondo* (world map) for installation somewhere in the community.[33] In the early 1460s, these two civic embellishments signified the conceptual change that lay at the heart of the Renaissance. The clock provided the means by which Pienza's inhabitants could place themselves within a uniform chronological continuum, and the map let them visualize themselves spatially, no longer occupying an isolated position but as part of a geographic totality. Could Columbus's expedition be far off?

The Renaissance urge to unify—the way in which paintings were composed or cities, such as Pope Pius's Pienza, were created, the desire to understand geographical relationships, to harmonize Christian and pagan philosophies, to calculate the passage of time, even how people identified and interacted with each other or how communities assigned fiscal responsibility—all these evidences of a period style may be linked, in turn, to the growth of centralized political authority within the various states of Europe.[34] Although Italy was home to a reinvigorated papacy and often subject to the monarchical moods of other European states, it had neither emperor nor king. That the spirit of absolutism was in the air north of the Alps while Italy was not itself subject to it might account for the Florentine ability to freely grasp the general concept of unity without being constrained by it. "As never before," writes Denys Hay, "the decades round 1500 witness in Italians a consciousness of Italian unity. The best minds of the period are, as it were, compelled to leave the narrow loyalty to a city or prince and see the larger loyalty to a country."[35]

With the reevaluation given to man during the Renaissance and the new philosophical and artistic recognition of his microcosmic role as the universal exemplar came a broadening interest in the world that evolved about the human centerpiece. Thus, as the new age progressed, there came increasing attention devoted to earthly human concerns (e.g., the growth of portraiture, genre, and still life painting) and to the nature over which man had been given dominion (landscape). Unity of vision was applied to all of creation. Leonardo's notebooks are full of proofs of his concern for the linkages that might demonstrate universal bondings. He not only drew flowers but saw the relationships between their symmetrical dynamics and the other elements of nature, even the most kinetic of them. Leonardo also was able to visualize emotional equations as seen in his transferral of human ferocity to equine expression in his drawings for the *Battle of Anghiari* (fig. 63).

Leonardo's composition for the central element of this unfinished and now obliterated battlepiece, the *Fight for the Standard,* is known from several copies including a spiritually faithful one by Peter Paul Rubens (fig. 64). It makes for an interesting comparison with the three painted panels executed some seventy years earlier by Paolo Uccello to record the Florentine victory at San Romano (fig. 65). Uccello has arranged his participants as if they were toy soldiers set against a scenic curtain. The effect is not medieval (although it consciously looks back to the pageantry of the International Gothic); while they are almost pedantically arranged within the spatial framework of a perspectival grid, the clarity of form is not naturalistic, and the emphasis is upon the individual warriors rather than the battle.[36] Leonardo's approach is quite different; he is interested in the combat as an event more than the combatants, and he masses the mounted soldiers in a broadly conceived impression of violence. For Leonardo, the individual elements are a means to an emotional end. It is a case of forest more than trees, and it signals the arrival of the wider and more encompassing vision we call the High Renaissance.

Such a swelling desire to see beyond the immediate and the particular was not limited to the Italians but was becoming pan-European. It can be found in the paintings of the great fifteenth-century Flemish artist Jan van Eyck, particularly in his ca. 1435 painting *The Madonna and Child with Chancellor Nicholas Rolin* (fig. 66). Here, too, the eye is drawn into a great unifying vista. One cannot help but think of the later ducal panels of Piero della Francesca, but there is no direct connection. The similarity of vision is there because the Fleming van Eyck and the Italian Piero were responding to the experiential demands of their day. The same interest in connecting the separate parts into a whole can be seen, later in the same century, in the landscape backgrounds of Hans Memling, Hugo van der Goes, Hieronymus Bosch, and, most especially, in the unified spatial recession of the Dutch painter Geertgen tot Sint Jans (fig. 67).

The ability to think in terms of totalities enabled Verrocchio to solve the problem of how to fill the vacated niche of the Guelph party at Orsanmichele in Florence. For this purpose the merchants' association that had acquired the space needed a statue of their St. Thomas, who is best known for having his doubts concerning the physical resurrection of Christ removed by touching the wounds of the risen Lord. Verrocchio needed to make Thomas part of a two-figure composition dominated by the presence of Christ yet still remain the focus of his niche by utilizing both physical and mental space. By placing the saint outside the niche upon the very convenient ledge, he made Thomas a transitional visitor from our world of rational doubt to the spiritual world of faith that is found in the niche-enshrined figure of the blessing Savior. Thomas spatially turns from our world to Christ's, and as his hand approaches the gaping wound, it hesitates and his drapery seems agitated with nervousness. The separate figures remain distinct but are merged into a single statement through both physical and psychological gesture. Verrocchio has achieved a unity of purpose without destroying personal individuality. This lesson in harmonious balance and spatial vision was not lost upon his prize pupil, Leonardo da Vinci. Just such a sense of compositional unity binds together the thirteen figures at the head table in the refectory of Santa Maria delle Grazie in Milan. It becomes part of how Leonardo and the High Renaissance that he helps to establish would visualize the world about us.

The wish to represent an encompassing view of nature is found in many of the drawings of Leonardo da Vinci dating from the late fifteenth and early sixteenth centuries, that is, from the very time of Columbus's explorations. The bird's-eye views that Leonardo renders are startling, and we must remember that for all his experiments with the idea of flight Leonardo could soar aloft only in his mind's eye. Even more amazing are his several imaginary views in which we look down upon vast landscapes; these are no mountain-view vistas but are maplike in character and almost satellite-like in their impact (fig. 68). Not until the second half of the twentieth century was man afforded the opportunity for such actual observation. I find it extraordinary that Leonardo could visualize in this fashion. Such drawings clearly are the product of the new connective thought processes of the Renaissance. Listen to the words of Leonardo:

> The eye is the master of astronomy, it makes geography, it advises and corrects all the human arts . . . the eye carries men to different parts of the world, it is the prince of mathematics . . . it has created architecture, and perspective, and divine painting . . . *it has discovered navigation.*[37]

Also typical, of course, is Leonardo's most celebrated painting, *The Last Supper,* painted while Columbus was making his second voyage to the new world. It is the first real example of the High Renaissance and is marked by a sense of physical and psychological integration previously unseen. Earlier, a comparison was made between it and the same subject painted by

Andrea del Castagno executed less than fifty years earlier. In Andrea's version each apostle seems locked into his own separate space like the successive ports of call of a medieval portolan chart. Leonardo's rendition is the Ptolemaic counterpart, exploring relationships and discovering human reactions.

Let me close this part of my discussion of the unifying spirit of the Renaissance with one final painting. It is an extraordinary historical panorama by the early-sixteenth-century German painter Albrecht Altdorfer (fig. 69). Altdorfer's *Battle of Issus* was painted only a little more than two decades after Columbus's death and seems to capture in an almost magical fashion the global, one might say cosmic, view that the Renaissance had made possible. In the present context, we need not bother to deal with the allegorical issues it presents, comparing the ancient Greek conqueror of the East with a contemporary Hapsburg emperor and his campaigns against the Turks. What is of lasting significance here is that great sweep out and beyond the horizon into infinite space. We see in that swirling mass of mountains, sea, clouds, sky, and sun, a new vision of a universal nature, not yet fully known and not yet ordered, but there to be explored, exploited, subdued, and structured: in many ways this is the vision of the Americas brought back to Europe through the explorations of Christopher Columbus and his successors, including the Florentine merchant-navigator, Amerigo Vespucci, after whom our new world has been named.

CHAPTER 6

Epilogue

The preceding chapter obviously has violated the conditions I established for my inquiry into the nature of the Renaissance. Mention of Jan van Eyck, Dürer, Copernicus, Gutenberg, and Altdorfer has taken the discussion north of the Alps, and the word *Renaissance,* as I defined it in the first chapter of this book, was not in the conceptual vocabulary of northern Europe during the fifteenth century.[1] Yet there were many points of congruity, despite the fact that the essential ingredient in the Italian-born Renaissance—the antique—was missing from its northern contemporary counterpart. What I continue to find truly extraordinary (and, so far, unexplainable) is that both Masaccio and Jan van Eyck embarked upon their amazing pictorial adventures at almost the same precise moment, oblivious of each other and separated by both geography and cultural climate. Certainly their revolutions in representation began and ended differently, but equally as certain is the fact that both masters cast aside a millennium of medievalisms and set off along new and analogous paths. Both artists questioned convention and explored new possibilities.[2] Both shared a newfound fascination for personal observation, experimentation, and attention to nature. While both Masaccio and van Eyck had rediscovered the concept of meliorism, they diverged in how they pursued their goals. The paths that they and their immediate successors followed remained separated but parallel for almost one hundred years. While the Italians revived and incorporated the lessons of antiquity, the northerners explored the wonders of nature and the delights of accurate and particularized depiction.

When all is said and done, however, artists in both regions rejected tradition and formula and focused their attention upon the earthly orbit as a means of attaining the heavenly realm. Consider, for instance, the fact that two-thirds of Jan van Eyck's paintings contain portraits and half of his preserved works are, in fact, individual portraits. This vividly demonstrates a new concern with the individual and a desire for personal memorializing. At the same time, there began in the north a growing, yet still fanciful, interest in the ancient past. Van Eyck himself was equated in his own day with the ubiquitous ancient Greek painter Apelles, and one of his portraits, likely of Philip the Good's court musician Gilles Binchois, is inscribed in pseudo-Greek with the name of the ancient court musician to Alexander the Great, Tymotheos. Thus, we may find in this painting a deliberate analogy between the ancient Apelles/Alexander/Tymotheos relationship and the modern-day correlation of Jan van Eyck/Duke Philip of Burgundy/Gilles Binchois. Here, in the as-yet-unhumanized north, we already have the sort of romanticized allusion to the antique that becomes so overt in the Medicean paintings of Botticelli (chap. 4). Yet the visual language that creates the ancient atmosphere in Italy is not there.[3] The ruins of antiquity were essentially absent in van Eyck's homeland, and there was no sympathetic lineage to connect the Fleming and the ancient Roman.

A more telling argument in favor of, if not the Renaissance, then at least a renascence in the north during the fifteenth century can be made through a comparison of two similarly composed portrait diptychs, the *Wilton Diptych* (fig. 70), painted by an anonymous French artist for the English king Richard II, and Jean Fouquet's *Melun Diptych* (fig. 71) of fifty years later.[4] This, of course, is really the exception that proves the rule, and we must remember that the sudden explosion of the antique into Fouquet's panels is a direct consequence of his visit to Rome in the Christian Jubilee Year of 1450. Fouquet stands alone in the north and others, even Rogier van der Weyden, who made the same pilgrimage journey, captured little of the new Italian (and antique) spirit. They kept true to their national character and context or reverted to it as soon as they got home. In any case, even if we see some of the same new vision in northern painting as in that of Italy during the fifteenth century, we most definitely do not see the same in the other arts. In Italy, the break with the medieval past took place along all the artistic fronts and proceeded apace. In the north, while one may marvel at the innovative freshness in the panels of Jan van Eyck, Robert Campin, Rogier van der Weyden, and their successors, the architecture of cathedrals and town halls remained firmly Gothic for decades, and the sculpture retained the expressive language of the International style.[5] There was a cultural lag in painting's sister arts, and this is telling. Clearly, the unifying character that we have seen as part of the Renaissance spirit in Italy was absent in the transalpine regions. But it was only to be expected that the two exploratory paths would eventually meet; they were going in the same direction and their juncture was as predictable as the intersection of the lines in a perspective diagram.

In truth, even in the art of painting, the ultimate Renaissance fusion came only when the previously nationalistic Italian concepts of intellectual humanism were transported into northern Europe—Albrecht Dürer and Desiderius Erasmus were part of the northern avant-garde who were receptive to the imports from the south. That the new spirit of the Renaissance had finally been carried across the Alps is made clear in the attitude of that region's first unmistakable Renaissance artist, Albrecht Dürer, who wrote of the "reawakening" of the antique spirit and whose own laborious effort to compose a treatise on the proportions of beauty was undertaken in emulation of ancient volumes that had done the same thing, volumes lost but reported in the writings of classical authors.[6]

Two examples from Dürer's graphic work illustrate the ways in which southern and antique ideas were absorbed into the visual vocabulary of the northern artist. The first is Dürer's drawing *The Slaying of Orpheus* of 1494 (fig. 72) and the second is the German's most celebrated image, the engraving *The Temptation of Adam and Eve* (fig. 73) of a decade later. Classical sources for the latter work are obvious and are oft cited. Dürer's Adam is magnificently dependent upon the ancient *Apollo Belvedere,* known since the late fifteenth century and already a part of the papal collection.[7] Of interest is the manner in which Dürer has fleshed out the physique of the somewhat effeminate Apollo (perhaps a Roman creation of the first century rather than a Hellenistic conception). His Eve, likewise, was of antique inspiration, her body being based upon a statue of the *Venus pudica* variety, of which the most famous was the *Medici Venus*—the same model that Botticelli had used for his *Arrival of Venus.* The other source, that for his Orpheus, is less apparent. Based upon the musculature and the spread of the legs, I believe that it had its source in the great Hellenistic fragment known as the *Belvedere Torso* (fig. 74), a seated Hercules by Apollonius of Athens and housed in the Palazzo Colonna in Rome since 1423.[8] Dürer may or may not have been aware of that work through someone's drawing of it, and Panofsky probably was correct in citing a mediocre Ferrarese engraving as the immediate source for his composition.[9] But whether the young Dürer knew of the existence of the Greek sculpture is not the point; his ultimate inspiration came from an ancient masterpiece. Dürer actually never did see either of the Belvedere sculptures or any other ancient monuments in Rome, because whatever plans he may have had for traveling further into Italy than Venice were thwarted on each of his trips to the peninsula in 1494 and 1505–7 by the presence of French invaders. The German's timing was off.

Erasmus of Rotterdam truly personified the mixture of medieval and modern ways of thinking and living; he was a monk, and later priest, who lived apart from religious confines and traditional duties and operated as an academic within the intellectual community of secular palaces, universities, and the general laity. Petrarch may have initiated this process of integration, but it was set into full motion by the Dutch scholar, who presaged the life of today's university researcher (or so we would like to think). It also was Erasmus who really was the first in the north to see an equality of value in the pagan ethical concepts of antiquity and the Christian teachings that rested upon scriptural authority. Erasmus possessed a global view of scholarly life as he moved with ease from his native Holland to England, Germany, Switzerland, and Italy. His was a world without limits and boundaries oblivious of national borders or ethnic restrictions. The extension of his intellectual reach was also beyond that enjoyed by earlier humanists; he well understood the market provided by the printing presses of Basel.

Interestingly enough, Erasmus also participated in the dissolution of the harmonious ideal of the Renaissance. The various pieces of the Western traditions had coalesced into the Renaissance and then, like a big bang, exploded in various new directions under the impact of their own weight and the revolution of the Reformation. The Neoplatonic, idealistic belief in the possible unification of all concepts, in the reconciliation of opposites, eventually was revealed as a marvelous but dysfunctional figment. In the same way the use of the printing press that, in the hands of Gutenberg, seemed to predict a further unification of thought also helped to break the universal power of the Church by allowing individuals to bring holy images and texts into their homes for personal devotion (and interpretation). While this personalizing of faith would seem to be in keeping with the movement initiated by St. Francis, it came to the aid of the German Augustinian Martin Luther and would spark the Protestant revolt. With a Bible at home, the pronouncements of the priest no longer had the same authority. Each person could read the Bible with discrimination and reach his own conclusions. Seeming opposites had, at first, unified; now they disassembled.

Shakespeare's Hamlet (2.2), who in one breath could proclaim the wondrous work that was man (chap. 3, this vol.), could in his next lines lose his confidence and moodily muse:

> And yet to me,
> What is this quintessence of dust?
> man delights not me;
> No, nor woman neither. . . .

Hamlet's doubting nature is indicative of the dissolution of the unified Renaissance ideal. Such a shattering of faith is to be found in the deliberate disharmonies of the Mannerists and in the dismemberment of the Western Church during the Reformation.

A comparison between Masaccio's distraught Adam from the Brancacci Chapel and the grieving St. John from Rosso Fiorentino's *Deposition* (fig. 75), painted just short of a hundred years later, illustrates the differences in mood and visual approach between the styles of the early Renaissance and Mannerism. Both figures hide their faces in mourning—one for the paradise that is lost and the other for the Messiah crucified. Yet what a change in attitude! Masaccio's Adam, reluctant as he is to face mortality (his dragging right leg a clear demonstration of his unwilling expulsion), enters the "real world" with nobility and physical ability, still created in the perfect image of God. Rosso's John, however, seems to wither and shrink from the scene, his body expressively attenuated. Colors and form echo the uncertainties of a new and much less confident era.

The same insertion of the irrational can be found in the curious inscription placed in 1521 upon the tomb of the painter Piero di Cosimo, whose mythological fantasies rivalled the imaginings of his Flemish contemporary, Hieronymus Bosch:

> If I was strange, and strange were my figures
> Such strangeness is a source of grace and of art;
> and whoever adds strangeness here and there to his style,
> gives life, force, and spirit to his paintings.[10]

Among the visual leitmotifs of the preceding chapters have been various treatments of the *Last Supper.* Despite the vast differences in perception and spatial context between the scene on the late-twelfth-century Pisan cross (chap. 2) and that of Leonardo's great *Last Supper,* they had one major element in common—a strongly felt (and conveyed) sense of the spiritual moment. The drama of the momentous occasion was visually told in each rendition, the one iconically, the other by visually involving us with the participants. Yet little more than three-quarters of a century after Leonardo put down his brushes, this sense of purpose was vanishing.

The case of Paolo Veronese's *Feast in the House of Levi* (fig. 76) may be somewhat unusual, but it is an indicator of a coming change in artistic motivation. Commissioned as a *Last Supper* for the refectory of the Venetian monastery of SS. Giovanni e Paolo, this painting (on canvas not on plaster due to the dampness of Venice) ran afoul of Counter Reformation censorship, and Veronese was hauled before the Holy Tribunal in 1573 to explain the painting's lack of religious focus and potential invitation to heresy. The records of that celebrated proceeding survive and are illuminating, not only of the potential perils to an artist but of a general shift in artistic direction. When asked the nature of his painting by the inquisitors, Veronese said that it was "a picture of the Last Supper that Jesus Christ took with His Apostles in the house of Simon."[11] Was he, we might wonder, deliberately feigning scriptural ignorance—playing the untutored and therefore innocent craftsman—or did he actually have so little biblical knowledge that he confused two distinct episodes in the Christian story? Interestingly, he was not corrected by his clerical judges. His interrogator then proceeded to note the presence of many an extraneous and profane element within the painting: a buffoon with a parrot, a tooth-picking apostle, a servant with a nosebleed, and, worst of all, German halberdiers. Veronese defended these genre elements by saying that they were simply ornamental additions to the central story. And then, his questioner came to the point:

> Are not the decorations which you painters are accustomed to add to paintings or pictures supposed to be suitable and proper to the subject and the principal figures or are they for pleasure—simply what comes to your imagination without any discretion or judiciousness?[12]

Veronese's reply was plain and prophetic: "I paint pictures as I see fit and as well as my talent permits."[13] Clearly, for Veronese, the religious experience had become but an excuse to display his exceptional gifts for rendering brilliant detail and coloristic sensuality. Little of the spiritual remained. So little did Veronese care for the religious context that he readily agreed to make a few changes and retitle the work *The Feast in the House of Levi,* actually an event more suitable to his gift for genre. Even more significant is the fact that his monastic patrons agreed to this alteration of subject without considering the iconographic effect within the spatial context of the refectory. Spiritual purpose finally has yielded to visual pleasure. Doctrine has given way to decoration.

Actually, Veronese's *Last Supper/Feast in the House of Simon/Feast in House of Levi* is one of the first great art-for-art's-sake creations of the modern era. The dual nature of one of Michelangelo's loveliest sculptures, the marble *David/Apollo,* now in the Bargello Museum in Florence (fig. 77), and the story of how Giovanni da Bologna's *Rape of the Sabine Woman* (fig. 78) got its name are other similar cases in point.

In the case of Michelangelo's statue in the Bargello, it probably started out life in 1527 as a David, in the tradition of similar works by Donatello and Verrocchio and his own gigantic *David* of 1501–4, intended to be read iconographically as the symbolic and watchful protector of the republican government of Florence. It remained unfinished when the Medici retook the city three years later, and Michelangelo promptly switched allegiances and began to transform his statue into an inoffensive Apollo; the bulge of marble on the youth's back, once intended for David's sling, would have been transformed into Apollo's quiver, and the head of Goliath beneath his foot was smoothed into a featureless Parnassian rock.

The equivocal nature of the *David/Apollo* was forced by circumstance. There was no such excuse in the case of Giovanni da Bologna's *Rape of the Sabine Woman,* which is even more overtly without implicit meaning. Really just a study in human form, structural difficulty, and compositional intricacy, it never received an identity until it was set up in the Loggia dei Lanzi in 1583. Only then was it baptized, ex post facto, by consensus. It was really meant to display the sculptor's technical virtuosity and proclaim Florence's leadership in the arts. Giovanni himself never settled upon a name for it, calling it either a Paris and Helen, or a Phineus and Andromeda, or a Pluto and Proserpina. Form had superseded message; affectation had replaced content. And Italy itself was now in danger of being culturally superseded. The creator of this equivocal Florentine sculptural composition was, of course, not native to the city (or even to the peninsula). Giovanni da Bologna, who occupies a pivotal position between Michelangelo and the Baroque's Bernini (chap. 1, this vol.), was a Frenchman, born Jean de Boulogne. His presence in late-sixteenth-century Florence demonstrates just how far and completely the Renaissance spirit born in that city almost two centuries earlier had spread. It also is symbolic of the fact that Florentine domination, even Italian domination, of the artistic movement had come to an end. The logical Renaissance conclusion had been reached: the urge to unify had done its work and had joined north and south together within a common international heritage of cultural transformation.

Notes

INTRODUCTION

1. From Jules Michelet, *Histoire de France* (Paris, 1855–67), 9:5, as given in Denys Hay, ed., *The Renaissance Debate* (New York: Holt, Rinehart, and Winston, 1965), 22.

2. Good surveys of the "new" approaches to art historical research can be found in Jonathan Harris, *The New Art History: A Critical Introduction* (London and New York: Routledge, 2001); Catherine Gallagher and Stephen Greenblatt, *Practicing New Historicism* (Chicago: University of Chicago Press, 2001); and Vernon Hyde Minor, *Art History's History,* 2nd ed., rev. (Upper Saddle River, NJ: Prentice-Hall, 2001), 140–222. The application of these methodologies is neatly demonstrated in Bradford R. Collins, ed., *Twelve Views of Manet's Bar* (Princeton: Princeton University Press, 1996).

3. The "new art history" has produced some interesting approaches but the object of these critical inquiries—what we, as art historians, supposedly, are all about—often gets lost in the verbal nuance. I regret that my discipline has succumbed to the intellectual seduction of the new literary criticism and that works of art are now being treated as artifacts.

4. Denys Hay, *The Italian Renaissance in Its Historical Background* (Cambridge: Cambridge University Press, 1970), 7–8.

5. On Wylie Sypher's use of Wölfflin, see his *Four Stages of Renaissance Style: Transformations in Art and Literature, 1400–1700* (Garden City, NY: Doubleday Anchor, 1955), esp. 18–34.

6. John Ruskin, *The Stones of Venice* (New York: John Wiley, 1880), 3:34–35. Emphasizing the continued religiosity of the Renaissance should no longer be necessary. Alexander Nagel, among others, has pointed this out in his review of Jörg Träger's *Renaissance und Religion: Die Kunst des Glaubens im Zeitalter Raphaels* in the *Art Bulletin* 82 (December 2000): 773–77. Nagel begins his commentary with the emphatic statement: "Richard Trexler said it three decades ago: 'The Pagan Renaissance is no more.' One hundred years of scholarship since Burckhardt had made it clear, Trexler declared, that 'Renaissance man

remained a Christian, even a pious one.' Since then sociohistorical and anthropological approaches to the Renaissance have only confirmed the pervasive presence of religious traditions and institutions in the life of the period."

7. Nicholas Pevsner, *An Outline of European Architecture* (Harmondsworth, Baltimore, and Victoria: Penguin, 1964), 182.

8. For the extensive bibliography of the *Primavera*'s iconography, see Umberto Baldini, *Primavera: The Restoration of Botticelli's Masterpiece* (New York: Harry N. Abrams, 1986), 113–14. See also the discussion in James Hall, *A History of Ideas and Images in Italian Art* (New York: Harper and Row Icon Editions, 1983), 263–66.

9. Arthur Field, *The Origins of the Platonic Academy of Florence* (Princeton: Princeton University Press, 1988), 194.

CHAPTER I

1. This cautionary advice is found in John Addington Symonds, *The Renaissance in Italy*, as quoted in Denys Hay, *Debate*, 71.

2. See references cited in the Introduction, n. 2, as well as Jean Howard, "The New Historicism in Renaissance Studies," *English Literary Renaissance* 16 (1986): 13–43.

3. William Hood, "The State of Research in Italian Renaissance Art," *Art Bulletin* 69 (June 1987): 174–86.

4. Lynn Thorndike, "Renaissance or Prenaissance," *Journal of the History of Ideas* 4 (1943): 65–74.

5. See, for instance, Charles Hope and Elizabeth McGrath, "Artists and Humanists," in *The Cambridge Companion to Renaissance Humanism*, ed. Jill Kraye (Cambridge: Cambridge University Press, 1996), 161–68, who play down the impact of antiquity upon the artists of the fifteenth century as well as the involvement of humanist scholars in establishing new criteria for the arts.

6. Howard Saalman, *Filippo Brunelleschi: The Buildings* (University Park and London: Pennsylvania State University Press, 1993), 422.

7. Giovanni Rucellai's praise of Brunelleschi is contained in his collected memoirs, *Zibaldone Quarasimile*, and is included in Isabelle Hyman, ed., *Brunelleschi in Perspective* (Englewood Cliffs, NJ: Prentice-Hall, 1974), 28.

8. Giorgio Vasari, *The Lives of the Painters, Sculptors, and Architects*, ed. William Gaunt (London: Dent; New York: Dutton, 1963), 1:18.

9. Jules Michelet, *Histoire de France* (Paris: 1876–78), 9:5 as given in Hay, *Debate*, 22.

10. One example of the outreach of an urban style into the countryside can be found in the new construction of bathing facilities at the many thermal spas throughout Tuscany and beyond. These rural medicinal retreats injected many of the architectural features of the Renaissance style into the hinterlands. See Charles R. Mack, "The Wanton Habits of Venus: Pleasure and Pain at the Renaissance Spa," *Explorations in Renaissance Culture* 26 (winter 2000): 257–76. Another such example may be found in the rural community of Corsignano, which was transformed between 1459 and 1464 into Renaissance Pienza by Pope Pius II. Pienza provides another example of the injection of urban style (primarily that of Florence and Rome) into the countryside. See the author's *Pienza: The Creation of a Renaissance City* (Ithaca and London: Cornell University Press, 1987). Pienza will receive further attention in chapter 5.

11. In his "Life of Leonardo," Giorgio Vasari (*Lives,* 2:164) says that "when it [Leonardo's cartoon] was finished and set up in the room, men and women, young and old, flocked to see it for two days, as if it had been a festival, and they marveled exceedingly."

12. As given in Hay, *Debate,* 10.

13. On this, see John Stephens, *The Italian Renaissance: The Origins of Intellectual and Artistic Change before the Reformation* (London and New York: Longman, 1990), 89.

14. Stephens, *Origins,* 89.

15. Giovanni da Bologna (Giambologna) was, of course, French by birth, but his active life was spent in Italy, primarily in the service of the Medici dukes of Florence. Further discussion of this artist is taken up in chapter 6.

16. It frequently is suggested that Italy, during the fifteenth century, was not, really, in a condition that might be thought conducive to momentous change. See Denys Hay, *The Italian Renaissance in Its Historical Background,* 67. Economically and politically the peninsula was beset—not yet recovered from the financial, agricultural, and industrial losses of the previous century, subject to frequent outbreaks of the plague that had decimated its urban population in 1348 and racked by constant warfare. Yet these negative factors seem not to have dampened innovation and intellectual inquiry; in fact they may have even been a stimulant. Or, more properly seen, they may have been unpleasant but really inconsequential (except, of course, to the individuals who suffered them) parallel events.

17. Michael Levey, *Florence: A Portrait* (Cambridge: Harvard University Press, 1996), 189.

18. As quoted in Hay, *Debate,* 63.

19. For additional commentary on the rather fuzzy nature of the architectural Renaissance, see Christine Smith, *Architecture in the Culture of Early Humanism: Ethics, Aesthetics, and Eloquence, 1400–1470* (Oxford: Oxford University Press, 1992), 57–79. The peculiar mixture of classical and medieval architectural elements is nicely explored in Howard Saalman's "The Palazzo Comunale in Montepulciano: An Unknown Work by Michelozzo," *Zeitschrift für Kunstgeschichte* 28 (1965): 1–65.

20. Leon Battista Alberti, *On Painting,* trans. and ed. John R. Spencer (New Haven and London: Yale University Press and Routledge and Kegan Paul, 1970), 40.

21. On this, see Charles Burroughs, *From Signs to Design: Environmental Process and Reform in Early Renaissance Rome* (Cambridge, MA, and London: MIT Press, 1990), 23–24.

22. Bernard Berenson, *Homeless Paintings of the Renaissance* (Bloomington: Indiana University Press, 1970), 49.

23. Professor Middeldorf's comment does not mean, however, that Milan should be seen as a cultural rival of Florence, only that it contains little-traveled artistic avenues that might be explored. The same, of course, is true of a number of other Italian urban centers.

24. Hood, *Art Bulletin,* 180.

25. Hood, *Art Bulletin,* 174.

26. Elizabeth G. Holt, ed., *A Documentary History of Art,* volume 1, *The Middle Ages and the Renaissance* (Garden City, NY: Doubleday Anchor, 1957), 206.

27. George Holmes, *The Florentine Enlightenment, 1400–1450* (London: Weidenfield and Nicholson, 1969), 99. The impact of the Byzantine diaspora upon the evolution of Florentine thought will be reviewed more extensively in chapter 3.

28. Holmes, *Enlightenment,* 98. Holmes's volume provides one of the most succinct, yet thorough, surveys of the intellectual and political climate of Florence at the initiation of the Renaissance movement.

29. Holmes, *Enlightenment,* 38.
30. Holmes, *Enlightenment,* 38.
31. Levey, *Florence,* 105.
32. As given in Hay, *Debate,* 62–63.

CHAPTER 2

1. For the Vivaldis' precocious voyage, see Ernest Wilkins, *A History of Italian Literature* (Cambridge: Harvard University Press, 1974), 25.

2. *"The Little Flowers" and the "Life of St. Francis" with the "Mirror of Perfection"* (London and Toronto: J. M. Dent; New York: E. P. Dutton, 1910), 311.

3. *Little Flowers,* 232–33.

4. This story is recounted in chapter 44 of the *Little Flowers.* In addition, see Francis of Assisi, *The Little Flowers of Saint Francis of Assisi,* trans. Abby Langdon Alger (Mount Vernon, NY: Peter Pauper Press, n.d.), 115.

5. Anonymous, *Meditations on the Life of Christ,* trans. and ed. Isa Ragusa and Rosalie Green (Princeton: Princeton University Press, 1961), 38.

6. The change in orientation was effected in 1215 consequent to liturgical modifications decreed at the Fourth Lateran Council. See Evelyn Welch, *Art and Society in Italy, 1350–1500* (Oxford and New York: Oxford University Press, 1997), 187–89, and Frederick Hartt, *History of Italian Renaissance Art: Painting, Sculpture, Architecture,* 4th ed., rev., David G. Wilkins (New York: Abrams; Englewood Cliffs, NJ: Prentice-Hall, 1993), 32–33.

7. On this, see Hans Belting and Christine Kruse, *Die Erfindung des Gemäldes: Das erste Jahrhundert der niederländischen Malerei* (Munich: Hirmer, 1994), 13, and the review of this book by Victor Stoichita and Didier Martens in the *Art Bulletin* 78 (December 1996): 733–35.

8. The rise of the mendicant and preaching orders was symbolic of a new social linkage between the religious and laity, uniting the monastic communities with the greater world they served.

9. This "commercial" view of Heaven was later supported by the opinion of the fifteenth-century Florentine humanist Giannozzo Manetti, who compared the daily balance sheet of a businessman to God's estimate of a person's life. See Arthur Field, *The Origins of the Platonic Academy of Florence* (Princeton: Princeton University Press, 1988), 65, as well as Edward Peragallo, *Origin and Evolution of Double Entry Bookkeeping: A Study of Italian Practice from the Fourteenth Century* (New York: 1938); Raymond de Roover, "The Development of Accounting Prior to Luca Pacioli According to the Account Books of Medieval Merchants," in *Studies in the History of Accounting,* ed. Ananias C. Littleton and B. S. Yamey (Homewood, IL: Richard D. Irwin, 1956), 115–39. Although the precise date of the first use of double-entry bookkeeping and where it took place are unknown, de Roover is emphatic that "double-entry book-keeping originated in Italy between 1250 and 1350" (139).

10. This passage from the *Legenda maior* of St. Bonaventure is given in Alastair Smart, *The Assisi Problem and the Art of Giotto* (Oxford: Clarendon, 1971), 286.

11. Bernard McGinn, *The Calabrian Abbot Joachim of Fiore in the History of Western Thought* (New York: Macmillan, 1985), 113.

12. On the "Francis as Christ" theme, see Henk van Os, "St. Francis of Assisi as a Second Christ in Early Italian Painting," *Simiolus* 7 (1974): 3–20.

13. On this, see Millard Meiss, *Painting in Florence and Siena after the Black Death* (New York: Harper and Row, 1964), esp. 70–73.

14. For St. Bridget, see Anthony Butkovich, *Revelations: Saint Birgitta of Sweden* (Los Angeles: Ecumenical Foundation of America, 1972), and for St. Catherine of Siena, see St. Catherine of Siena (Caterina Benincasa), *Saint Catherine of Siena as Seen in Her Letters,* trans. and ed. Vida Scudder (London: J. M. Dent; New York: C. P. Dutton, 1905).

15. On this topic, see Joseph Polzer, "Christ Judge, Saviour, Advocate, Franciscan Devotion, and the Doubting Thomas," in *Essays Presented to Myron P. Gilmore, II: History of Art, History of Music* (Florence: La Nuova Italia, 1978), 301–10. Polzer believes that "this new subject matter documents a new status being given to empirical proof of theological truth. Before the thirteenth century, with its Saint Thomas Aquinas who acknowledged natural philosophy as the harmonious complement of faith, with its Saint Francis who was enraptured by a nature, no longer the container of lust, but the epiphany of God, this equation would have been impossible" (308).

16. Meiss, *Painting in Florence and Siena,* 112.

17. Leon Battista Alberti, *On Painting,* trans. and ed. J. R. Spencer (New Haven and London: Yale University Press), 78.

18. St. Bonaventura, *The Mind's Road to God,* trans. George Boas (Indianapolis: Bobbs-Merrill, 1953), 43–44.

19. The authorship of these frescoes is a point of intense debate. For some of the arguments, see Bruce Cole, *Giotto and Florentine Painting, 1280–1375* (New York: Harper and Row, 1976), 146–60, and Smart, *The Assisi Problem.* Caution encourages an interim attribution to a "St. Francis Master" but, for those who challenge the traditional association with Giotto himself, attention might be given the mysterious Maestro Stefano, mentioned in the Second Commentary of Lorenzo Ghiberti. See Creighton E. Gilbert, *Italian Art, 1400–1500: Sources and Documents* (Evanston: Northwestern University Press, 1992), 78, and, later, in the anonymously written *Codice magliabechiano,* ed. Carl Frey (Berlin: G. Grote'sche, 1892), 54, and again by Giorgio Vasari, *Lives,* 1:94–97. Ghiberti says that this Stefano (to whom no known paintings have been attributed) worked at Assisi and that his murals "are marvelous, and done with great learning." Vasari claims Stefano was a pupil of Giotto and goes so far as to say that "he so far surpassed his master himself that he was deservedly considered the best of the painters up to that time as his works clearly prove" (94). Supposedly, Maestro Stefano's son was the painter Giottino.

20. Samuel Y. Edgerton, *The Renaissance Rediscovery of Linear Perspective* (1975; reprint, New York, Evanston, San Francisco, and London: Harper and Row, 1976), 16–18.

21. The comparison I am using here was also noted by Edgerton and published by him in "Florentine Interest in Ptolemaic Cartography as Background for Renaissance Painting," *Journal of the Society of Architectural Historians* 33 (December 1974): 276–77.

22. See further discussion of this Renaissance view of Florence in chapter 5 and commentary on its execution and impact in chapter 5, note 27. Another striking contrast between the medieval way of seeing and that demanded by the new and unifying mind of the Renaissance can be found in how the city of Rome was to be represented. In a drawing dated 1433 and now preserved in New York's Metropolitan Museum of Art, the distinctive topography of the papal city is conveyed through a series of monuments recognizable to the

pilgrim. Although somewhat more accurate in its arrangement of the buildings of Rome than the emblematic portrayal of Florence executed eight decades earlier, it still belongs to the medieval tradition of assembling architectural components into an impression rather than re-creating an accurate, site-specific, and spatially related reconstruction of a unified reality. Only a few years later, such an old-fashioned recollection of Roman monuments was not sufficient for Alberti, who carefully prepared a measured map of the city—the first such attempt at coherent mapmaking since the days of the geographer Ptolemy. Alberti's map of Rome was part of his *Descriptio urbis Roma* of ca. 1443, no longer extant. It was, evidently, a milestone of topographical study. For this contribution of Alberti to the development of cartography, see especially Edgerton, *Linear Perspective,* 115–18, and Charles Burroughs, "Alberti and Rome," in *Leon Battista Alberti,* ed. Joseph Rykwert and Anne Engel (Milan: Olivetti/Electa, 1994), 134–57.

23. The sculptural fragments from the Capuan gateway are conserved in the Museo Campano in Capua. Related to them is the royal portrait head (either of Frederick II or his son Manfred) in the Berlin Museum. Indicative of the revivalist spirit in the air and akin to these obvious attempts to imitate the ancient manner are the Visitation figures from the west front of Rheims Cathedral in France, with features that also must be derived from actual appreciative study of ancient sculptures.

24. A certain measure of inconsistency is apparent in the execution of the Brancacci Chapel. This is due to the fact that three artists actually were involved in the task. The third participant (Filippino Lippi) was accidentally involved, brought in to complete the project after work on it had been suspended. Masolino and Masaccio were a team from the beginning and, although approaching the assignment from divergent stylistic positions, produced, all things considered, a remarkably harmonious result. This was, in part, due to the fact that instead of each assuming a responsibility for an entire wall (which only would have drawn attention to their differences), they alternated their responsibilities, not only horizontally but vertically as well.

25. Cennino d'Andrea Cennini, *Il Libro dell'Arte: The Craftsman's Handbook,* trans. Daniel V. Thompson Jr. (New Haven: Yale University Press, 1936), 5–6. On Cennini's use of sfumato, see Hellmut Wohl, *The Aesthetics of Italian Renaissance Art: A Reconsideration of Style* (Cambridge: Cambridge University Press, 1999), 78.

26. Leonardo Bruni, *Laudatio Florentinae urbis* (1404), as quoted in Hans Baron, *The Crisis of the Early Renaissance,* 2nd ed., rev. (Princeton: Princeton University Press, 1966), 207, and in Edgerton, *Linear Perspective,* 36. Bruni was representative of the stoical/Ciceronian/Aristotelian brand of philosophy that typified the Florentine school of rhetorical humanism during the first half of the quattrocento. In many respects this approach was at variance with the Aristotelian scholasticism upon which late medieval theology was grounded. The second generation of Florentine philosophers, inspired by a new wave of Greek émigrés and whose Florentine pupils were best represented by Marsilio Ficino, turned in the direction of Neoplatonism through which they sought an accommodation with traditional Christianity (see chap. 3, this vol.). For a more complete, yet succinct, historical synopsis of the philosophic positions of the early Renaissance, consult George Holmes, *The Florentine Enlightenment, 1400–1450* (London: Weidenfield and Nicholson, 1969).

27. From Bruni's *Laudatio,* as quoted in Baron, *Crisis,* 207.

28. As given in Baron, *Crisis,* 200–201. Bruni's description of Florence as the center of a series of concentric rings of walls, suburbs, villas, and dependent communities is derived

in its origins from a description of the legendary lost Atlantis imagined by Plato in his *Critias.* The inspiration for Bruni's ekphrastic eloquence came from his instruction in rhetoric under Manuel Chrysoloras in the Florentine studio. See Christine Smith, *Architecture in the Culture of Early Humanism: Ethics, Aesthetics, and Eloquence, 1400–1470* (Oxford: Oxford University Press, 1992), 177, and Benjamin B. Kohl and Roland G. Witt with Elizabeth B. Welles, eds., *The Earthly Republic: Italian Humanists in Government and Society* (Philadelphia: University of Pennsylvania Press, 1978), 141. Coluccio Salutati came to the same geometric conclusions about Florence when he also lauded the circular plan of the city, radiating out from the Duomo and the Palazzo Vecchio and reaching past its churches and monasteries to the hillside villas beyond its encircling walls. He, too, saw in the configuration of Florence a mirror of its social harmony. See Bram Kempers, *Painting, Power, and Patronage: The Rise of the Professional Artist in the Italian Renaissance* (London: Allen Lane/Penguin, 1992), 212.

29. John Shearman, "Masaccio's *Pisa Altar-piece:* An Alternative Reconstruction," *Burlington Magazine* 108 (1966): 449–55.

30. Holt, *Documentary,* 1:285.

31. Edgerton, "Ptolemaic Cartography." A rather different interpretation regarding the role Brunelleschi might have played in the formative stages of the Renaissance has been presented in Howard Saalman's biography of the architect. But one should not disregard the way in which Brunelleschi was viewed in his own day. Filarete, for instance, extolled Brunelleschi's contribution by saying, "I bless the soul of Filippo di Ser Brunellesco, Florentine citizen, famous and worthy architect and subtle imitator of Daedalus. He has revived in our city of Florence this ancient style of building in such a way that today in churches as in public and private buildings no other style is used" (as presented in Holt, *Documentary,* 1:247). Filarete's praise, of course, also conflicts with my early Christian interpretation of Brunelleschi's inspiration; the fact that he was thought to have revived the "ancient style of building" is what really counts in how we see his role. For Toscanelli, see Gustavo Uzielli, *La vita e tempi di Paolo dal Pozzo Toscanelli* (Rome: Ministerio della pubblica istruzione, 1894), and Paul Lawrence Rose, *The Italian Renaissance of Mathematics: Studies on Humanists and Mathematicians from Petrarch to Galileo* (Geneva: Librairie Droz, 1975), 29–31.

32. Edgerton, "Ptolemaic Cartography," 275.

33. Edgerton, "Ptolemaic Cartography," 275.

34. Edgerton, "Ptolemaic Cartography," 285.

35. A discussion of the several possible systems Brunelleschi might have employed in designing the facade of the Innocenti can be found in Charles R. Mack, "Brunelleschi's Hospital of the Innocents: Of Proportions and Intentional Fallacies," *Studies in Iconography* 5 (1979): 31–44.

36. Charles R. Mack, "Brunelleschi's Spedale degli Innocenti Rearticulated," *Architectura* 11, no. 2 (1981): 60–69.

37. Holt, *Documentary,* 1:282.

38. The passage from the *Laudatio* is quoted in Smith, *Architecture,* 178. Also see Kohl and Witt, *Earthly Republic,* 141.

39. See chapter 5, this volume, for a further discussion of the Florentine tax system and how it might be viewed as part of the overall context of the Renaissance.

40. Robert Zwijnenberg, *The Writings and Drawings of Leonardo da Vinci: Order and Chaos in Early Modern Thought,* trans. Caroline A. van Eck (Cambridge, New York, and

Melbourne: Cambridge University Press, 1999), 110–11. As Zwijnenberg points out, Leonardo actually utilized both systems in his creative process—thereby melding the particular with the encompassing, the medieval with the Renaissance.

CHAPTER 3

1. Voltaire's disparagement comes from his *Essay on Universal History,* as quoted in Hay, *Debate,* 13. See chapter 1 for Ruskin's views on the Renaissance.

2. From Charles Homer Haskins, *Renaissance of the Twelfth Century* (Cambridge, MA: Harvard University Press, 1927), as quoted in Hay, *Debate,* 78.

3. Haskins, as quoted in Hay, *Debate,* 79.

4. Haskins, as quoted in Hay, *Debate,* 80. See also R. L. Benson, G. Constable, and C. D. Lanham, eds., *Renaissance and Renewal in the Twelfth Century* (Cambridge, MA: Clarendon, 1982).

5. Haskins, as quoted in Hay, *Debate,* 80.

6. From Lynn Thorndike, "Renaissance or Prenaissance?" *Journal of the History of Ideas* 4 (1945): 65–74, as given in Hay, *Debate,* 90. Such uniformity was, however, not applied uniformly. The renovation project undertaken by Pope Pius II at Pienza is a case in point. On this see especially Christine Smith, *Architecture in the Culture of Early Humanism: Ethic, Aesthetics, and Eloquence, 1400–1470* (Oxford: Oxford University Press, 1992), 98–126.

7. As given in Stephens, *Origins,* 86.

8. On Jeanne d'Evreaux's book of hours, see Richard Randall, "Frog in the Middle," *Metropolitan Museum of Art Bulletin* 16 (1958): 269–75, and Kathleen Morand, *Jean Pucelle* (Oxford: Clarendon, 1962).

9. On this see Paul Oskar Kristeller, *Renaissance Thought: The Classic, Scholastic, and Humanist Strains* (New York: Harper and Row, 1965), 8–20, 110–11, 120–24; his "The Classics and Renaissance Thought," as presented in Hay, *Debate,* 108; and the informative treatment given in Liana De Girolami Cheney, *Quattrocento Neoplatonism and Medici Humanism in Botticelli's Mythological Paintings* (Lanham, MD: University Press of America, 1995), 12–13. Also see A. Campana, "The Origin of the Word Humanist," *Journal of the Courtauld and Warburg Institutes* 9 (1960): 60. While classical texts were rediscovered or reappreciated with the coming of the Renaissance, how they were utilized was often conditioned by the presence of medieval precedent. A case in point is the emphasis upon the moralizing value that could be attached to pagan subject matter.

10. The earlier humanists had concentrated upon Latin-based scholarship to which they, later, added a competency in Greek. They ignored and even disdained exercises in speculative philosophy. This, they felt, lay in the purview of the Scholastics. Only after midcentury did the philosophical disciplines make inroads with the Florentine humanists, thereby indicating a conjunction of secular and theological learning (yet another example of Renaissance fusion). See Arthur Field, *The Origins of the Platonic Academy of Florence* (Princeton: Princeton University Press, 1988), 64–66.

11. Holt, *Documentary,* 1:248.

12. Holt, *Documentary,* 1:248.

13. For a discussion of the Studio, see Jonathan Davies, *Florence and Its University during the Early Renaissance* (Leiden and Boston: Brill, 1998). Certainly the Florentine Studio

never did acquire the academic prominence of the universities of Bologna or Padua or Pisa. Cheney (*Botticelli,* 13) points out, however, that it was only in Florence that one could find a curriculum in Greek. Curiously, despite the universalism sweeping the era, the universities themselves lost much of their dynamic. It should be noted, to the discomfort of those of us dependent upon the scholastic environment, that the intellectual life of Florence functioned admirably throughout the Renaissance without the benefit of having a major university of its own.

14. On this, see Field, *Origins,* 109–10.

15. As reported in 1492 by the Vatican librarian and chancery official Paolo Cortese and given in Smith, *Architecture,* 134.

16. Smith, *Architecture,* 135.

17. See Smith, *Architecture,* 143.

18. Michael Baxandall, *Giotto and the Orators: Humanist Observers of Painting in Italy and the Discovery of Pictorial Composition* (Oxford: Clarendon, 1971), 26, and Smith, *Architecture,* 144. Such a correlation between the visual and literary arts was echoed, of course, in the passage from Antonio Filarete's treatise quoted earlier in this chapter.

19. Smith, *Architecture,* 145.

20. The home-based conversations of the Renaissance humanists or the later salons of eighteenth- and nineteenth-century European society have now been replaced by the online chatroom.

21. As discussed in Smith, *Architecture,* 179.

22. On Michelozzo's curious melding of architectural languages, see Howard Saalman, "The Palazzo Comunale in Montepulciano: An Unknown Work by Michelozzo," *Zeitschrift für Kunstgeschichte* 28 (1965): 6–10. Alberti's reputation for architectural purity is attested to by Pope Pius, whose sole mention of him in his *Memoirs of a Renaissance Pope: The Commentaries of Pius II,* trans. Florence A. Gragg, ed. Leona C. Gabel (New York: Capricorn, 1959), 316, is as "a scholar and a very clever archaeologist." For a thoroughgoing treatment of Alberti's life and career, see Anthony Grafton, *Leon Battista Alberti: Master Builder of the Italian Renaissance* (New York: Hill and Wang, 2000) and the review of this book by Alina Payne in the *Art Bulletin* 85 (June 2003): 387–90.

23. Smith, *Architecture,* 126.

24. Smith, *Architecture,* 126. This explanation of changes in standards would seem to have a modern parallel in the debate between formalist and contextualist art historians.

25. Smith, *Architecture,* 126. On the nature of Renaissance Neoplatonism, see James Hankins, *Plato in the Renaissance,* 2 vols. (New York: Columbia University Press, 1990).

26. The turning point from Aristotelian humanism to that oriented toward Neoplatonism may have come with the arrival of the Greek scholars accompanying Byzantine emperor John III Paleologus and the Orthodox patriarch to the reconciliation council held in Florence in 1439. The Greek contingent was dominated by Platonists, chief among them Giorgios Gemistos Plethon, who remained behind for a time after the entourage had left, long enough to have had a strong impact upon Cosimo de' Medici. Also among that group was Argyropoulos, who obtained a position at the university and took up permanent residency in Florence in 1456 following the fall of Constantinople.

27. Field, *Origins,* 112–13. The medieval tendency had been to separate and even oppose Aristotle and Plato. The discovery of new texts and the more critical analysis of the actual positions of the two philosophers (encouraged by Byzantine scholarship) argued against this traditional polarization and tended to view the ancient teachers in a more rec-

oncilable fashion, seeing them as utilizing different approaches toward a common end. On this philosophical transformation, see Field, *Origins,* 138.

28. It was, of course, this sense of philosophical unity that Raphael was to represent in his fresco in the Vatican apartments known as *The School of Athens,* which we have come to see as a visual demonstration of the spirit of the High Renaissance.

29. Late in life it is not uncommon for those who have concentrated their interests upon the accumulation of wealth to refocus their attention upon the Hereafter. And so, it would seem, it was with Cosimo de' Medici, but instead of renouncing the world of the flesh in favor of a purely Christian affirmation of faith, he gravitated toward a classically inspired philosophical transition. Cosimo, through his protégé, Marsilio Ficino, replaced an Aristotelian interest with a Platonic one. For arguments against the significance of Florence's Neoplatonic Academy, see James Hankins, "Cosimo de' Medici and the Platonic Academy," *Journal of the Warburg and Courtauld Institutes* 53 (1990): 144–62, and his "The Myth of the Platonic Academy of Florence," *Renaissance Quarterly* 45 (1992): 549–53.

30. As presented in Field, *Origins,* 165–67.

31. Field, *Origins,* 170. Once again, Raphael's *Stanza della Segnatura* with the facing murals of the *Disputa* and the *School of Athens* comes to mind.

32. Field, *Origins,* 194.

33. Field, *Origins,* 203.

34. Field, *Origins,* 219–20.

35. Field, *Origins,* 231.

36. A good explanation of Ficino's philosophic position is found in chapter 9 of the second volume of Charles Edward Trinkhaus, *In Our Image and Likeness: Humanity and Divinity in Italian Humanist Thought* (London: Constable, 1970).

37. Field, *Origins,* 198.

38. Field, *Origins,* 86.

39. On this see Poggio Bracciolini, *Two Renaissance Book Hunters: The Letters of Poggius Bracciolini to Nicholaus de Niccolis,* trans. and ed. Phyllis Gordon (New York: Columbia University Press, 1974).

40. On the antiquarian pursuits of Petrarch's friends, see Roberto Weiss, *The Renaissance Discovery of Classical Antiquity* (Oxford: Basel Blackwell, 1969), 49, 51–53.

41. For the survival of Vitruvius's text, see chapter 4, note 66.

42. Poggio Bracciolini, *Two Renaissance Book Hunters: The Letters of Poggius Bracciolini to Nicholaus de Niccolis,* trans. and ed. Phyllis Gordon (New York: Columbia University Press, 1974), 118. For a consideration of the typology of Renaissance villas in the Tuscan region see especially Amanda Lillie, "The Humanist Villa Revisited," in *Languages and Images of Renaissance Italy,* ed. Alison Brown (Oxford: Clarendon, 1995), 193–215.

43. Vespasiano da Bisticci, *Renaissance Princes, Popes, and Prelates: The Vespasiano Memoirs. Lives of Illustrious Men of the Fifteenth Century,* intro. Myron Gilmore, trans. William George and Emily Waters (New York, Evanston, IL, and London: Harper and Row, 1963), 401.

44. Vespasiano, *Lives,* 199.

45. Vespasiano, *Lives,* 397.

46. Vespasiano, *Lives,* 401.

47. Vespasiano, *Lives,* 399. Niccolò's "sedentary" approach to geographical investigation seems to retain a medieval flavoring akin to the medical doctors who still practiced

according to the traditions of Galen rather than through actual observation and experimentation.

48. Poggio Bracciolini, *Book Hunters,* 49. A more insistent questioning of the humanist movement was raised by the Dominican monk Giovanni Dominici, whose *Lucula Noctis,* written at the dawn of the fifteenth century, challenged the pagan intrusion into the Christian tradition. See Holmes, *Enlightenment,* 31–33.

49. John Pope-Hennessy, *Italian Renaissance Sculpture* (New York: Random House, 1985), 1.

50. The fact that certain members within the Florentine intelligentsia were aware of the cultural *rinascita* (at least in certain respects) does not mean that they could have made stylistic distinctions between a "Gothic" Gentile da Fabriano and a "Renaissance" Andrea del Castagno, much less between a Masolino and a Masaccio. They were too close to the problem; the terms *Gothic* and *Renaissance* were not yet so clearly defined in respect to the visual arts, and such stylistic niceties were not yet understood. The professional art historian had yet to be invented.

51. In designing San Lorenzo, Brunelleschi may well have emulated (in a more enlarged and modernized form) the architectural language of the older church it replaced. That building, in turn, may have reflected the late antique/early Christian design of the celebrated basilica of San Lorenzo fuori le Mura in Rome.

52. One does wonder, however, if he had analyzed the dome of the Pantheon in sufficient detail to realize that it had been constructed in separate wedges and not as a whole, wedges that were held together by internal horizontal arches and the stepped rings of the exterior. Perhaps he applied an adaptation of these structural lessons to his solution for the cupola of the Florentine Cathedral with its sectional construction, cross ribs, and wooden chain girdle. Could his speculations at the Roman Pantheon even have produced his scheme of movable construction platforms that proved so essential in the construction of the cupola?

53. For this, see Smith, *Architecture,* 65.

54. *Aeneas Silvius Piccolomini (Pius II), Selected Letters of Aeneas Silvius Piccolomini,* trans. and ed. Albert R. Baca, San Fernando Valley State College Renaissance Editions 2 (Northridge, CA: San Fernando State College, 1969), 43. Pope Pius's own names, both given and chosen, were an exercise in Early Renaissance classicism and symbolism. That he had been given the name of the Virgilian hero by his father was no accident, and that he selected the name "Pius" as his papal designator was no fluke. The Piccolomini family had been exiled from their native Siena just as had the Trojan hero, and the papal name was then chosen less as a memorial to an obscure early pope than a literary conceit combining a papal name with the Virgilian complement of the "pious Aeneas." Once again, Christian traditions (the name of the early pope) combine with the classical (the Virgilian phrase) to produce Pope Pius as the pious Aeneas. In much the same way Cardinal Giuliano della Rovere, upon his election to the papacy, chose to use the latinized version of his given name, recalling not only an earlier pope but also the Roman imperator whose own family (like the della Rovere) had used the oak as their emblem (also connected with the mighty Jupiter and thus a reference to the family's divine origins). On this see Laura A. Voight, "Livia's Garden Room at Prima Porta," unpublished paper presented in Session IIB of the 2003 Meeting of the Southeastern College Art Conference held in Raleigh, North Carolina.

55. As quoted in Field, *Origins,* 251.

56. Seznec, Panofsky, and others have demonstrated how, in order for there to have been a true Renaissance, it was first necessary for the pagan gods to become disengaged from their biblical metamorphoses (Perseus from St. George, Hercules from Samson, etc.). In the same way, it was necessary to the rebirth of ancient philosophy for Aristotle and Plato to become disentangled from their Christian envelope through a strict reading of the original texts in the Studio instructions of John Argyropoulos. Earlier, his Byzantine predecessor in Florence, John Chrysoloras, had introduced a purist approach to the study of classical rhetoric. See Field, *Origins,* 107–26.

57. Robert Zwijnenberg, *The Writings and Drawings of Leonardo da Vinci: Order and Chaos in Early Modern Thought,* trans. Caroline A. van Eck (Cambridge, New York, and Melbourne: Cambridge University Press, 1999), 45.

58. Charles Hope and Elizabeth McGrath, "Artists and Humanists," in *The Cambridge Companion to Renaissance Humanism,* ed. Jill Kraye (Cambridge: Cambridge University Press, 1996), 170, have pointed out that the area of closest cooperation between humanists and painters lay in the area of iconography. "In a more general way, humanist ideals, and in particular devotion to classical precedent, played a fundamental part in the gradual transformation of art from an almost exclusive involvement with the production of religious imagery into an activity embracing portraiture, secular history, classical mythology, and allegory."

59. On Botticelli's *Lama Adoration,* see Rab Hatfield, *Botticelli's "Uffizi Adoration": A Study in Pictorial Content* (Princeton: Princeton University Press, 1976).

60. On these issues, see Denys Hay, *The Italian Renaissance in Its Historical Background,* 126–28, and the discussion presented in Evelyn Welch, *Art and Society in Italy, 1350–1500* (Oxford and New York: Oxford University Press, 1997), 277–80, as well as Hans Baron, "Franciscan Poverty and Civic Wealth as Factors in the Rise of Humanistic Thought," *Speculum* 13 (1938): 1–37.

61. Field, *Origins,* 25.

62. As quoted in Anthony Grafton, *Leon Battista Alberti: Master Builder of the Italian Renaissance* (New York: Hill and Wang, 2000), 59–60.

63. Rucellai's memoirs have been published as *Il Zibaldone Quaresimile.* Viewpoints concerning the palace's dates of construction and its architect vary; on these see Charles R. Mack, "The Rucellai Palace: Some New Proposals," *Art Bulletin* 56 (December 1974): 517–29; Kurt Forster, "Discussion: The Palazzo Rucellai and Questions of Typology in the Development of Renaissance Buildings," *Art Bulletin* 58 (March 1976): 109–13; Brenda Preyer, "The Rucellai Palace," in *Giovanni Rucellai ed il suo Zibaldone, II: A Florentine Patrician and His Palace,* ed. F. W. Kent, A. Perosa, B. Preyer, P. Sanpaolesi, and R. Salvini (London: University of London, 1981), 155–225; Howard Saalman, "Review of *Giovanni Rucellai ed il suo Zibaldone,*" *Journal of the Society of Architectural Historians* 47 (1988): 82–90; and Marvin Trachtdenberg, who revisits the debate in his "Review Essay: Renaissance Stories," *Journal of the Society of Architectural Historians* 59 (2000): 383.

64. Franco Borsi, *Leon Battista Alberti* (Milan: Electa Editrice, 1975), 59.

65. See Hans Baron's essay "Cicero and the Roman Civic Spirit in the Middle Ages and Early Renaissance," first published in the *Bulletin of the John Rylands Library* 22 (1938) and excerpted in Hay, *Debate,* 102.

66. Baron as given in Hay, *Debate,* 102.

67. Marsilio Ficino, *Opera Omnia* (Turin: Bottega d'Erasmo, 1959), 22–23.

68. Such an analogy had been made during the Middle Ages, of course. St. Bonaventura had called man a microcosm. See his book *The Mind's Road to God,* trans. George Boas (Indianapolis: Bobbs-Merrill, 1953), 15. Both the interpretation and the implication to be drawn from the correlation were quite different. For the distinctly different interpretation of man's role in the Middle Ages, see the interesting commentary in Zwijnenberg, *Leonardo,* 104.

69. This overwhelming passion for unity is to be found, for instance, in Pico della Mirandola's acceptance of cabalistic literature: "When I had read them through with the greatest diligence and with unwearying toil, I saw in them (as God is my witness) not so much the Mosaic as the Christian religion. . . . But in those parts which concern philosophy you really seem to hear Pythagoras and Plato, whose principles are so closely related to the Christian faith. . . . Taken altogether, there is absolutely no controversy between ourselves and the Hebrews on any matter." Pico della Mirandola, "On the Dignity of Man," in *The Renaissance Philosophy of Man,* ed. Ernst Cassirer, Paul Oskar Kristeller, and John Herman Randall Jr. (Chicago and London: University of Chicago Press, 1948), 252.

70. For a discussion of Renaissance mathematics and their impact upon the arts, see Mark A. Petersen, "The Geometry of Piero della Francesca," *Mathematical Intelligencer* 19, no. 3 (1997): 33–40.

71. Pico's praise of numbers is found in his *Conclusiones Nongentae,* as quoted in Paul Lawrence Rose, *The Italian Renaissance of Mathematics: Studies on Humanists and Mathematicians from Petrarch to Galileo* (Geneva: Librairie Droz, 1975), 9. Much the same belief in the power of a divine reckoning was argued, ca. 1450, by the character "Idiota" in Nicholas of Cusa's play of the same name. Idiota claims that the ability to measure was God's greatest gift to humanity and that the essence of the celestial knowledge might be found in the units of measurement and in the harmonies of geometric proportions. On this, see Samuel Y. Edgerton, *The Renaissance Rediscovery of Linear Perspective* (1975; reprint, New York, Evanston, San Francisco, and London: Harper and Row Icon Editions, 1976), 36–37.

72. A progression toward a mathematical solution to the spiritual problems of life is precisely the argument also followed in Alberti's treatise on the *Tranquility of the Soul.* See Smith, *Architecture,* 15.

73. In chapter 1 of book 3 of his treatise on architectural practice and design, Vitruvius describes the human-based symmetry fundamental to the architectural practice of the Greeks:

> In the human body the central point is naturally the navel. For if a man be placed flat on his back, with his hands and feet extended, and a pair of compasses centered at his navel, the fingers and toes of his two hands and feet will touch the circumference of a circle described therefrom. And just as the human body yields a circular outline, so too a square figure may be found from it. For if we measure the distance from the soles of the feet to the top of the head, and then apply that measure to the outstretched arms, the breadth will be found to be the same as the height.

The Roman architect goes on to note that "since nature has designed the human body so that its members are duly proportioned to the frame as a whole, it appears that the ancients had good reasons for their rule, that in perfect buildings the different members must be in exact, symmetrical relations to the whole general scheme." See Vitruvius, *Ten Books on*

Architecture, trans. Morris Hicky Morgan (Cambridge: Harvard University Press, 1914), 73.

74. As given in Cassirer, *The Renaissance Philosophy of Man,* 123.

75. A number of these ideas are explored by Charles Carman in the third chapter of his *Images of Human Ideals in Italian Renaissance Art,* Studies in Art History 2 (Lewiston, Queenston, and Lampeter: Edwin Mellen Press, 2000), 69–90, which is entitled "Leonardo's Vitruvian Man: A Renaissance Microcosm."

76. This also is the conclusion of Charles Carman (*Images,* 132), who speaks of "that emblem of mankind . . . who has moved himself to reach the circle of divinity while still framed within the square of earthliness." It might be pointed out that it seems a misnomer to call Leonardo a humanist. In his understanding of man, he seems to stand apart from the other Renaissance personalities. Despite his memorable illustration of Vitruvius, Leonardo's world is not homocentric. Leonardo is much more the naturalist, and he appears to regard man as a part of the universal system.

77. Levey, *Early Renaissance,* 121–22.

78. Cassirer, Paul Oskar Kristeller, and John Herman Randall Jr., eds., *The Renaissance Philosophy of Man,* 224–25. Pico's fascination with the Jewish mystery texts, the *Cabala,* had as its ultimate goal a reconciliation of Judaic and Christian beliefs in much the same way as the revival and reintroduction of Platonism was aimed at a merger of Greco-Roman concepts with Christian doctrine.

79. The harmonizing mandate given to the artist is enunciated in Marsilio Ficino's discussion of the doctrine of love. According to Ernst Cassirer, *The Individual and the Cosmos in Renaissance Philosophy,* trans. Mario Domandi (Philadelphia: University of Pennsylvania Press, 1972), 135: "The theodicy of the world given by Ficino in his doctrine of Eros had . . . become the true theodicy of art. For the task of the artist, precisely like that of Eros, is always to join together things that are separate and opposed."

80. As quoted in Holt, *Documentary,* 1:137.

81. Holt, *Documentary,* 1:137–38. For a general discussion of the relationship of art to rhetoric see Stephens, *Origins,* 89–91.

82. Hope and McGrath, "Artists and Humanists," 161, list four principal cross-influences between Renaissance artists and humanists at work: (1) humanist ideals could have influenced artists to emulate the antique; (2) artists could have made humanists aware of ancient art and aesthetics; (3) humanists might have introduced new, classically based standards for the discussion and criticism of the arts; and (4) humanists could have been involved in artistic production. See also "The Influence of Humanistic Ideas," in Stephens, *Origins,* 88–102, for a further discussion of the relation of the artist to the poet and the revival of creativity as an artistic virtue.

83. Leon Battista Alberti, *On Painting,* trans. and ed. John R. Spencer (New Haven and London: Yale University Press), 91.

84. Alberti's advice (*On Painting,* 81) to painters may also have inspired Botticelli's handling of the draperies in both the *Primavera* and the *Arrival of Venus:*

> As I have noted, movements should be moderated and sweet. They should appear graceful to the observer rather than a marvel of study. However, where we should like to find movement in the draperies, cloth is by nature heavy and falls to the earth. For this reason it would be well to place in the picture the face of the wind Zephyrus or Austrus who blows from the clouds making the draperies move in the wind. Thus you will see with what grace the bodies, where they are struck by the

wind, show the nude under the draperies in suitable parts. In other parts the draperies blown by the wind fly gracefully through the air.

85. Alberti, *On Painting,* 91.

86. As quoted in Holt, *Documentary,* 1:215–16. In this desire, Alberti echoes the advice of Vitruvius concerning the education of the architect: "Let him be educated, skillful with the pencil, instructed in geometry, know much history, and have followed the philosophers with attention." Vitruvius, *The Ten Books,* 5.

87. From book 3 of Alberti's *On Painting,* as given in Holt, *Documentary,* 1:216. For Pamphilus, see J. J. Pollitt, *The Art of Greece, 1400–31 B.C.* (Englewood Cliffs, NJ: Prentice-Hall, 1965), 162–63.

88. Holt, *Documentary,* 1:277–78. At the same instant, Leonardo also claimed for painting an equivalency with philosophy. Leonardo, of course, had Plutarch in mind, who, in turn, quoted Simonides' comment about painting being mute poetry and poetry being verbalized poetry. On this see Vernon Hyde Minor, *Art History's History,* 2nd ed., rev. (Upper Saddle River, NJ: Prentice-Hall, 2001), 39.

CHAPTER 4

1. Erwin Panofsky, "Artist, Scientist, Genius: Notes on the 'Renaissance Dämmerung,'" in *The Renaissance: A Symposium, 1952* (New York: Metropolitan Museum of Art, 1953), 90.

2. Christine Smith, *Architecture in the Culture of Early Humanism: Ethics, Aesthetics, and Eloquence, 1400–1470* (Oxford: Oxford University Press, 1992), 136.

3. Sometime in the early 1300s, the Florentine Guild of Doctors and Apothecaries opened its roles to painters, who also ground their pigments in the same way that the medical professionals prepared their herbs. In 1339, the painters founded their own quasi-official association, the Confraternity of St Luke; guild membership, however, continued to remain obligatory.

4. From book 2 of Leon Battista Alberti, *On Painting,* trans. and ed. John R. Spencer (New Haven and London: Yale University Press), 64.

5. As given in Robert Zwijnenberg, *The Writings and Drawings of Leonardo da Vinci: Order and Chaos in Early Modern Thought,* trans. Caroline A. van Eck (Cambridge, New York, and Melbourne: Cambridge University Press, 1999), 71.

6. Alberti, *On Painting,* 40.

7. This story is recounted in the *Commentaries* of Lorenzo Ghiberti and given in Holt, *Documentary,* 1:165–66.

8. On this see the comments in Stephens, *Origins,* 271ff. Although Renaissance reason shed increasing light upon the darker superstitions of the Middle Ages, it did not erase the dark side in its entirety. One is reminded of later witch-hunts and of that wonderfully evocative tale of the supernatural recounted by Benvenuto Cellini, who, with a priest as his medium, conjured up the host of Hades in the arena of the Roman Colosseum. For this see his *Life of Benvenuto Cellini,* trans. Anne MacDonell (London: J. M. Dent; New York: E. P. Dutton, 1926), 98–101. See also André Chastel, *Myth of the Renaissance* (Geneva: Skira, 1969).

9. John R. Spencer, "Volterra, 1466," *Art Bulletin* 48 (1966), 96.

10. Possible evidence of a knowledge or, at least, a recognition of Etruscan art can be found as far back as the days of Giotto. The character of that great master has been tarnished by the suspicion of anti-Semitism, a charge largely based upon the "stereotypical" ethnic features he has given to the face of Judas in the frescoed scene in the Scrovegni (Arena) Chapel illustrating that fallen apostle's pact to betray Jesus. Such features, however, are also to be found on painted and terracotta representations of the demonic deities of the Etruscan underworld, Charun and Tuchulcha. With their pointed beards and prominent hook noses, the type seems a plausible source for the physiognomy of Giotto's Judas as well as for the ancestral prototypes for the Christian conception of Satan. Could Giotto have seen such an Etruscan example and have used it for his Judas, thereby emphasizing his diabolic metamorphosis? For some examples of the Etruscan deities, see Nigel Spivey, *Etruscan Art* (London: Thames and Hudson, 1997), 162–67.

11. George Holmes, *The Florentine Enlightenment, 1400–1450* (London: Weidenfield and Nicholson, 1969), 20, and L. Bertalot, "Cincius Romanus und seine Briefe," *Quellen und Forschungen aus Italiensichen Archiven und Bibliotheken* 21 (1929–30): 224–25.

12. Smith, *Architecture,* 203.

13. For information on the survival of antique sculptures and how they were appreciated during the Renaissance, see Charles R. Mack, "Botticelli's *Venus:* Antique Allusions and Medicean Propaganda," *Explorations in Renaissance Culture* 28 (2002): 230, n. 24, as well as Phyllis Pray Bober and Ruth Olitsky Rubenstein, *The Renaissance Artist and Antique Sculpture: A Handbook of Sources* (New York and London: Harvey Miller/Oxford University Press, 1986).

14. Holmes, *Enlightenment,* 22.

15. See, for instance, the comments made in 1444 by Alberto Averardo de' Alberti, who wrote Giovanni de' Medici from Rome that "there are many splendid palaces, houses, tombs, and temples, and other edifices in infinite number, but all are in ruins; much porphyry and marble from ancient buildings, and every day these marbles are destroyed by being burnt for lime in scandalous fashion." Janet Ross, *Lives of the Early Medici as Told in Their Correspondence* (London: Chatto, 1910), 47.

16. Poggio Bracciolini, *Two Renaissance Book Hunters: The Letters of Poggius Bracciolini to Nicholaus de Niccols,* trans. and ed. Phyllia Gordon (New York: Columbia University Press, 1974), 114.

17. Ruth Rubinstein, "Pius II and Roman Ruins," *Renaissance,* II, The Society for Renaissance Studies (Oxford: Oxford University Press, 1988), 2:199.

18. Rubinstein, "Pius II and Roman Ruins," 199.

19. Holmes, *Enlightenment,* 191–92. Apparently, judging by Pope Pius's later actions, Pope Eugenius's efforts in regard to the pillaging of the Colosseum had little success. That the monuments of ancient Rome continued to have a precarious existence is attested to in Raphael's famous report of 1518–19 to Pope Leo X on the antiquities of Rome. In it Raphael chides Leo's predecessors by noting that they "have demolished the ancient temples, statues, triumphal arches, and other magnificent buildings! . . . How many have reduced ancient pillars and marble ornaments to lime! The new Rome, which we now see standing in all its beauty and grandeur, adorned with palace, churches, and other buildings, is built throughout with the lime obtained in this way from ancient marbles," as quoted in Hans Baron, *The Crisis of the Early Renaissance,* 2nd rev. ed. (Princeton: Princeton University Press, 1966), 313. Clearly the Renaissance approach to the monumental presence of antiq-

uity was inconsistent and often lacking in archaeological focus. The appreciation for the ancient past was more likely to express itself in emulation than in conservation.

20. Rubinstein, "Pius II and Roman Ruins," 198.

21. Peter Holliday, "Time, History, and Ritual on the Ara Pacis Augustae," *Art Bulletin* 72 (1990): 542–44.

22. Pienza receives further attention in the following chapter. On the transformation of Pope Pius's birthplace, see Charles R. Mack, *Pienza: The Creation of a Renaissance City* (Ithaca and London: Cornell University Press, 1987), and the pope's own description given in his journal, Aeneas Silvius Piccolomini, *Memoirs of a Renaissance Pope: The Commentaries of Pius II,* trans. Florence A. Gragg and ed. Phyllis C. Gabel (New York: Capricorn, 1959), esp. 102, 282–92. On other aspects of the papal renewal of Pienza, also see Nicholas Adams, "The Construction of Pienza (1459–1464) and the Consequences of Renovatio," in *Urban Life in the Renaissance,* ed. Susan Zimmerman and Roland F. E. Weissman (Newark: University of Delaware Press; London and Toronto: Associate University Presses, 1989), 50–79, and the author's "Pienza beyond the Monumental" appearing as a chapter in a forthcoming monograph devoted to Pienza to be published under the sponsorship of the Seaside Pienza Institute for Town Building and Land Stewardship.

23. Pius II, *Memoirs,* 102.

24. Alberti, *On Painting,* 72. In this treatise, Alberti says the art of painting consists of (1) circumscription [draughtsmanship], (2) composition, and (3) the reception of light [coloration and chiaroscuro]. According to Charles Hope and Elizabeth McGrath, "Artists and Humanists," in *The Cambridge Companion to Renaissance Humanism,* ed. Jill Kraye (Cambridge: Cambridge University Press, 1996), 166–67, Alberti "was well aware that composition was a technical term for rhetoric, which referred to the creation of sentences out of their component parts—words and clauses. His extension of the term from individual figures [something already done by Cennini in discussing the elements in a figure] to the combination of figures that made up a story may well be novel; and it is clear too that he was recommending a specific kind of story, in which all the individual elements contributed to an overall effect." Alberti saw in both the arts of rhetoric and painting the unification of the parts into the whole.

25. Alberti, *On Painting,* 73.

26. Michael Baxandall, *Painting and Experience in Fifteenth-Century Italy* (London, Oxford, and New York: Oxford University Press, 1972), 42–43.

27. Vasari, *Lives,* 2:276. The significance of this anecdote is discussed in Phyllis Pray Bober and Ruth Rubinstein, *Handbook,* 31–32.

28. The front of this sarcophagus depicts a battle between Dionysus and Amazons. Said to have been found in 1240 in a field below the Pieve di Santa Maria (now the Cathedral), this work of the second century is now housed in the Museo Diocesano of Cortona. See Bober and Rubinstein, *Handbook,* 180–81. Also see Piero Scapecchi, *Cortona: arte, storia e cultura* (Genoa: Sagep, 1980), 54, and Philancy N. Holder, *Cortona in Context: The History and Architecture of an Italian Hilltown to the Seventeenth Century* (Clarksville, TN: HP Publishing, 1992), 43–44.

29. Alberti, *On Painting,* 73. This relief is perhaps identical to the one on a sarcophagus formerly in the Palazzo Sciarra in Rome (present whereabouts unknown). See Bober and Rubinstein, *Handbook,* 146–48.

30. Alberti, *On Painting,* 74.

31. Given in Hay, *The Italian Renaissance in Its Historical Background,* 11, and W. H. Woodward, *Studies in Education during the Age of the Renaissance, 1400–1600* (Cambridge: Cambridge University Press, 1906), 67.

32. On the discovery of the antique and its use in the Renaissance, consult Leonard Barkan, *Unearthing the Past: Archaeology and Aesthetics in the Making of the Renaissance* (New Haven: Yale University Press, 2000); Bober and Rubinstein, *Handbook;* and Roberto Weiss, *The Renaissance Discovery of Classical Antiquity* (Oxford: Basel Blackwell, 1969).

33. On the origins of the term, see Thorndike, "Renaissance or Prenaissance," *Journal of the History of Ideas* 4 (1943): 67–68.

34. On this, see especially Hugh Ross Williamson, *Lorenzo the Magnificent* (London: Michael Joseph, 1974), 87–91.

35. Michael Levey, *Florence: A Portrait* (Cambridge: Harvard University Press, 1966), 6.

36. Baron, *Crisis,* 193.

37. The phrasing used by Lorenzo il Magnifico is of more than passing interest since it combines the structure of the Latin antique and the Tuscan trecento. On this see Charles Dempsey, *The Portrayal of Love: Botticelli's Primavera and Humanist Culture at the Time of Lorenzo the Magnificent* (Princeton: Princeton University Press, 1992), 161, and the essay by Pierre Francastel, "La fête mythologique au Quattrocento: Expression littéraire et visualisation plastique," in his *Oeuvres II: La réalité figurative: Eléments structurels de la sociologie et de l'art* (Paris: Gonthier, 1965), 229–52.

38. On Alberti's literary fraud, see Anthony Grafton, *Leon Battista Alberti: Master Builder of the Italian Renaissance* (New York: Hill and Wang, 2000), 3–6.

39. On such matters, see Elisabeth MacDougall, *Fountains, Statues, and Flowers: Studies in Italian Gardens of the Sixteenth and Seventeenth Centuries* (Washington, DC: Dumbarton Oaks, 1994), 30.

40. On the history of the *Laocoön,* see Nancy De Grummond's essay in her *Encyclopedia of the History of Classical Archaeology* (Westport, CT: Greenwood Press, 1996), 660–62. See also Bober and Rubinstein, *Handbook,* 152–55.

41. Alberti, *On Painting,* 90–91.

42. The same great Roman ruin also may have inspired the appearance of the Florentine civic loggia, the Loggia della Signoria.

43. Apostolos Athanasakis, *The Homeric Hymns* (Baltimore and London: Johns Hopkins University Press, 1976), 55. Popularly called the *Nascita di Venere* or *The Birth of Venus,* the painting actually depicts the goddess's arrival on human shores.

44. I discussed this topic in a paper presented at the Fourth International Congress on Fifteenth-Century Studies held in Antwerp in July 2000, which, in expanded form, was published as "Botticelli's *Venus:* Antique Allusions and Medicean Propaganda," in *Explorations in Renaissance Culture* 28 (2002): 207–37.

45. J. J. Pollitt, *The Art of Greece, 1400–31 BC: Source and Documents* (Englewood Cliffs, NJ: Prentice-Hall, 1965), 165–66.

46. Pollitt, *Greece,* 166.

47. Pollitt, *Greece,* 167.

48. Creighton Gilbert, *Italian Art, 1400–1500: Sources and Documents* (Englewood Cliffs, NJ: Prentice-Hall, 1992), 93.

49. Bram Kempers, *Painting, Power, and Patronage: The Rise of the Professional Artist*

in the Italian Renaissance (London: Allen Lane/Penguin, 1992), 205, who quotes Lorenzo's testimony that "I was received with great show of respect and came away with two statues, one of Augustus and the other of Agrippa, which the pope presented to me as gifts." The tradition of a Roman foundation of Florence had been given added authority by Poliziano, who claimed to have found historical documentation for that event. On this, see Eve Borsook and J. Offerhaus, *Francesco Sassetti and Ghirlandaio at Santa Trinità, Florence: History and Legend in a Renaissance Chapel* (Doornspijk: Davaco, 1981), 53.

50. See Mack, "Venus," 224–26.

51. Levey, *Florence,* 105, and the life of Niccolò in Vespasiano da Bisticci, *Renaissance Princes, Popes, and Prelates: The Vespasiano Memoirs; Lives of Illustrious Men of the Fifteenth Century,* intro. Myron Gilmore, trans. William George and Emily Waters (New York, Evanston, and London: Harper and Row, 1963), 403. See also E. H. Gombrich, "From the Revival of Letters to the Reform of the Arts: Niccolò Niccoli and Filippo Brunelleschi," in *Essays in the History of Art Presented to Rudolf Wittkower,* ed. D. Fraser, H. Hibbard, and M. Lewine (London: Phaidon, 1967), 71–82.

52. Holmes, *Enlightenment,* 30.

53. Holmes, *Enlightenment,* 32–34. It was not until the end of the fifteenth century that the strident protests of Fra Girolamo Savonarola would demand attention from the citizenry of Florence.

54. On this, see Alison Cole, *Virtue and Magnificence: Art of the Renaissance Courts* (New York and Englewood Cliffs, NJ: Harry N. Abrams and Prentice-Hall, 1995), 70.

55. On the program of Nicholas V, see Charles R. Mack, "Nicholas V and the Rebuilding of Rome: Reality and Legacy," in *Light on the Eternal City,* Papers in the History of Art 2, ed. Helmut Hager and Susan Munshower (University Park: Pennsylvania State University, 1987), 30–56, and "Bernardo Rossellino, L. B. Alberti, and the Truth about Nicholas V's Rome," *Southeastern College Art Conference Review* 10, no. 2 (1982): 60–69; Charles Burroughs, *From Sign to Design: Environmental Process and Reform in Early Renaissance Rome* (Cambridge: MIT Press, 1990); and Carroll William Westfall, *In This Most Perfect Paradise: Alberti, Nicholas V, and the Invention of Conscious Urban Planning in Rome, 1447–55* (University Park: Pennsylvania State University Press, 1974). For a rather different view concerning Pope Nicholas and humanism, see Manfredo Tafuri, "Cives esse non licere: The Rome of Nicholas V and Leon Battista Alberti," *Harvard Architectural Review* 6 (1987). A solid synopsis is presented in Burroughs, "Alberti e Roma," in *Leon Battista Alberti,* ed. Joseph Rykwert and Anne Engel (Milan: Olivetti/Electa, 1994), 134–57.

56. C. Ugurgieri Bererdenga, *Pio II Piccolomini con notizie su Pio III e altri membri della famiglia* (Florence: Olschki, 1973), 338.

57. Wylie Sypher, *Four Stages of Renaissance Style: Transformations in Art and Literature, 1400–1700* (Garden City, NY: Doubleday Anchor Book, 1955), 57.

58. As given in James S. Ackerman, *The Architecture of Michelangelo* (Harmondsworth: Penguin, 1971), 37.

59. Charles R. Mack, *Pienza: The Creation of a Renaissance City* (Ithaca and London: Cornell University Press, 1987), 48.

60. Antonio Manetti, *The Life of Brunelleschi,* trans. Catherine Enggass, ed. Howard Saalman (University Park and London: Pennsylvania State University Press, 1970), 50.

61. Samuel Y. Edgerton, "Florentine Interest in Ptolemaic Cartography as Background for Renaissance Painting, Architecture, and the Discovery of America," *Journal of the Society of Architectural Historians* 33 (1974): 278.

62. This passage is contained in the preface of part 3 of Vasari's *Lives,* 1:151.

63. Paolo Uccello's obsession with perspective is recounted in Vasari, *Lives,* 2:239. The literature on Renaissance perspective is quite extensive, but see John White, *Birth and Rebirth of Pictorial Space* (London: Faber, 1967); Joan Gadol, *Leon Battista Alberti: Universal Man of the Renaissance* (Chicago: University of Chicago Press, 1969); and, more recently, J. Elkins, "Piero della Francesca and the Renaissance Proof of Linear Perspective," *Art Bulletin* 69 (1987): 220–30.

64. Edgerton, "Ptolemaic Cartography," 275–76.

65. In his introduction to book 7 of his *Ten Books on Architecture,* Vitruvius discusses the writings on art and architecture left by the Greeks and, in so doing, notes that both Democritus and Anaxagoras had shown how "given a centre in a definite place, the lines should naturally correspond with due regard to the point of sight and the divergence of the visual rays, so that by this deception a faithful representation of the appearance of buildings might be given in painted scenery, and so that, though all is drawn on a vertical flat facade, some parts may seem to be withdrawing into the background, and others to be standing out in front." See Vitruvius, *The Ten Books on Architecture,* trans. Morris Hickey Morgan (Cambridge: Harvard University Press, 1914), 198. For a consideration of the significance of Vitruvius's text and its impact on Renaissance aesthetics, see the thoughtful essay by Philipp Fehl, "Patronage through the Ages," in *The Great Ideas Today; Part I: A Symposium on Culture and Society* (New York: Encyclopedia Britannica, 1977), 74–90.

66. Toscanelli (1397–82) would have been only about twenty years of age at the time during which he could have imparted perspectival ideas to the older Brunelleschi. The discovery of the text of Vitruvius in 1418 might have occurred too late to have been of any use in inspiring Brunelleschi, whose perspective inventions took place sometime shortly after 1415, I believe. However, copies of Vitruvius were known already, one of which was in Florence by the second half of the thirteenth century. Boccaccio owned his own copy. Although Vitruvius had been copied since Carolingian days, the treatise was neither appreciated nor utilized. On the survival of Vitruvius during the Middle Ages, see Carol Krinsky, "Seventy-eight Vitruvius Manuscripts," *Journal of the Warburg and Courtauld Institutes* 30 (1967): 36–70, as well as L. A. Ciapponi, "Il *De architectura* di Vitruvio nel primo umanesimo," *Italia mediovale e umanistica* 3 (1960): 59–99, and Erwin Panofsky, *Renaissance and Renascences in Western Art* (New York: Harper and Row Torchbook, 1960), 178–79. For a discussion as to whether Brunelleschi "invented" or "discovered" perspective, see Zwijnenberg, *Leonardo,* 113–15.

67. The panels have vanished but were inspected by Antonio Manetti and extensively described by him in his *Life of Brunelleschi,* 42, 44.

68. Zwijnenberg, *Leonardo,* 128, believes that "we can conclude that there are at least two phenomena that have made it possible for linear perspective to become such a very important artistic resource. One is the direct knowledge of and familiarity with the tradition of practical geometry that Early Renaissance artists possessed; the other is the change in attitude toward works of art that gave the personality of the artist and the spectator more scope. Together, they constitute the background for the practical application of linear perspective in the visual arts."

69. Alberti, *Painting,* 58. The only known example of the application of scientific perspective in antiquity, based upon a single vanishing point, is to be found in an architectural fresco in the so-called House of Livia on the Palatine Hill in Rome. Otherwise, the charming but spatially jumbled depictions found in the Boscoreale Villa (now in the Metropoli-

tan Museum) are the norm. I find this absence of (or disinterest in) spatial accuracy mystifying in a culture that seems so preoccupied with the definition and control of space, as both conquerors and as builders.

70. Alberti, *Painting,* 51.

71. From Muratori, *Rerum ital. script.* 25, cols. 299c–300a, as trans. by Spencer in Alberti, *Painting,* 106.

72. Bruce Cole, *Masaccio and the Art of the Early Renaissance* (Bloomington: Indiana University Press, 1980), 139. This is also the view of Samuel Y. Edgerton, *The Renaissance Discovery of Linear Perspective* (1975; reprint, New York, Evanston, San Francisco, and London: Harper and Row Icon Editions, 1976), 56, who notes: "Linear perspective has come to be regarded as unaesthetic, since it implies the primacy of objective realism over true artistic subjectivity . . . however, perspective was not embraced by its first practitioners for any such reason. 'Realism' in fifteenth-century eyes was as metaphysical as it was physical. Therefore perspective rules were accepted by these early artists because it gave their depicted scenes a sense of harmony with natural law, thereby underscoring man's moral responsibility within God's geometrically ordered universe."

CHAPTER 5

1. Portions of the material in this chapter have been published in Charles Mack, "Fictive Spaces for Monastic Places: Art and Architecture in Fifteenth-Century Florence," *Arris* 2 (2001): 30–43. For another approach to this theme see William Hood, "Creating Memory: Monumental Painting and Cultural Definition," in *Language and Painting in Renaissance Italy,* ed. Allison Brown (Oxford: Clarendon, 1995), 157–69.

2. Tertullian, *Disciplinary, Moral, and Ascetical Works,* trans. Rudolph Arbesmann, Sister Emily Joseph Daly, and Edwin A. Quain (New York: Fathers of the Church, 1959), 21.

3. Wolfgang Braunfels, *Monasteries of Western Europe: The Architecture of the Orders* (London: Summer, 1972), 37–46.

4. On the history and architecture of this cloister, see Charles Mack, "Studies in the Architectural Career of Bernardo di Matteo Ghamberelli Called Rossellino, 1409–1464," diss., University of North Carolina at Chapel Hill, 1972, 116–36.

5. Vasari, *Lives,* 2:13.

6. Thomas à Kempis, *The Imitation of Christ* (New York: Walter J. Black, 1932), 153.

7. Anthony Butkovich, *Iconography: St. Brigitta of Sweden* (Los Angeles: Ecumenical Foundation of America, 1969), 43–45.

8. Vasari, *Lives,* 2:13.

9. For information on the cloister, see Piero Sanpaolesi, "Costruzioni dal primo Quattrocento nella Badia Fiorentina," *Rivista d'Arte* 41 (1956): 11–29.

10. The treatment recalls that given large-scale paintings in ancient Greece that frequently were designed to be viewed through the porticoed screen of a stoa. For some ancient examples of such stoa- and portico-related placements, see J. J. Pollitt, *The Art of Greece, 1400–31 B.C.: Sources and Documents* (Englewood Cliffs, NJ: Prentice-Hall, 1965), 105, 108, 170. A surviving indication of this Grecian technique may be found in the celebrated *Odyssey Landscapes* now in the Vatican Museums in which the episodes unfurl behind a line of simulated pilaster strips. Some would see this cycle as a Roman reproduc-

tion of a Greek original; others believe it to be the work of Hellenistic decorators in Roman employ. For a general discussion, see George M. A. Hanfmann, *Roman Art: A Modern Survey of the Art of Imperial Rome* (New York: W. W. Norton, 1975), 268–70.

11. On Fra Angelico's frescoes at San Marco, see William Hood, *Fra Angelico at San Marco* (New Haven: Yale University Press, 1993), and Paolo Morachiello, *Fra Angelico: The San Marco Frescoes,* trans. Eleanor Daunt (London: Thames and Hudson, 1996).

12. Caterina Benincasa, *St. Catherine of Siena as Seen in Her Letters,* trans. and ed. Vida D. Scudder (London: J. M. Dent; New York: E. P. Dutton, 1905), 137. Saint Catherine expressed this same passionate sentiment in a letter of ca. 1375 to Monna Agnese Malavolti (43): "Now then, I want that you should wholly destroy your own will, that it may cling to nothing but Christ crucified."

13. Thomas à Kempis, *Imitation of Christ,* 151.

14. Thomas à Kempis, *Imitation of Christ,* 171.

15. Hindsight gives perspective and often can lead to metaphoric interpretation. From our historic vantage point we can see Brunelleschi's and Alberti's spatial constructions, the reintroduction of Ptolemaic cartography, and a multitude of such quattrocento innovations as symbolic of a new and encompassing worldview. It is likely, on the other hand, that those who first invented and employed such procedures did not. They saw them in practical terms as technical processes and could not step away to grasp their integrated significance.

16. Ironically, while an impetus toward a universal vision and homogeneity typified the fifteenth century in Italy and gave definition to the Renaissance as a period style, the visual arts actually began to lose their contextual identity within the changing social structure. For medieval society, the function and expression of art was at one with the purposeful program of Christianity. The spirit of the Renaissance ushered in the beginnings of the separation of art from its culture, the start of an artistic divorce that would lead to the eventual estrangement of art from the normal patterns of life. A good example of this modern development may be found in an article by Richard Woodward, "The Perfect Painting," *New York Times Magazine* (20 February 1994): 36, in which he discusses a recent survey concerning people's attitudes about art. One of the respondents replied: "I'm glad that it [art] exists, but I don't necessarily like it in my house." The same, of course, is true of religion itself; while classically inspired inquiry led to the formulation of rational laws for governance, representation, discourse, conduct, navigation, etc., the heavenly connection began to disengage.

17. That a new focus upon the individual was born with the Renaissance (or just prior to it) cannot be denied and would seem to contradict my emphasis upon the period's determination to amalgamate and unify. How, for instance, can the appearance of specifically rendered painted and sculpted portraits be reconciled with the overall tendency of the period to subordinate parts within the whole? How can this seeming dichotomy be resolved? Perhaps the desire to make the pieces of the puzzle fit forces the issue too much, and this may be but the exception that proves the rule. On the other hand, it is possible that it was first necessary to have a more precise concept of individuality before that individuality could become collective; the trees needed definition, as it were, before the forest could be seen. In much the same way, the distorted memory of old pagan gods had to be put to rest before they could be reborn with classical precision.

18. For a general discussion of the Florentine *catasto,* see Michael Levey, *Florence: A Portrait* (Cambridge: Harvard University Press, 1996), 100, and Rufus Graves Mather, *Excavating Buried Treasure* (Cambridge: Harvard University Press, 1945), 32–40.

19. See Donald R. Kelley, ed., *Versions of History from Antiquity to the Present* (New Haven and London: Yale University Press, 1991), 236–46. There are many examples of increasing temporal recognition during the Renaissance. One such is found in the way in which Botticelli unifies text and image in the illustrations he prepared for Dante's *Inferno*. In cantos 28 and 29, the repetition of figures leads the eye of the reader/viewer through the progressive series of events. On this see an unpublished paper presented by Barbara Watts in Session IIB of the 2003 Meeting of the Southeastern College Art Conference held in Raleigh, North Carolina.

20. Giovanni Villani (ca. 1276–1348) published his *Chroniche fiorentine* between 1333 and 1341 before falling victim to the plague.

21. Hellmut Wohl's comments about the Renaissance concept of time in *The Aesthetics of Italian Renaissance Art: A Reconsideration of Style* (Cambridge: Cambridge University Press, 1999), 241–42, are particularly cogent and worth quoting at some length:

> One of the dimensions of the transformations in art and in writing about art between the early fifteenth and the later sixteenth century is that of historical time. Chrysoloras wrote about Roman relief [sculpture] as the record of a civilization separated from his own time by the space of history. No historical space separated Vasari from the images of Roman antiquity in Salviati's frescoes of Furius Camilius in the Sala dell'Udienza in the Palazzo Vecchio for in them the antique was subsumed into the present. Quattrocento artists and humanists looked at the monuments of antiquity across the space of historical time as records of a distant past that they admired and endeavored to emulate. Mantegna and the masters of the ornate classical style, such as Ripanda in his frescoes of the life of Trajan in the bishop's palace at Ostia strove above all for archaeological accuracy and fidelity. Salviati and the masters of the Roman grand manner, by contrast, invested the antique with movement and inner life, re-creating "the deeds of the Romans" not only "as they really were" but as if they were taking place in front of our eyes, fusing the past with the present and suspending historical time by transposing antiquity into the here and now.

See also the comments of Erwin Panofsky, *Renaissance and Renascences in Western Art* (New York: Harper and Row Torchbook, 1960), 108:

> In the Italian Renaissance the classical past began to be looked upon from a fixed distance, quite comparable to the "distance between the eye and the object" in that most characteristic invention of this very Renaissance, focused perspective. As in focused perspective, this distance prohibited direct contact—owing to the interposition of an ideal "projection plane"—but permitted a total and rationalized view. Such a distance is absent from both medieval renascences [those of the Carolingian and of the twelfth century].

22. On this topic, see Donald J. Wilcox, *The Development of Florentine Humanist Historiography in the Fifteenth Century* (Cambridge: Harvard University Press, 1969).

23. James Ackerman, "Architectural Practice in the Italian Renaissance," *Journal of the Society of Architectural Historians* 13 (September 1954): 3–11.

24. On this see Christian Bec, *L'umanismo civile: Alberti, Salutati, Bruni, Bracciolini e altri trattatisti del '400* (Turin: Paravia, 1975).

25. Guillaume Dufy's motet *Nuper rosarum flores* composed for the consecration of the Florentine Cathedral in 1436 was derived from the twelfth-century form. It was polyphonic and not yet harmonic. By "harmonic," as Alberti described it, was meant the concordance of opposites between the tenor voice and the superius—a musical expression of Alberti's principle of congruity. See C. Warren, "Brunelleschi's Dome and Dufay's Motet," *Musical Quarterly* 59 (1973): 92–105.

26. Typesetting fixed words in a specific location, and by comparison the varied calligraphy of the medieval scriptorium seems unstructured and aimless. Printing also introduced fixed margins and other elements of internal visual organization that reinforced the argument of the text. In many respects the printed page was akin to a Ptolemaic map or a painting done in accordance with a perspective grid.

27. The *Chain View of Florence* also has been attributed to a Lucantonio degli Uberti. See Joseph Rykwert and Anne Engel, *Leon Battista Alberti* (Milan: Olivetti/Electa, 1994), 30, fig. 3. The *Chain View of Florence* also provided the visual information for Hartmann Schedel's rendition of Florence included in his celebrated "Nuremberg Chronicle" of 1493, a project upon which the young Albrecht Dürer also worked and through which he might have acquired some of his taste for things Italian.

28. Jay A. Levenson, *Prints of the Italian Renaissance* (Washington, DC: National Gallery of Art, 1973), 6.

29. Christiane J. Hessler, "Piero della Francescas Panorama," *Zeitschrift für Kunstgeschichte* 55 (1992): 165.

30. Angelo Poliziano, *Detti piacevoli,* ed. Tiziano Zaneto (Rome: Istituto della Enciclopedia italiana, 1983), 44, and discussed in Alison Brown, "Cosimo de' Medici's Wit and Wisdom," in *Cosimo 'il Vecchio' de' Medici, 1389–1464: Essays in Commemoration of the 600th Anniversary of Cosimo de' Medici's Birth,* ed. Francis Ames-Lewis (Oxford: Clarendon, 1992), 103.

31. Pius II (Aeneas Silvius Piccolomini), *Memoirs of a Renaissance Pope: The Commentaries of Pius II,* trans. Florence A. Gragg, ed. Leona C. Gabel (New York: Capricorn, 1959), 285.

32. Pius II, *Memoirs,* 321.

33. On these two events, see Nicholas Adams, "The Construction of Pienza (1459–1464) and the Consequences of Renovatio," in *Urban Life in the Renaissance,* ed. Susan Zimmerman and Ronald F. E. Weismann (Newark: University of Delaware Press; London and Toronto: Associated University Presses), 70–71, and Charles R. Mack, *Pienza: The Creation of a Renaissance City* (Ithaca and London: Cornell University Press, 1987), 113.

34. Caution must be taken not to turn the Renaissance interest in unity into a Baroque passion. The Renaissance tendency was to arrange, in an additive fashion, the separate parts into a totality, while the Baroque aimed at a more sweeping distillation.

35. Hay, *The Italian Renaissance in Its Historical Background,* 172.

36. Of the three panels once in the Palazzo Medici (two of which were probably a commission from Cosimo for the old family palace that preceded the present building), that now in the Uffizi seems the most interesting and puzzling. Victims of the struggle have fallen like chess pieces along the directional lines of the spatial grid, and Uccello has painted them in unnatural hues of pinks and blues. His color rationale has yet to be suitably explained.

37. As given in Edgerton, *The Renaissance Rediscovery of Linear Perspective* (1975; reprint, New York, Evanston, San Francisco, and London: Harper and Row Icon Editions,

1976), 92. The expansive vision of Leonardo so well demonstrated in these aerial views illustrates the "synoptic view" of the true philosopher as discussed in Robert Zwijnenberg, *The Writings and Drawings of Leonardo da Vinci: Order and Chaos in Early Modern Thought,* trans. Caroline A. van Eck (Cambridge, New York, and Melbourne: Cambridge University Press, 1999), 110–11.

CHAPTER 6

1. A brief but useful consideration of the diffusion of Renaissance concepts into the north of Europe is given in the final chapter of Denys Hay, *The Italian Renaissance in Its Historical Background,* 179–203.

2. Craig Harbison in *The Mirror of the Artist: Northern Renaissance Art in Its Historical Context* (Englewood Cliffs, NJ, and New York: Prentice-Hall and Harry N. Abrams, 1995), 7, has pointed to the word *discovery,* saying that "the art of the Northern Renaissance is, to a great extent, based on that simple point—discovery of the world and of the self." Indeed, northerners did reawaken to themselves and to the world about them at about the same time as did their Italian counterparts. Many of the same stimuli were present in both locales as the Middle Ages entered its state of transformation. What was missing in the transalpine regions, of course, was an appreciated connection to an antique past.

3. Erwin Panofsky, *Early Netherlandish Painting: Its Origins and Character* (Cambridge: Harvard University Press, 1953), 196. Also see Millard Meiss, "Jan van Eyck and the Italian Renaissance," published in his book *The Painter's Choice: Problems in the Interpretation of Renaissance Art* (New York, Hagerstown, San Francisco, and London: Harper and Row, 1976), 9–35.

4. One might also compare the *Wilton Diptych* with van Eyck's *Madonna and Child with Chancellor Rolin* as a demonstration of the self-confidence of the new age; while the king of England (despite the fact that his nation's flag is planted in Heaven) has need of saintly sponsors, the Burgundian bureaucrat apparently needs no introduction.

5. This conclusion is verified by the contents of the basic textbooks used in college surveys of Italian and Northern Renaissance art. In the former, the concentration is divided among the three major arts; in the latter, it almost exclusively rests upon the development of painting (and the print).

6. André Chastel, *Myth of the Renaissance* (Geneva: Skira, 1969), 230–31.

7. A convenient synopsis of the history of the *Apollo Belvedere* can be found in the essay by Philipp Fehl in *An Encyclopedia of the History of Classical Archaeology,* ed. Nancy De Grummond (Westport, CT: Greenwood, 1996).

8. Although the finding of the *Belvedere Torso* is frequently reported as having taken place during the papacy of Julius II, it actually had been known for a much longer period of time. By the 1420s, the torso was in the possession of the Colonna family where it was noted by Ciriaco d'Ancona; by 1500, the torso was in the possession of the Roman sculptor Andrea Bregno; and at some point prior to 1530 it had passed into the papal collection and was on display in the little Belvedere courtyard. The torso of the Adam in Jacopo della Quercia's *Expulsion from Paradise* of 1418–19 from the *Fonte Gaia* in the Campo of Siena also may reflect a familiarity with the *Belvedere Torso.* On the history of this sculpture and its impact, consult Nancy De Grummond's essay in her *Encyclopedia of the History of Classical Archaeology,* 146–48. Also see Bober and Rubinstein, *Handbook,* 166–68.

9. Erwin Panofsky, *The Life and Art of Albrecht Dürer,* 4th ed. (Princeton: Princeton University Press, 1955), 32.

10. Giancarlo Maiorino, *Portrait of Eccentricity: Archimbolo and the Mannerist Grotesque* (University Park: Pennsylvania State University Press, 1991), 62.

11. Elizabeth G. Holt, ed., *A Documentary History of Art,* volume 2, *Michelangelo and the Mannerists, the Baroque, and the Eighteenth Century* (Garden City, NY: Doubleday Anchor, 1958), 69.

12. Holt, *Documentary,* 2:69.

13. Holt, *Documentary,* 2:69.

Selected Bibliography

Ackerman, James S. "Architectural Practice in the Italian Renaissance." *Journal of the Society of Architectural Historians* 13 (September 1954): 3–11.

———. *The Architecture of Michelangelo.* Harmondsworth: Penguin, 1971.

Adams, Nicholas. "The Construction of Pienza (1459–1464) and the Consequences of Renovatio." In *Urban Life in the Renaissance,* ed. Susan Zimmerman and Ronald F. E. Weissman, 50–79. Newark: University of Delaware Press; London and Toronto: Associated University Presses, 1989.

Alberti, Leon Battista. *On Painting.* Trans. and ed. J. R. Spencer. New Haven and London: Yale University Press, 1966.

Antal, Friedrich. *Florentine Painting and Its Social Background.* London: Routledge and Kegan Paul, 1948.

Athanasakis, Apostolos. *The Homeric Hymns.* Baltimore and London: Johns Hopkins University Press, 1976.

Baldini, Umberto. *Primavera: The Restoration of Botticelli's Masterpiece.* New York: Harry N. Abrams, 1986.

Barkan, Leonard. *Unearthing the Past: Archaeology and Aesthetics in the Making of the Renaissance.* New Haven: Yale University Press, 2001.

Barnes, Maude Fiero. *Renaissance Vistas.* Freeport, NY: Books for Libraries Press, 1968.

Baron, Hans. *The Crisis of the Early Renaissance.* 2nd ed., rev. Princeton: Princeton University Press, 1966.

———. "Franciscan Poverty and Civic Wealth as Factors in the Rise of Humanistic Thought." *Speculum* 13 (1938): 1–37.

———. "Towards a More Positive Evaluation of the Fifteenth-Century Renaissance." *Journal of the History of Ideas* 4 (1943): 21–49.

Baxandall, Michael. "Guarino, Pisanello, and Manuel Chrysoloras." *Journal of the Warburg and Courtauld Institutes* 28 (1965): 183–204.

———. *Giotto and the Orators: Humanist Observers of Painting in Italy and the Discovery of Pictorial Composition.* Oxford: Clarendon, 1971.

———. *Painting and Experience in Fifteenth Century Italy: A Primer in the Social History of Pictorial Style.* London: Oxford University Press, 1972.

Bec, Christian. *L'Umanismo civile: Alberti, Salutati, Bruni, Bracciolini e altri trattatisti del '400.* Turin: Paravia, 1975.

Becker, Marvin. *Florence in Transition.* 2 vols. Baltimore: Johns Hopkins University Press, 1967.

Belting, Hans. *Likeness and Presence: A History of the Image before the Era of Art.* Trans. E. Jephcolt. Chicago: University of Chicago Press, 1994.

Belting, Hans, and Christine Kruse. *Die Erfindung des Gemäldes: Das erste Jahrhundert der niederländischen Malerie.* Munich: Hirmer Verlag, 1994.

Benson, R. L., G. Constable, and C. D. Lanham, eds. *Renaissance and Renewal in the Twelfth Century.* Cambridge, MA: Clarendon, 1982.

Berenson, Bernard. *Homeless Paintings of the Renaissance.* Bloomington: Indiana University Press, 1970.

Bertolet, L. "Cincius Romanus und seine Briefe." *Quellen und Forschungen aus Italienischen Archiven und Bibliotheken* 21 (1929–30): 209–51.

Blunt, Anthony. *Artistic Theory in Italy.* 1940; reprint, Oxford: Clarendon, 1963.

Bober, Phyllis Pray, and Ruth Rubinstein. *The Renaissance Artist and Antique Sculpture: A Handbook of Sources.* New York: Harvey Miller; London: Oxford University Press, 1986.

Bonaventura, Saint (Giovanni da Fidenza). *The Mind's Road to God.* Trans. George Boas. Indianapolis: Bobbs-Merrill, 1953.

Borsi, Franco. *Leon Battista Alberti.* Milan: Electa Editrice, 1975.

Borsook, Eve, and J. Offerhaus. *Francesco Sassetti and Ghirlandaio at Santa Trinità, Florence: History and Legend in a Renaissance Chapel.* Doornspijk: Davaco, 1981.

Braunfels, Wolfgang. *Monasteries of Western Europe: The Architecture of the Orders.* London: Thames and Hudson, 1972.

Brown, Alison. "Cosimo de' Medici's Wit and Wisdom." In *Cosimo 'il Vecchio' de' Medici, 1389–1464: Essays in Commemoration of the 600th Anniversary of Cosimo de' Medici's Birth,* ed. Francis Ames-Lewis, 95–113. Oxford: Clarendon, 1992.

Brucker, Gene A. *Renaissance Florence.* Rev. ed. Berkeley, Los Angeles, and London: University of California Press, 1983.

Burckhardt, Jacob. *Civilization of the Renaissance in Italy.* Trans. S. C. G. Middlemore. 2 vols. New York: Harper Torchbook, 1958.

Burke, Peter. *Tradition and Innovation in Renaissance Italy: A Sociological Approach.* London: Fontana, 1974.

Burroughs, Charles. "Alberti e Roma." In *Leon Battista Alberti,* ed. Joseph Rykwert and Anne Engel, 134–57. Milan: Olivetti/Electa, 1994.

———. *From Sign to Design: Environmental Process and Reform in Early Renaissance Rome.* Cambridge and London: MIT Press, 1990.

Butkovich, Anthony. *Iconography: St. Birgitta of Sweden.* Los Angeles: Ecumenical Foundation of America, 1969.

———. *Revelations: Saint Birgitta of Sweden.* Los Angeles: Ecumenical Foundation of America, 1972.

Campana, A. "The Origin of the Word Humanist." *Journal of the Courtauld and Warburg Institutes* 9 (1960): 60.

Canfield, G. B. "The Florentine Humanists' Concept of Architecture in the 1430s and Filippo Brunelleschi." In *Scritti di storia dell'arte in onore di Federico Zeri,* 1:112–21. Venice: Electa, 1984.

Carman, Charles H. *Images of Humanist Ideals in Italian Renaissance Art.* Studies in Art History 2. Lewiston, Queenston, and Lampeter: Edwin Mellen Press, 2000.

Cassirer, Ernst. *The Individual and Cosmos in Renaissance Philosophy.* Trans. Mario Domandi. Philadelphia: University of Pennsylvania Press, 1972.

———. "Some Remarks on the Originality of the Renaissance." *Journal of the History of Ideas* 4 (1943): 49–56.

Cassirer, Ernst, Paul Oskar Kristeller, and John Herman Randall Jr., eds. *The Renaissance Philosophy of Man.* Chicago and London: University of Chicago Press, 1948.

Catherine of Siena, Saint (Caterina Benincasa). *Saint Catherine of Siena as Seen in Her Letters.*Trans. and ed. Vida Scudder. London: J. M. Dent; New York: C. P. Dutton, 1905.

Cellini, Benvenuto. *The Life of Benvenuto Cellini.* Trans. Anne MacDonell. London: J. M. Dent; New York: E. P. Dutton, 1926.

Cennini, Cennino d'Andrea. *Il Libro dell'Arte: The Craftsman's Handbook.* Trans. Daniel V. Thompson Jr. New Haven: Yale University Press, 1936.

Chastel, André. *Age of Humanism in Europe.* New York: McGraw-Hill, 1964.

———. *Myth of the Renaissance.* Geneva: Skira, 1969.

Chastel, André, Cecil Grayson, Marie Boas Hall, Denys Hay, Walter Ullman, Charles Trinkaus, Paul Oskar Kristeller, Nicolai Rubinstein, and Charles B. Schmitt. *The Renaissance: Essays in Interpretation.* New York and London: Methuen, 1982.

Cheney, Liana De Girolami. *Quattrocento Neoplatonism and Medici Humanism in Botticelli's Mythological Paintings.* Lanham, MD: University Press of America, 1995.

Ciapponi, L. A. "Il *De architectura* di Vitruvio nel primo umanesimo." *Italia mediovale e umanistica* 3 (1960): 59–99.

Codice magliabechiano. Ed. Carl Frey. Berlin: G. Grote'sche, 1892.

Cole, Alison. *Virtue and Magnificence: Art of the Renaissance Courts.* New York: Harry N. Abrams; Englewood Cliffs: Prentice-Hall, 1995.

Cole, Bruce. *Giotto and Florentine Painting, 1280–1375.* New York: Harper and Row, 1976.

———. *Italian Art, 1250–1550: The Relation of Renaissance Art to Life and Society.* New York: Harper and Row Icon Editions, 1987.

———. *Masaccio and the Art of the Early Renaissance.* Bloomington: Indiana University Press, 1980.

———. *The Renaissance Artist at Work.* New York: Harper and Row, 1983.

Collins, Bradford R., ed. *Twelve Views of Manet's Bar.* Princeton: Princeton University Press, 1996.

Coulton, G. G. *The Fate of Medieval Art in the Renaissance and Reformation.* Oxford: Blackwell, 1928.

Davies, Jonathan. *Florence and Its University during the Early Renaissance.* Education and Society in the Middle Ages and Renaissance, 8. Leiden and Boston: Brill, 1998.

Davis, Margaret. *Piero della Francesca's Mathematical Treatises.* Ravenna: Longo Editore, 1971.

Dempsey, Charles. *The Portrayal of Love: Botticelli's Primavera and Humanist Culture at the Time of Lorenzo the Magnificent.* Princeton: Princeton University Press, 1992.

Edgerton, Samuel Y., Jr. "Florentine Interest in Ptolemaic Cartography as Background for Renaissance Painting, Architecture, and the Discovery of America." *Journal of the Society of Architectural Historians* 33 (December 1974): 274–92.

———. *The Heritage of Giotto's Geometry: Art and Science on the Eve of the Scientific Revolution.* Ithaca and London: Cornell University Press, 1991.

———. *The Renaissance Rediscovery of Linear Perspective.* 1975; reprint, New York, Evanston, San Francisco, and London: Harper and Row Icon Editions, 1976.

Elkins, J. "Piero della Francesca and the Renaissance Proof of Linear Perspective." *Art Bulletin* 69 (1977): 220–30.

Encyclopedia of the History of Classical Archaeology. Ed. Nancy De Grummond. Westport, CT: Greenwood Press, 1996.

Fehl, Philipp. "Patronage through the Ages." In *The Great Ideas Today: Part I: A Symposium on Culture and Society,* 74–90. New York: Encyclopedia Britannica, 1977.

Fengler, Christine Knapp. "Lorenzo Ghiberti's *Second Commentary:* The Translation and Interpretation of a Fundamental Renaissance Treatise on Art." Diss., University of Wisconsin, 1974.

Ferguson, Wallace K. *The Renaissance in Historical Thought: Five Centuries of Interpretation.* Boston: Houghton Mifflin, 1948.

Field, Arthur. *The Origins of the Platonic Academy of Florence.* Princeton: Princeton University Press, 1988.

Field, J. V. *The Invention of Infinity: Mathematics as Art in the Renaissance.* Oxford: Oxford University Press, 1997.

Forster, Kurt. "Discussion: The Palazzo Rucellai and Questions of Typology in the Development of Renaissance Buildings." *Art Bulletin* 58 (1976): 109–13.

Francastel, Pierre. "La fête mythologique au Quattrocento: Expression littéraire et visualisation plastique." In P. Francastel, *La réalité figurative: Eléments structurels de la sociologie et de l'art,* 229–52. Paris: Gonthier, 1965.

Fryde, E. B. *Humanism and Renaissance Historiography.* London: Hambledon, 1983.

Gadol, Joan. *Leon Battista Alberti: Universal Man of the Renaissance.* Chicago: University of Chicago Press, 1969.

Gallagher, Catherine, and Stephen Greenblatt. *Practicing New Historicism.* Chicago: University of Chicago Press, 2001.

Gebhart, Emile. *Mystics and Heretics in Italy at the End of the Middle Ages.* London: G. Allen and Unwin, 1922.

Ghiberti, Lorenzo. *I Commentari.* Ed. Ottavio Morisani. Naples: R. Ricciardi, 1947.

Gilbert, Creighton. *Italian Art, 1400–1500: Sources and Documents.* Englewood Cliffs, NJ: Prentice-Hall, 1992.

———. *Poets Seeing Artists' Work: Instances in the Italian Renaissance.* Florence: Leo S. Olschki, 1991.

Goldthwaite, Richard A. *The Building of Renaissance Florence: An Economic and Social History.* Baltimore and London: Johns Hopkins University Press, 1980.

———. *Private Wealth in Renaissance Florence.* Princeton: Princeton University Press, 1968.

———. *Wealth and the Demand for Art in Italy.* Baltimore and London: Johns Hopkins University Press, 1993.

Gombrich, E. H. "From the Revival of Letters to the Reform of the Arts: Niccolo Niccoli and Filippo Brunelleschi." In *Essays in the History of Art Presented to Rudolf Wittkower,* ed. D. Fraser, H. Hibbard, and M. Lewine, 71–82. London: Phaidon, 1967.

Grafton, Anthony. *Leon Battista Alberti: Master Builder of the Italian Renaissance.* New York: Hill and Wang, 2000.

Hall, James. *A History of Ideas and Images in Italian Art.* New York: Harper and Row Icon Editions, 1983.

Hall, Marie Boas. *The Scientific Renaissance, 1450–1630.* New York: Dover, 1994.

Hanfmann, George M. A. *Roman Art: A Modern Survey of the Art of Imperial Rome.* New York: W. W. Norton, 1975.

Hankins, James. "Cosimo de' Medici and the Platonic Academy." *Journal of the Warburg and Courtauld Institutes* 53 (1990): 144–62.

———. "The Myth of the Platonic Academy of Florence." *Renaissance Quarterly* 45 (1992): 549–53.

———. *Plato in the Renaissance.* 2 vols. New York: Columbia University Press, 1990.

Harbison, Craig. *The Mirror of the Artist: Northern Renaissance Art in Its Historical Context.* Englewood Cliffs, NJ and New York: Prentice-Hall and Harry N. Abrams, 1995.

Harris, Jonathan. *The New Art History: A Critical Introduction.* London and New York: Routledge, 2001.

Hartt, Frederick. "Art and Freedom in Quattrocento Florence." In *Marsyas: Studies in the History of Art.* Suppl. 1: *Essays in Memory of Karl Lehmann,* New York: New York University Institute of Fine Arts, 1964:114–31.

Haskins, Charles Homer. *Renaissance of the Twelfth Century.* Cambridge: Harvard University Press, 1927.

Hatfield, Rab. *Botticelli's Uffizi "Adoration": A Study in Pictorial Content.* Princeton: Princeton University Press, 1976.

Hay, Denys. *The Italian Renaissance in Its Historical Background.* Cambridge: Cambridge University Press, 1970.

———, ed. *The Renaissance Debate.* European Problem Studies. New York: Holt, Rinehart, and Winston, 1965.

Helton, Tinsley, ed. *The Renaissance: A Reconsideration of the Theories and Interpretations of the Age.* Westport, CT: Crestwood Press, 1961.

Herlihy, David, and Christine Klapish-Zuber. *Tuscans and Their Families: A Study of the Florentine Catasto of 1427.* New Haven and London: Yale University Press, 1985.

Hessler, Christiane J. "Piero della Francescas Panorama." *Zeitschrift für Kunstgeschichte* 55 (1992): 161–79.

Heuzinga, J. *The Waning of the Middle Ages: A Study of the Forms of Life, Thought, and Art in France and the Netherlands in the Fourteenth and Fifteenth Centuries.* Garden City, NY: Doubleday Anchor, 1954.

Holder, Philancy N. *Cortona in Context: The History and Architecture of an Italian Hilltown to the Seventeenth Century.* Clarksville, TN: HP Publishing, 1992.

Holliday, Peter. "Time, History, and Ritual on the Ara Pacis Augustae." *Art Bulletin* 72:542–57.

Holmes, George. *Florence, Rome, and the Origins of the Renaissance.* Oxford: Clarendon, 1986.

———. *The Florentine Enlightenment, 1400–1450.* London: Weidenfield and Nicholson, 1969.

Holt, Elizabeth G., ed. *A Documentary History of Art.* Volume 1, *The Middle Ages and the Renaissance.* Garden City, NY: Doubleday Anchor, 1957.

———. *A Documentary History of Art: Volume II; Michelangelo and the Mannerists, the Baroque and the Eighteenth Century.* Garden City, NY: Doubleday Anchor, 1958.

Hood, William. "Creating Memory: Monumental Painting and Cultural 'Definitions.'" In

Language and Images of Renaissance Italy, ed. Olson Brown, 151–69. Oxford: Clarendon, 1995.

———. *Fra Angelico at San Marco.* New Haven: Yale University Press, 1993.

———. "The State of Research in Italian Renaissance Art." *Art Bulletin* 69 (June 1987): 174–86.

Hope, Charles, and Elizabeth McGrath. "Artists and Humanists." In *The Cambridge Companion to Renaissance Humanism,* ed. Jill Kraye, 161–88. Cambridge: Cambridge University Press, 1996.

Howard, Jean. "The New Historicism in Renaissance Studies." *English Literary Renaissance* 16 (1986): 13–43.

Hyman, Isabelle, ed. *Brunelleschi in Perspective.* Englewood Cliffs, NJ: Prentice-Hall, 1979.

Jenkins, A. D. Fraser. "Cosimo dei Medici's Patronage of Architecture and the Theory of Magnificence." *Journal of the Warburg and Courtauld Institutes* 33 (1970): 162–70.

Kelley, Donald, ed. *Versions of History from Antiquity to the Enlightenment.* New Haven: Yale University Press, 1991.

Kempers, Bram. *Painting, Power, and Patronage: The Rise of the Professional Artist in the Italian Renaissance.* London: Allen Lane/Penguin, 1992.

Kohl, Benjamin G., and Roland G. Witt, with Elizabeth B. Welles, eds. *The Earthly Republic: Italian Humanists in Goverment and Society.* Philadelphia: University of Pennsylvania Press, 1978.

Krautheimer, Richard. "Alberti and Vitruvius." *The Renaissance and Mannerism. Studies in Western Art: Acts of the Twentieth International Congress of the History of Art,* II, 42–52. Princeton: Princeton University Press, 1963.

Krinsky, Carol. "Seventy-eight Vitruvius Manuscripts." *Journal of the Warburg and Courtauld Institutes* 30 (1967): 36–70.

Kristeller, Paul Oskar. *Renaissance Thought: The Classic, Scholastic, and Humanistic Strains.* New York: Harper and Row, 1965.

———. *Renaissance Thought II: Papers on Humanism and the Arts.* New York: Harper and Row, 1965.

Land, Norman. *The Viewer as Poet: The Renaissance Response to Art.* University Park: Pennsylvania State University Press, 1994.

Larner, John. *Culture and Society in Italy, 1290–1420.* London: Batsford, 1971.

Lehmann, Karl, and Phyllis Williams Lehmann. *Samothracian Reflections: Aspects of the Revival of the Antique.* Princeton: Princeton University Press, 1973.

Lemaitre, Alain J., and Erich Lessing. *Florence and the Renaissance: The Quattrocento.* Paris: Terrail, 1995.

Levenson, Jay. *Prints of the Italian Renaissance.* Washington: National Gallery of Art, 1973.

Levey, Michael. *Early Renaissance.* Harmondsworth, Baltimore, and Ringwood: Penguin, 1967.

———. *Florence: A Portrait.* Cambridge: Harvard University Press, 1996.

———. *High Renaissance.* Harmondsworth, Baltimore, and Ringwood: Penguin, 1975.

Lillie, Amanda. "The Humanist Villa Revisited." In *Language and Images of Renaissance Italy,* ed. Alison Brown, 193–215. Oxford: Clarendon, 1995.

"The Little Flowers" and the "Life of St. Francis" with the "Mirror of Perfection." London and Toronto: J. M. Dent; New York: E. P. Dutton, 1910.

Lopez, Robert S. *The Three Ages of the Italian Renaissance.* Boston and Toronto: Little, Brown, 1970.

MacDougall, Elisabeth Blair. *Fountains, Statues, and Flowers: Studies in Italian Gardens of the Sixteenth and Seventeenth Centuries.* Washington, DC: Dumbarton Oaks, 1994.

Mack, Charles R. "Bernardo Rossellino, L. B. Alberti, and the Truth about Nicolas V's Rome." *Southeastern College Art Conference* 10, no. 2 (1982): 60–69.

———. "Botticelli's *Venus:* Antique Allusions and Medicean Propaganda." *Explorations in Renaissance Culture* 28 (2002): 207–37.

———. "Brunelleschi's Hospital of the Innocents: Of Proportions and Intentional Fallicies." *Studies in Iconography* 5 (1979): 31–44.

———. "Nicholas V and the Rebuilding of Rome: Reality and Legacy." In *Light on the Eternal City,* ed. Hellmut Hager and Susan Munshower. Papers in Art History II, 30–56. University Park, PA: Pennsylvania State University, 1987.

———. *Pienza: The Creation of a Renaissance City.* Ithaca and London: Cornell University Press, 1987.

———. "The Rucellai Palace: Some New Proposals." *Art Bulletin* 56 (1974): 517–29.

———. "Studies in the Architectural Career of Bernardo di Matteo Ghamberelli, Called Rossellino." Diss., University of North Carolina at Chapel Hill, 1972.

Maiorino, Giancarlo. *Portrait of Eccentricity: Archimbolo and the Mannerist Grotesque.* University Park: Pennsylvania State University Press, 1991.

Manchester, William. *A World Lit Only by Fire: The Medieval Mind and the Renaissance: Portrait of an Age.* Boston, New York, Toronto, and London: Little, Brown, 1992.

Manetti, Antonio. *The Life of Brunelleschi.* Trans. Catherine Enggass and ed. Howard Saalman. University Park and London: Pennsylvania State University Press, 1970.

Manetti, Giannozzo. *De dignitate et excellentia hominis.* Padua: Antenore, 1975.

Martines, Lauro. *Power and Imagination: City-States in Renaissance Italy.* New York: Alfred A. Knopf, 1979.

Mather, Rufus Graves. *Excavating Buried Treasure.* Cambridge: Harvard University Press, 1945.

McGinn, Bernard. *The Calabrian Joachim of Fiore in the History of Western Thought.* New York: Macmillan, 1985.

Meditations on the Life of Christ. Trans. and ed. Isa Ragusa and Rosalie Green. Princeton: Princeton University Press, 1961.

Meiss, Millard. *The Painter's Choice: Problems in the Interpretation of Renaissance Art.* New York, Hagerstown, San Francisco, and London: Harper and Row, 1976.

———. *Painting in Florence and Siena after the Black Death: The Arts, Religion, and Society in the Mid–Fourteenth Century.* New York: Harper and Row, 1964.

Michelet, Jules. *Histoire de France.* Lausanne: Rencontre, 1965–67.

Minor, Vernon Hyde. *Art History's History.* 2nd ed., rev. Upper Saddle River, NJ: Prentice-Hall, 2001.

Moorman, J. *A History of the Franciscan Order from Its Origins to the Year 1517.* Oxford: Clarendon, 1968.

Morachiello, Paolo. *Fra Angelico: The San Marco Frescoes.* Trans. Eleanor Daunt. London: Thames and Hudson, 1996.

Morand, Kathleen. *Jean Pucelle.* Oxford: Clarendon, 1962.

Muratori, Ludovico, ed. *Rerum italicarum scriptores.* Milan, 1734.

Nagel, Alexander. Review of Jörg Traeger's *Renaissance und Religion: Die Kunst des Glaubens im Zeitalter Raphaels. Art Bulletin* 82 (December 2000): 773–77.

Norman, Dianna, ed. *Italian Art and Society: Siena, Florence, and Padua: Art, Society, and Religion, 1280–1400.* New Haven: Yale University Press, 1995.

Os, Henk van. "St. Francis of Assisi as a Second Christ in Early Italian Painting." *Simiolus* 7 (1974): 3–20.

Panofsky, Erwin. "Artist, Scientist, Genius: Notes on the 'Renaissance Dämmerung.'" In *The Renaissance: A Symposium, 1952.* New York: Metropolitan Museum of Art, 1953.

———. *Early Netherlandish Painting: Its Origins and Character.* Cambridge: Harvard University Press, 1953.

———. *The Life and Art of Albrecht Dürer.* 4th ed. Princeton: Princeton University Press, 1955.

———. *Renaissance and Renascences in Western Art.* New York: Harper and Row Torchbook, 1960.

———. *Studies in Iconology: Humanistic Themes in the Art of the Renaissance.* New York: Harper and Row Icon Editions, 1972.

Paoletti, John T., and Gary M. Radke. *Art in Renaissance Italy.* New York: Harry N. Abrams; Englewood Cliffs, NJ: Prentice-Hall, 1997.

Peragallo, Edward. *Origin and Evolution of Double Entry Bookkeeping: A Study of Italian Practice from the Fourteenth Century.* New York: American Institute Publishing, 1938.

Pevsner, Nikolaus. *An Outline of European Architecture.* Harmondsworth, Baltimore, and Victoria: Penguin, 1964.

Pius II (Aeneas Silvius Piccolomini). *Memoirs of a Renaissance Pope: The Commentaries of Pius II.* Trans. Florence A. Gragg and ed. Leona C. Gabel. New York: Capricorn, 1959.

Poggio Bracciolini. *Two Renaissance Book Hunters: The Letters of Poggius Bracciolini to Nicholaus de Niccolis.* Trans. and ed. Phyllis Gordon. New York: Columbia University Press, 1974.

Poliziano, Angelo. *Detti piacevoli.* Ed. Tiziano Zaneto. Rome: Istituto della Enciclopedia italiana, 1983.

Pollitt, J. J. *The Art of Greece, 1400–31 BC: Sources and Documents.* Englewood Cliffs, NJ: Prentice-Hall, 1965.

Polzer, Joseph. "Christ Judge, Saviour, Advocate, Franciscan Devotion, and the Doubting Thomas." In *Essays Presented to Myron P. Gilmore, II: History of Art, History of Music,* 301–10. Florence: La Nuova Italia, 1978.

Pope-Hennessy, John. *Italian Renaissance Sculpture.* New York: Random House, 1985.

Preyer, Brenda. "The Rucellai Palace." In F. W. Kent, A. Perosa, B. Preyer, P. Sanpaolesi, and R. Salvini, *Giovanni Rucellai ed il suo Zibaldone, II: A Florentine Patrician and His Palace,* 155–225. London: University of London, 1981.

Randall, Richard. "Frog in the Middle." *Metropolitan Museum of Art Bulletin* 16 (1958): 269–75.

Roover, Raymond de. "The Development of Accounting Prior to Luca Pacioli According to the Account Books of Medieval Merchants." In *Studies in the History of Accounting,* ed. Ananias C. Littleton and B. S. Yamey, 114–74. Homewood, IL: Richard D. Irwin, 1956.

Rose, Paul Lawrence. "Humanist Culture and Renaissance Mathematics." *Studies in the Renaissance* 20 (1973): 46–106.

———. *The Italian Renaissance of Mathematics: Studies on Humanists and Mathematicians from Petrarch to Galileo.* Geneva: Librairie Droz, 1975.

Ross, Janet. *Lives of the Early Medici as Told in Their Correspondance.* London: Chatto, 1910.

Rubinstein, Ruth. "Pius II and Roman Ruins." In *Renaissance* II, The Society for Renaissance Studies, 2:197–203. Oxford: Oxford University Press, 1988.

Rucellai, Giovanni. *Giovanni Rucellai ed il suo Zibaldone, I: "Il Zibaldone Quaresimale," Pagine scelte.* Ed. Alessandro Perosa. London: University of London, 1960.

Ruskin, John. *The Stones of Venice.* 3 vols. New York: John Wiley and Sons, 1880.

Rykwert, Joseph, and Anne Engel, eds. *Leon Battista Alberti.* Milan: Olivetti/Electa, 1994.

Saalman, Howard. *Filippo Brunelleschi: The Buildings.* University Park: Pennsylvania State University Press, 1993.

———. "The Palazzo Comunale in Montepulciano: An Unknown Work by Michelozzo." *Zeitschrift für Kunstgeschichte* 28 (1965): 1–65.

———. "Review of *Giovanni Rucellai ed il suo Zibaldone.*" *Journal of the Society of Architectural Historians* 47 (1988): 82–90.

Sanpaolesi, Piero. "Costruzioni del primo Quattrocento nella Badia Fiorentina." *Rivista d'Arte* 41 (1956): 11–29.

Scapecchi, Piero. *Cortona: arte, storia e cultura.* Genoa: Sagep, 1980.

Shearman, John. "Masaccio's *Pisa Altar-piece:* An Alternative Reconstruction." *Burlington Magazine* 108 (1966): 449–55.

———. *Only Connect: Art and the Spectator in the Italian Renaissance.* Princeton: Princeton University Press, 1992.

Singleton, Charles S., ed. *Art, Science, and History in the Renaissance.* Baltimore: Johns Hopkins University Press, 1967.

Smart, Alaistair. *The Assisi Problem and the Art of Giotto.* Oxford: Clarendon, 1971.

Smith, Christine. *Architecture in the Culture of Early Humanism: Ethics, Aesthetics, and Eloquence, 1400–1470.* Oxford: Oxford University Press, 1992.

Spencer, John R. "Volterra, 1466." *Art Bulletin* 48 (1966): 95–96.

Spivey, Nigel. *Etruscan Art.* London: Thames and Hudson, 1997.

Stephens, John. *The Italian Renaissance: The Origins of Intellectual and Artistic Change before the Reformation.* London and New York: Longman, 1990.

Stinger, Charles L. *The Renaissance in Rome.* Bloomington: Indiana University Press, 1985.

Struever, N. *The Language of History in the Renaissance.* Princeton: Princeton University Press, 1970.

Sypher, Wylie. *Four Stages of Renaissance Style: Transformations in Art and Literature, 1400–1700.* Garden City, NY: Doubleday Anchor Book, 1955.

Tafuri, Manfredo. "Cives esse non linere: The Rome of Nicholas V and Leon Battista Alberti. Elements towards a Historical Revision." *Harvard Architectural Review* 6 (1977): 61–75.

Tertullian. *Disciplinary, Moral, and Ascetical Works.* Trans. Rudolph Arbesmann, Sister Emily Joseph Daly, and Edwin A. Quain. New York: Fathers of the Church, 1959.

Thode, Henry. *Francesco d'Assisi e le origini dell'arte del Rinascimento in Italia.* Rome: Donzelli, 1993.

Thomas à Kempis. *The Imitation of Christ.* New York: Walter J. Black, 1932.

Thorndike, Lynn. "Renaissance or Prenaissance." *Journal of the History of Ideas* 4 (1943): 65–74.

Trachtenberg, Marvin. "Review Essay: Renaissance Stories." *Journal of the Society of Architectural Historians* 59 (2000): 380–85.

Traeger, Jörg. *Renaissance und Religion: Die Kunst des Glaubens im Zeitalter Raphaels.* Munich: Beck, 1997.

Trexler, Richard. "Florentine Religious Experience: The Sacred Image." *Studies in the Renaissance* 19 (1972): 7–41.

Trinkaus, Charles Edward. *In Our Image and Likeness: Humanity and Divinity in Italian Humanist Thought.* 2 vols. London: Constable, 1970.

———. *The Scope of Renaissance Humanism.* Ann Arbor: University of Michigan Press, 1983.

Turner, A. Richard. *Renaissance Florence: The Invention of a New Art.* New York: Abrams; Saddle River, NJ: Prentice-Hall, 1997.

———. *The Vision of Landscape in Renaissance Italy.* Princeton: Princeton University Press, 1966.

Urgurgieri della Bererdenga, C. *Pio II Piccolomini con notizie su Pio III e altri membri della famiglia.* Florence: Olschki, 1973.

Uzielli, Gustavo. *La vita e i tempi di Paolo dal Pozzo Toscanelli.* Rome: Ministerio della pubblica istruzione, 1894.

Vasari, Giorgio. *The Lives of the Painters, Sculptors, and Architects.* Ed. William Gaunt. London: Dent; New York: Dutton, 1963.

Verdon, Timothy, and J. Henderson. *Christianity and the Renaissance: Image and Religious Imagination in the Quattrocento.* Syracuse: Syracuse University Press, 1990.

Vespasiano da Bisticci. *Renaissance Princes, Popes, and Prelates: The Vespasiano Memoirs; Lives of Illustrious Men of the Fifteenth Century.* Intro. Myron Gilmore and trans. William George and Emily Waters. New York, Evanston, and London: Harper and Row, 1963.

Vitruvius. *The Ten Books on Architecture.* Trans. Morris Hickey Morgan. Cambridge: Harvard University Press, 1914.

Wackernagel, Martin. *The World of the Florentine Renaissance Artist: Projects and Patrons, Workshops and Art Market.* Trans. A. Luchs. Princeton: Princeton University Press, 1981.

Warren, C. "Brunelleschi's Dome and Dufay's Motet." *Musical Quarterly* 59 (1973): 92–105.

Weiss, Roberto. *The Renaissance Discovery of Classical Antiquity.* Oxford: Basil Blackwell, 1969.

Welch, Evelyn. *Art and Society in Italy, 1350–1500.* Oxford and New York: Oxford University Press, Oxford History of Art, 1997.

Westfall, Carroll William. *In This Most Perfect Paradise: Alberti, Nicholas V, and the Invention of Conscious Urban Planning in Rome, 1447–55.* University Park: Pennsylvania State University Press, 1974.

White, John. *Birth and Rebirth of Pictorial Space.* London: Faber, 1967.

Wightman, W. *Science in Renaissance Society.* London: Hutchinson, 1972.

Wilcox, D. *The Development of Florentine Humanist Historiography in the Fifteenth Century.* Cambridge: Harvard University Press, 1969.

Williamson, Hugh Ross. *Lorenzo the Magnificent.* London: Michael Joseph, 1974.

Wittkower, Rudolf. *Architectural Principles in the Age of Humanism.* London: Alec Tiranti, 1962.

Wohl, Hellmut. *The Aesthetics of Italian Renaissance Art: A Reconsideration of Style.* Cambridge: Cambridge University Press, 1999.

Wood, Christopher W. *Albrecht Altdorfer and the Origins of Landscape.* Chicago: University of Chicago Press, 1993.

Woodward, W. H. *Studies in Education during the Age of the Renaissance, 1400–1600.* Cambridge: Cambridge University Press, 1906.

Zwijnenberg, Robert. *The Writings and Drawings of Leonardo da Vinci: Order and Chaos in Early Modern Thought.* Trans. Caroline A. van Eck. Cambridge, New York, and Melbourne: Cambridge University Press, 1999.

Index

Plates

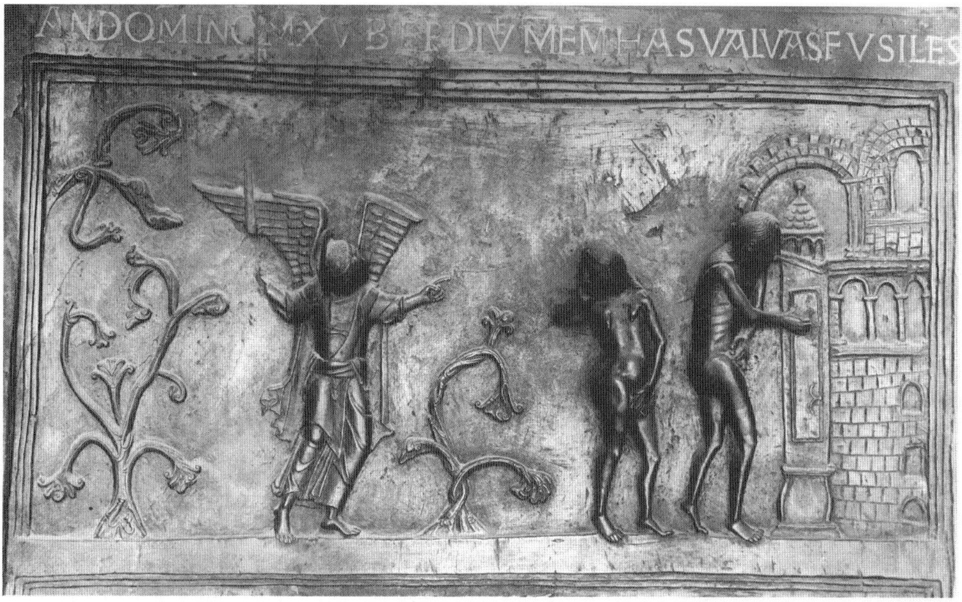

Fig. 1. *Expulsion of Adam and Eve from Paradise,* ca. 1015, Doors of St. Michael's, Hildesheim, Germany. (Photo: Foto Marburg/Art Resource, New York.)

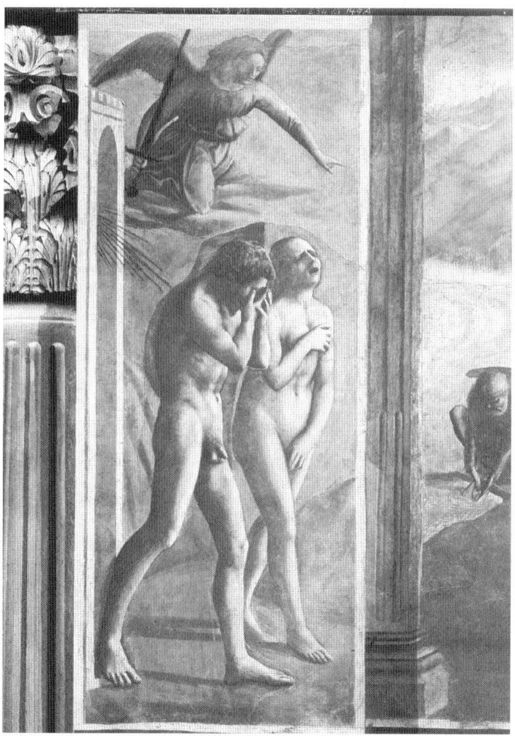

Fig. 2. Masaccio, *Expulsion of Adam and Eve from Paradise,* ca. 1425, Brancacci Chapel, Church of Santa Maria del Carmine, Florence. (Photo: Scala/Art Resource, New York.)

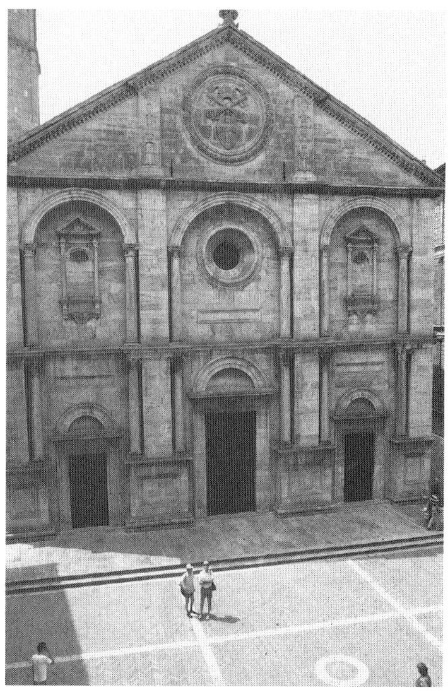

Fig. 3. Bernardo Rossellino, Facade of the Pienza Cathedral, 1459–63. (Photo: author.)

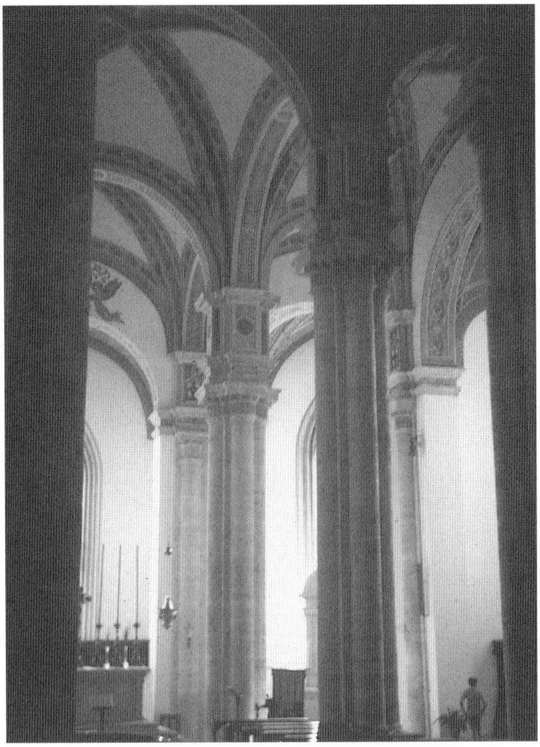

Fig. 4. Bernardo Rossellino, Interior of the Pienza Cathedral, 1459–63. (Photo: author.)

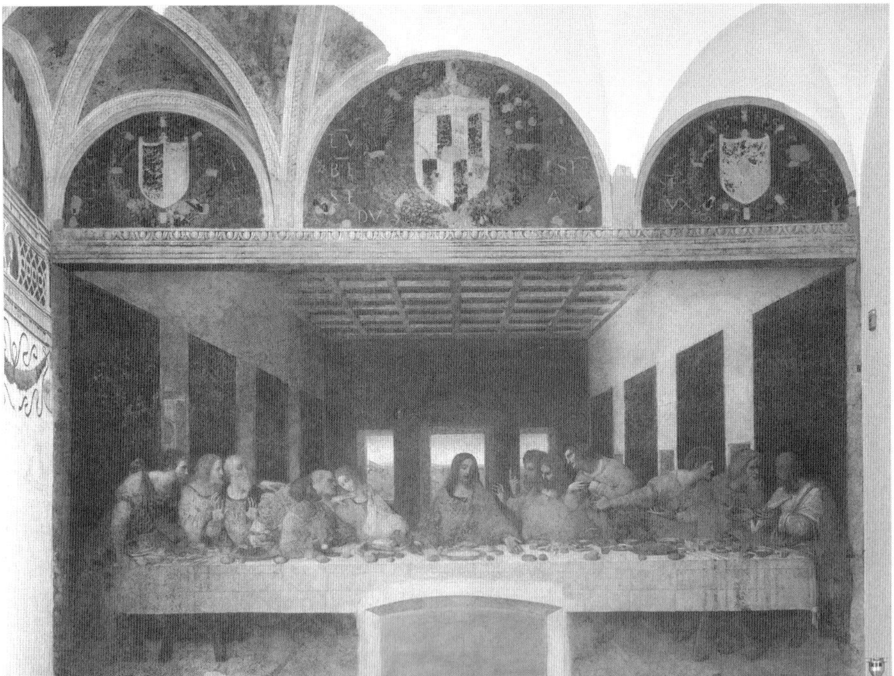

Fig. 5. Leonardo da Vinci, *The Last Supper,* 1495–98, Refectory of the Monastery of Santa Maria delle Grazie, Milan. (Photo: Scala/Art Resource, New York.)

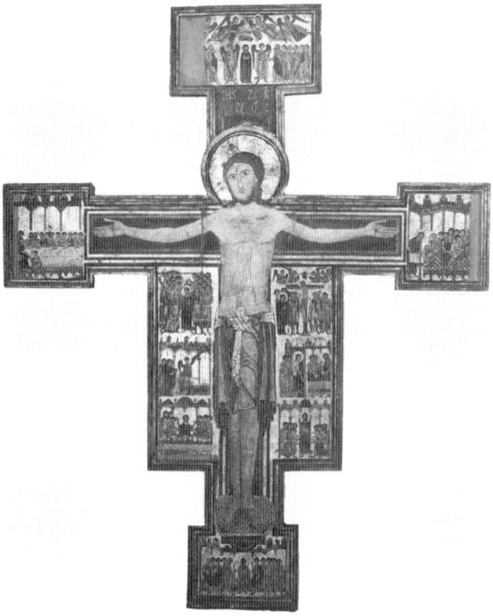

Fig. 6. Anonymous Pisan artist, *Pisa Cross #15,* late twelfth century, Museo Civico, Pisa. (Photo: Alinari/Art Resource, New York.)

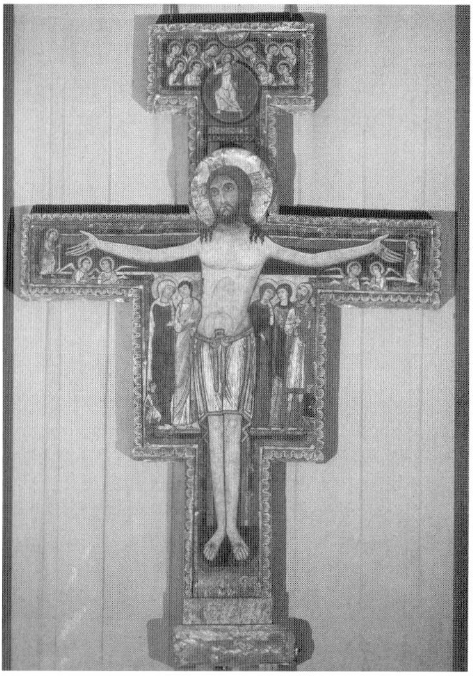

Fig. 7. Anonymous artist, *Cross of San Damiano,* late twelfth century, Basilica of Santa Chiara, Assisi. (Photo: Scala/Art Resource, New York.)

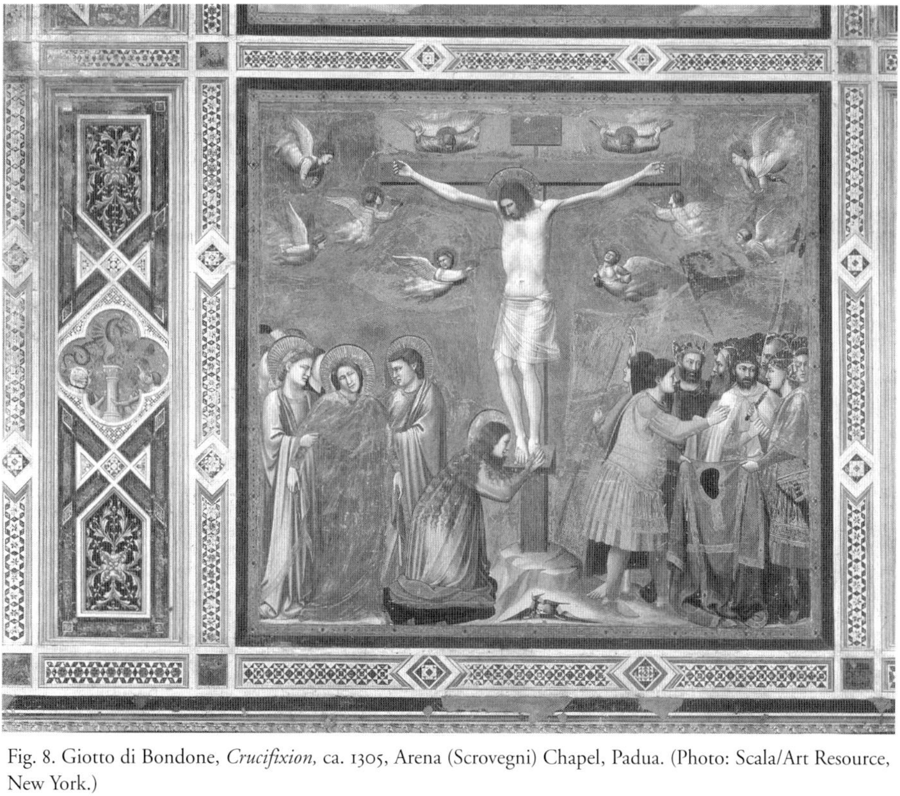

Fig. 8. Giotto di Bondone, *Crucifixion,* ca. 1305, Arena (Scrovegni) Chapel, Padua. (Photo: Scala/Art Resource, New York.)

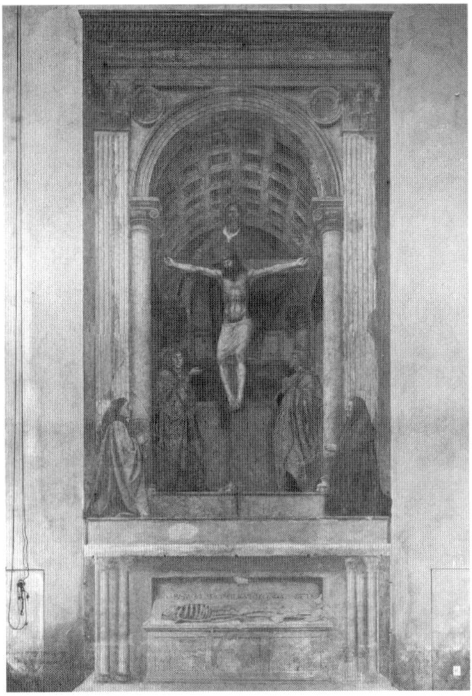

Fig. 9. Masaccio, *Trinity Fresco,* ca. 1427, Church of Santa Maria Novella, Florence. (Photo: Scala/Art Resource, New York.)

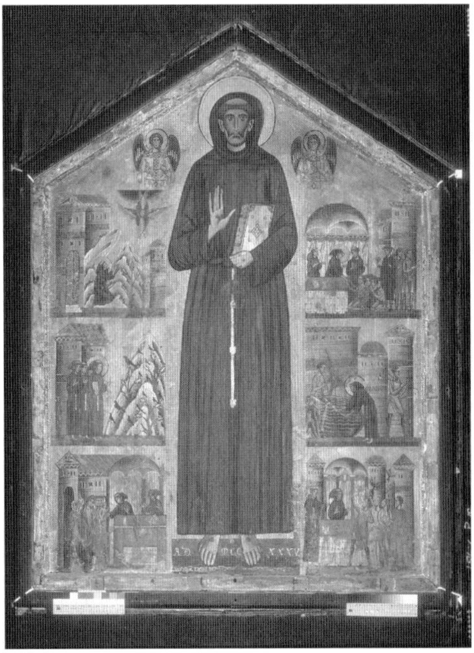

Fig. 10. Bonaventura Berlinghieri, *Altarpiece of St. Francis,* 1235, Church of San Francesco, Pescia. (Photo: Scala/Art Resource, New York.)

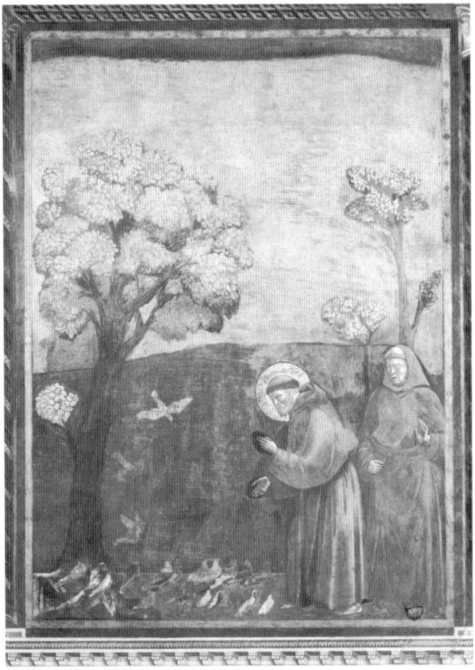

Fig. 11. St. Francis Master, *St. Francis Preaching to the Birds,* early fourteenth century, Upper Church of San Francesco, Assisi. (Photo: Scala/Art Resource, New York.)

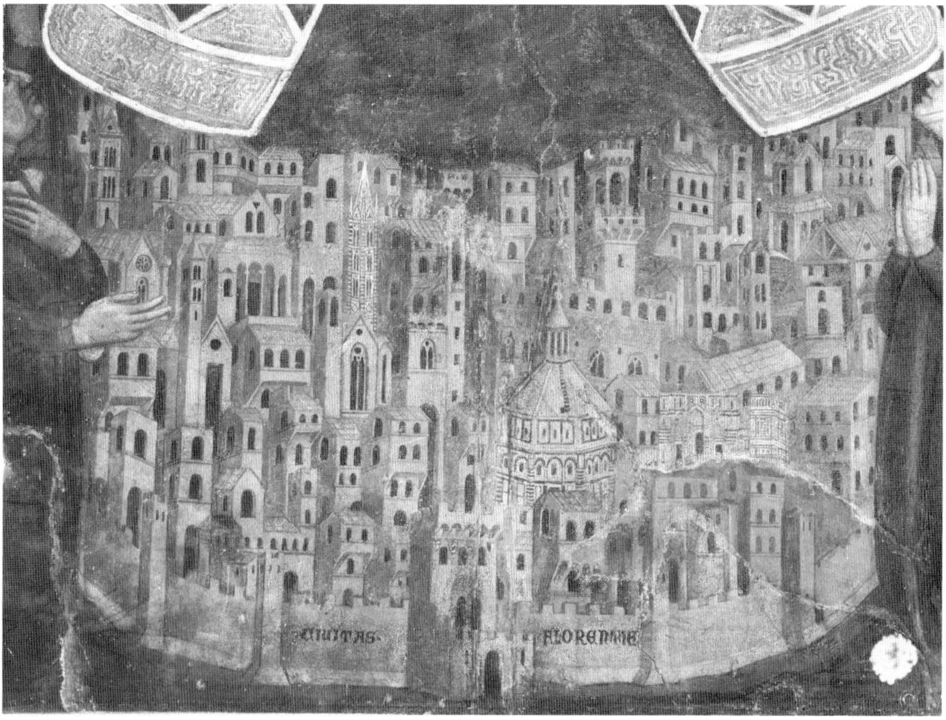

Fig. 12. Anonymous Florentine artist, Detail of the *Misericordia Fresco* from the Loggia del Bigallo, 1352, Council Chamber, Misericordia Palace, Florence. (Photo: Alinari/Art Resource, New York.)

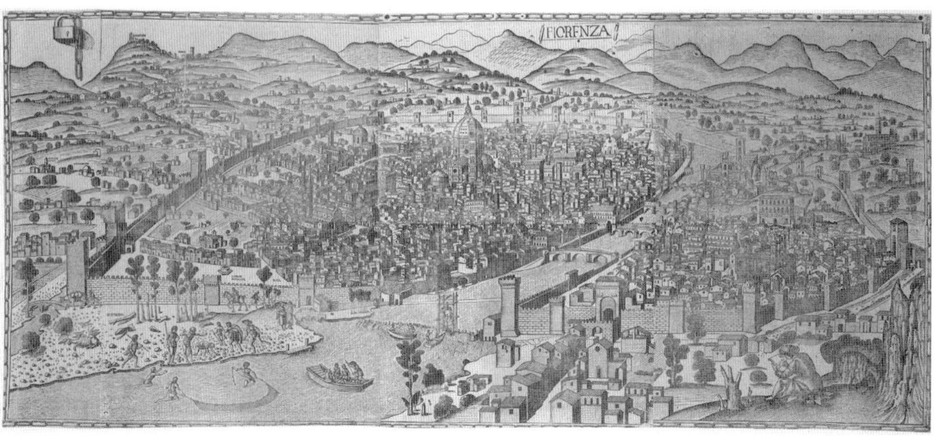

Fig. 13. Florentine artist (Francesco Rosselli?), *"Della Catena" View of Florence,* 1470s, Kupferstichkabinett, Staatliche Museen zu Berlin. (Photo: Bildarchiv Preußischer Kulturbesitz/Art Resource, New York.)

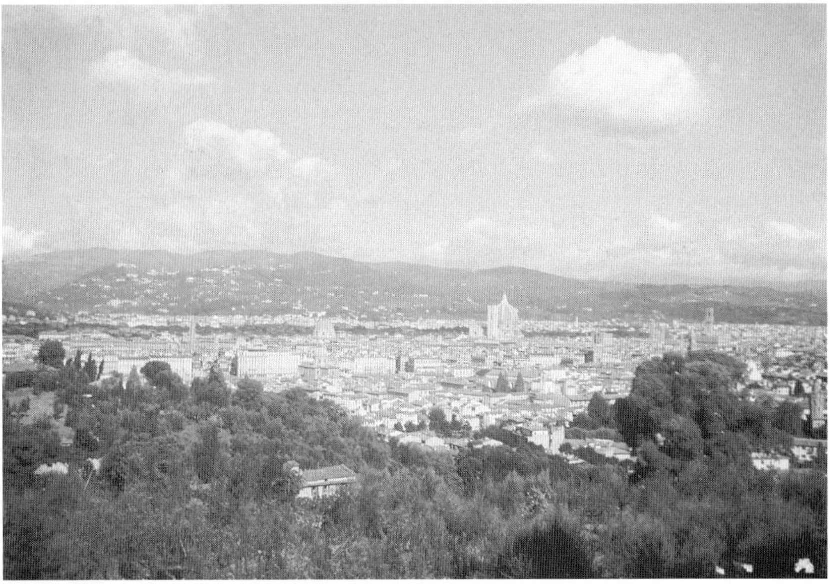

Fig. 14. Present-day view of Florence from the Costa San Giorgio. (Photo: author.)

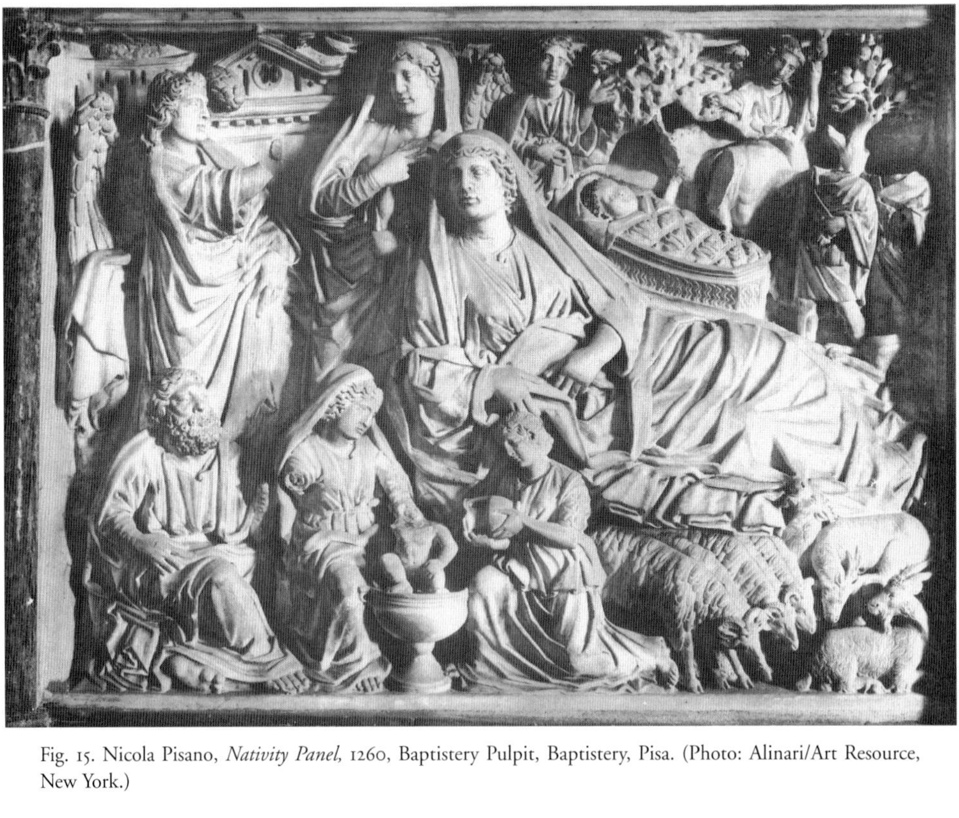

Fig. 15. Nicola Pisano, *Nativity Panel,* 1260, Baptistery Pulpit, Baptistery, Pisa. (Photo: Alinari/Art Resource, New York.)

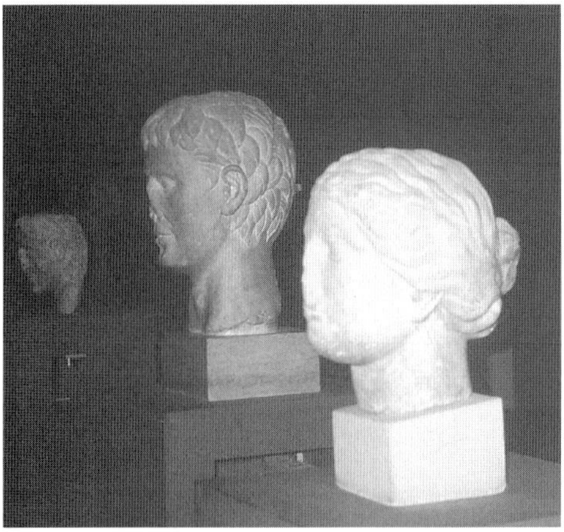

Fig. 16. Medieval heads in the "antique manner" from the Gate of Capua, 1234–39. (Photo: author.)

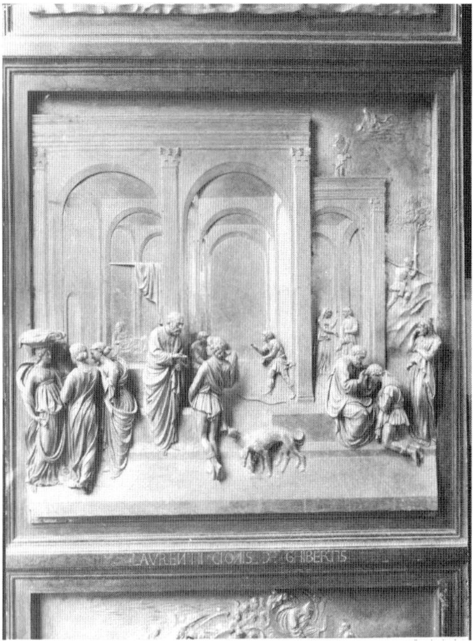

Fig. 17. Lorenzo Ghiberti, *Jacob and Esau Panel,* 1435, East Doors, Baptistery, Florence. (Photo: Alinari/Art Resource, New York.)

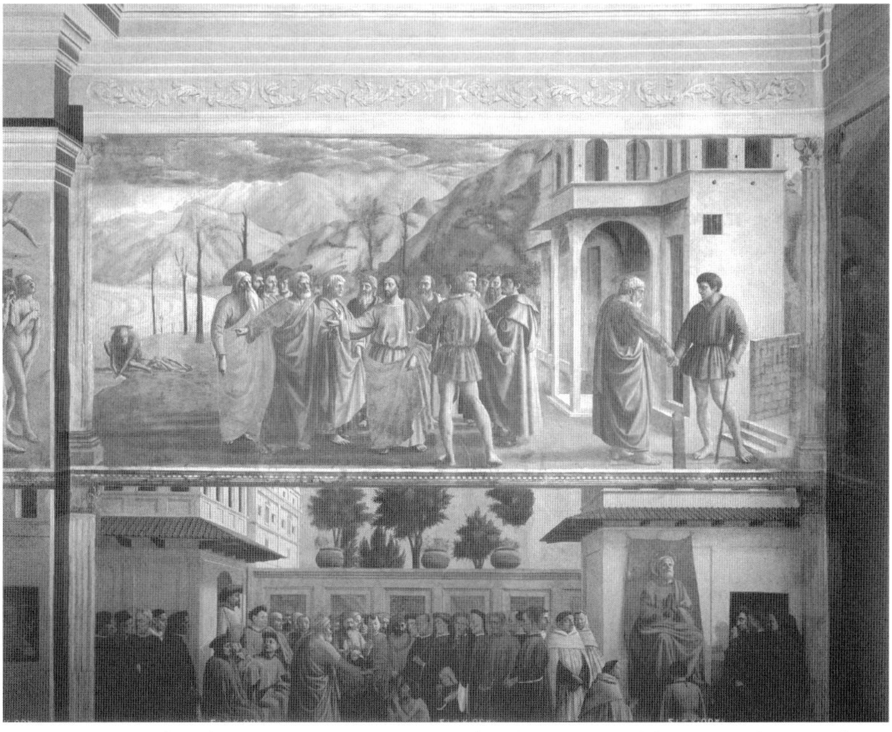

Fig. 18. Masaccio, *The Tribute Money,* ca. 1425, Brancacci Chapel, Santa Maria del Carmine, Florence. (Photo: Scala/Art Resource, New York.)

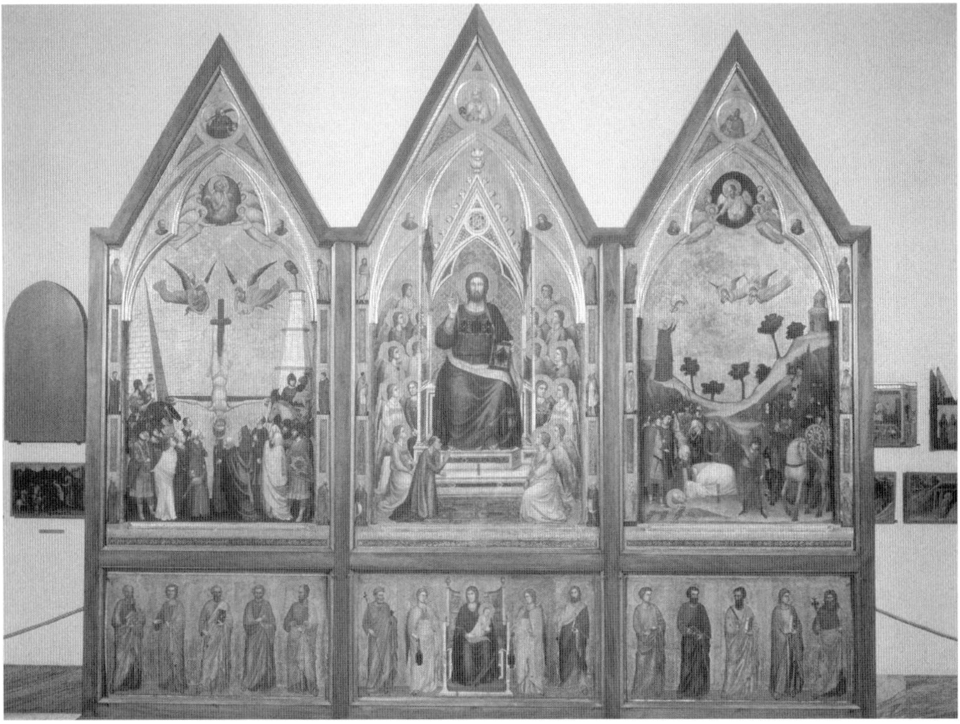

Fig. 19. Giotto di Bondone, *Stefaneschi Altarpiece,* ca. 1330, Pinacoteca, Vatican Museums. (Photo: Scala/Art Resource, New York.)

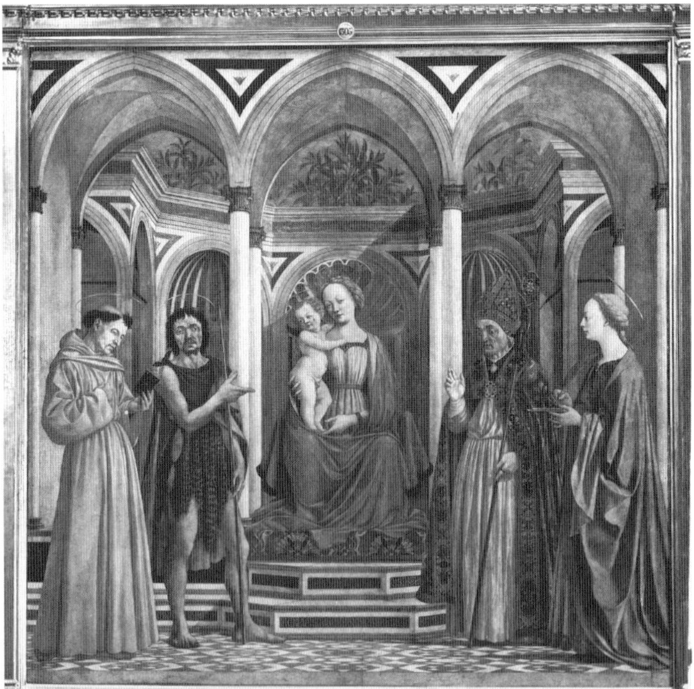

Fig. 20. Domenico Veneziano, *St. Lucy Altarpiece,* ca. 1450, Galleria degli Uffizi, Florence. (Photo: Alinari/Art Resource, New York.)

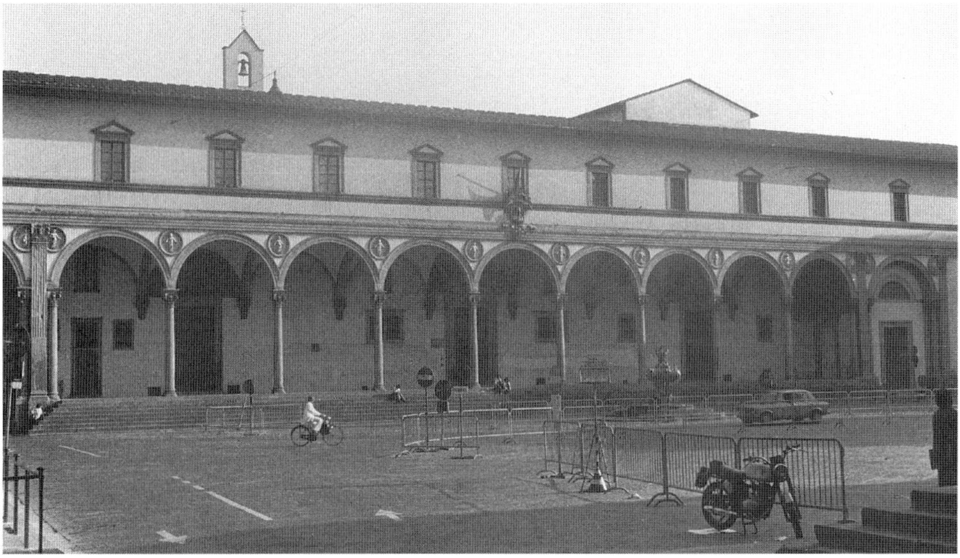

Fig. 21. Brunelleschi, Loggia Facade of the Hospital of the Innocents, begun 1419, Florence. (Photo: author.)

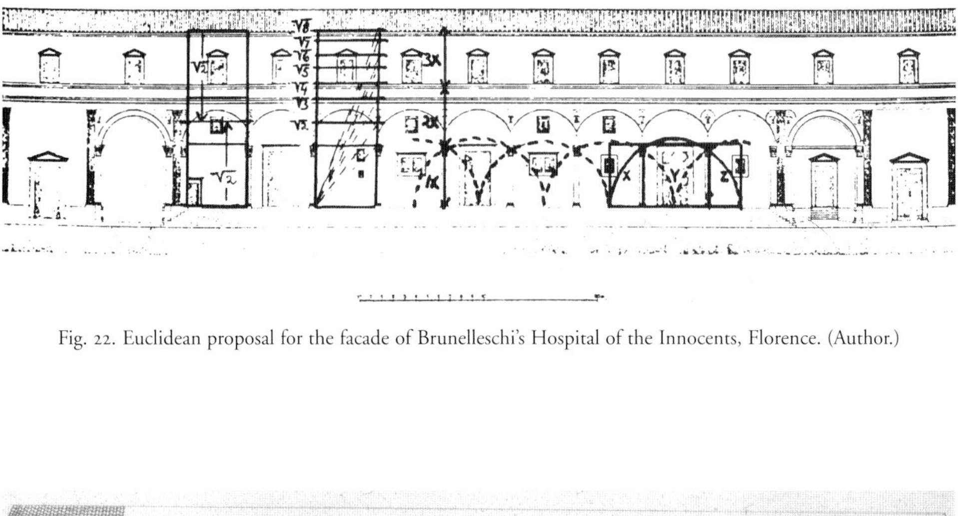

Fig. 22. Euclidean proposal for the facade of Brunelleschi's Hospital of the Innocents, Florence. (Author.)

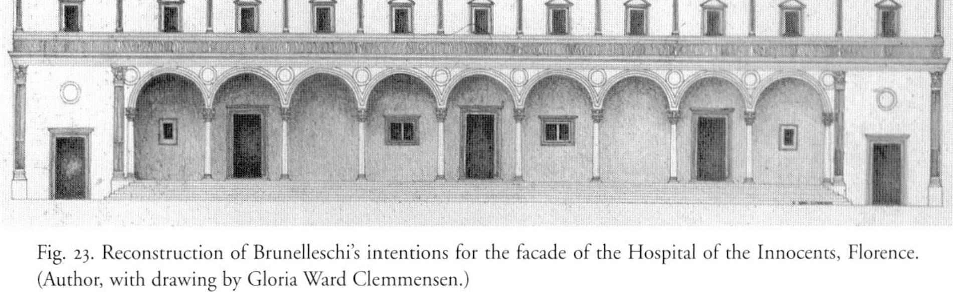

Fig. 23. Reconstruction of Brunelleschi's intentions for the facade of the Hospital of the Innocents, Florence. (Author, with drawing by Gloria Ward Clemmensen.)

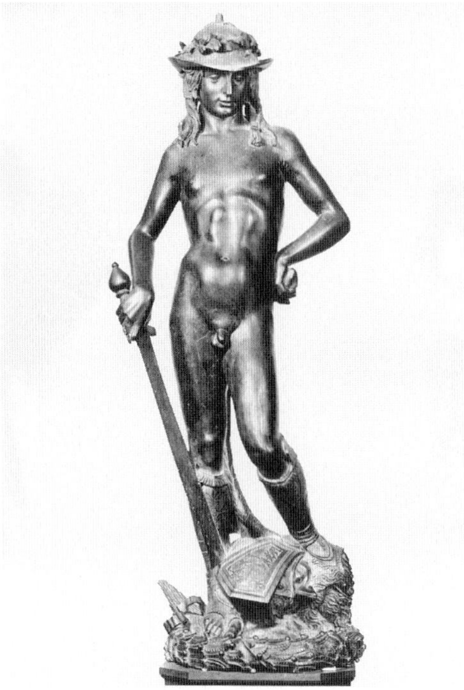

Fig. 24. Donatello, *Bronze David,* ca. 1435–45, Museo Nazionale Bargello, Florence. (Photo: Alinari/Art Resource, New York.)

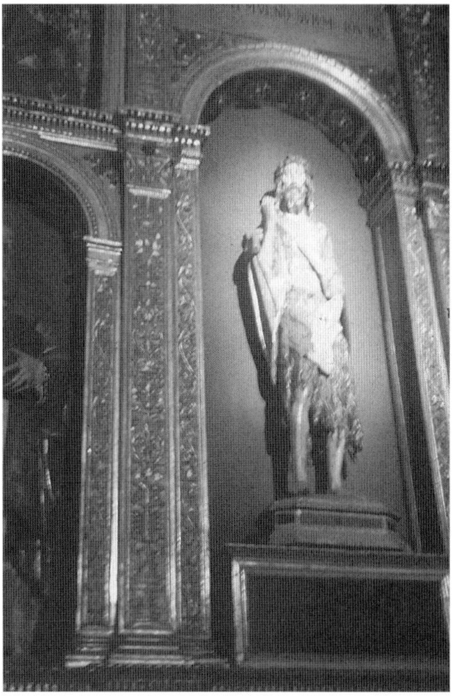

Fig. 25. Donatello, *John the Baptist,* 1435, Church of the Frari, Venice. (Photo: author.)

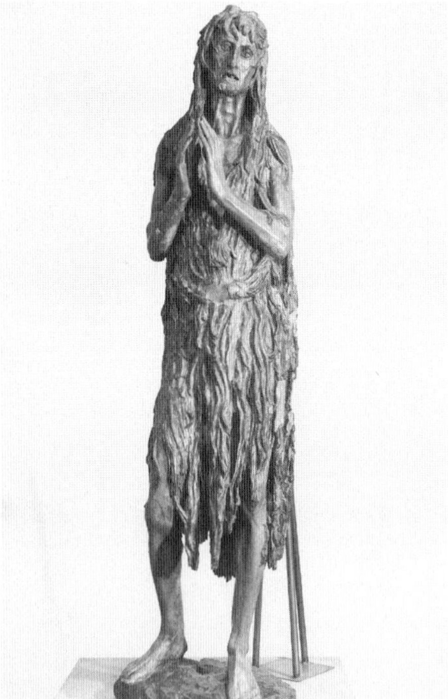

Fig. 26. Donatello, *Mary Magdalene,* ca. 1435 or ca. 1450, Museo dell'Opera del Duomo (formerly Baptistery), Florence. (Photo: Alinari/Art Resource, New York.)

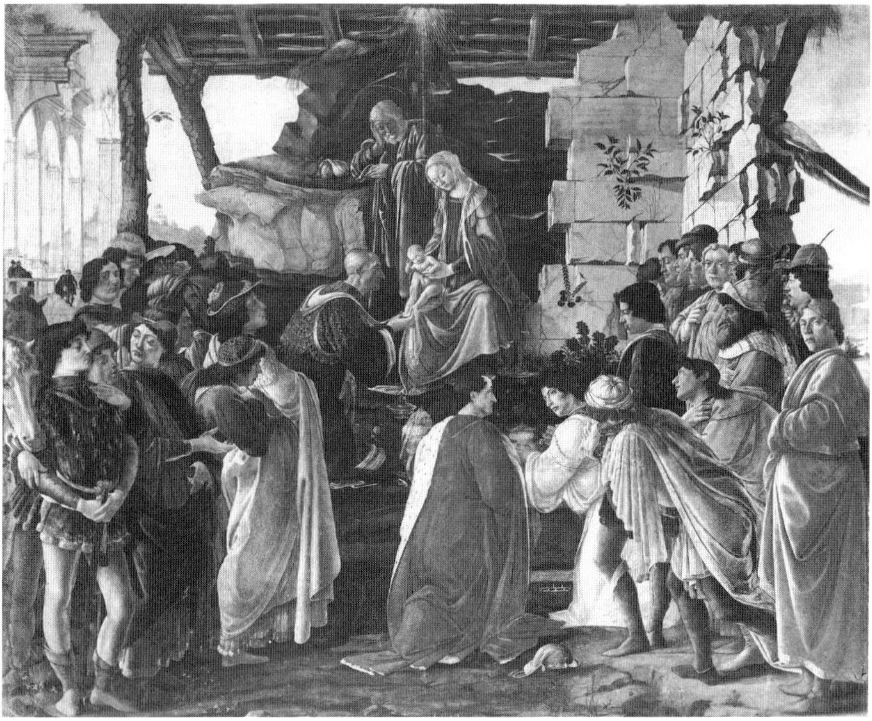

Fig. 27. Sandro Botticelli, *Guaspare del Lama Adoration Altarpiece (Adoration of the Magi),* early 1470s, Uffizi Gallery, Florence. (Photo: Alinari/Art Resource, New York.)

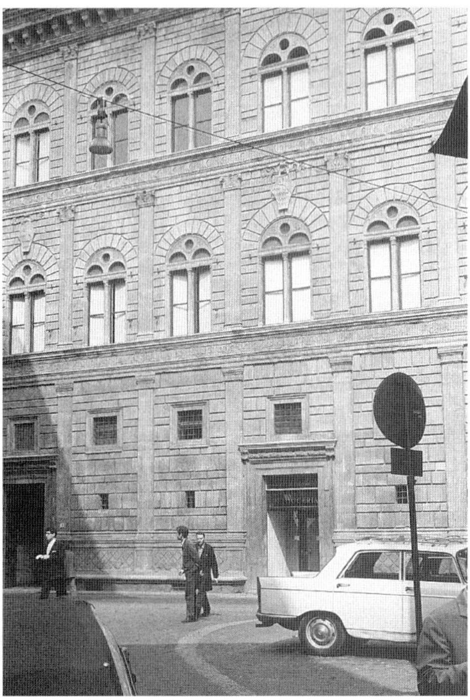

Fig. 28. Bernardo Rossellino or L. B. Alberti, facade of the Palazzo Rucellai, ca. 1460, Florence. (Photo: author.)

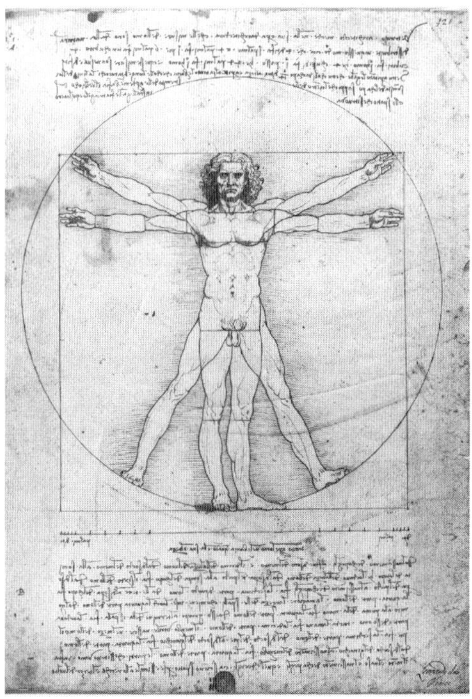

Fig. 29. Leonardo da Vinci, *Vitruvian Man (Self-Portrait in Circle and Square),* 1485–90, Accademia, Venice. (Photo: Alinari/Art Resource, New York.)

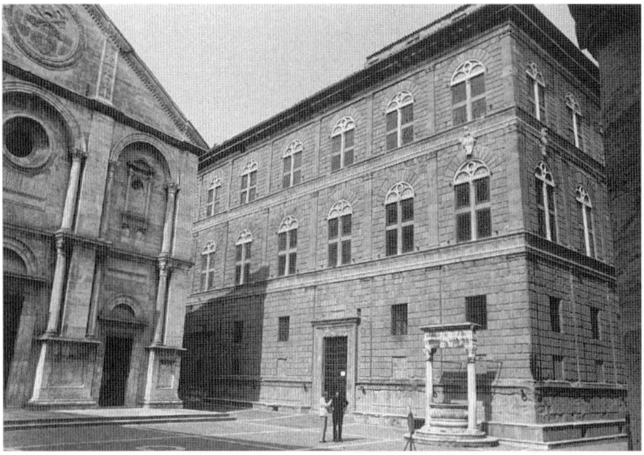

Fig. 30. Bernardo Rossellino, Cathedral Square, 1462, Pienza. (Photo: author.)

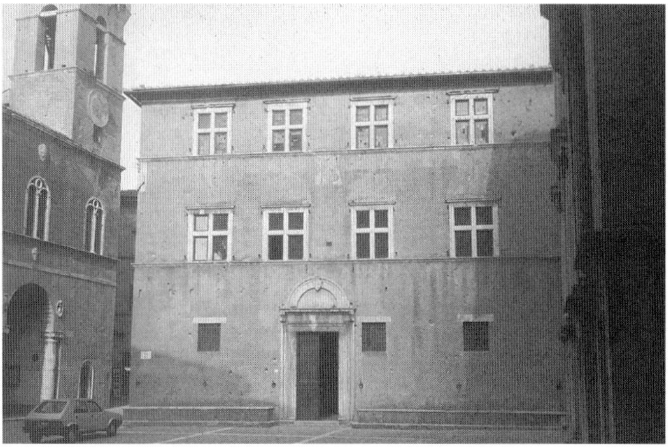

Fig. 31. Bernardo Rossellino, Bishop's Palace of Cardinal Rodrigo Borgia, 1462–64, Pienza. (Photo: author.)

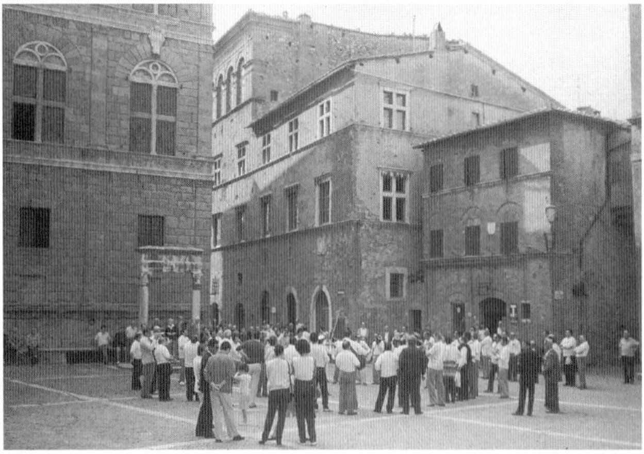

Fig. 32. Bernardo Rossellino, Palazzo Ammannati with its belvedere loggia, 1460–68, Pienza. (Photo: author.)

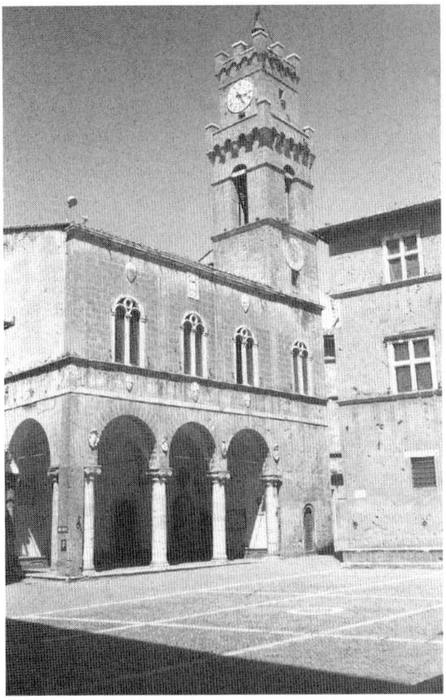

Fig. 33. Palazzo Communale, 1462–63, Pienza. (Photo: author.)

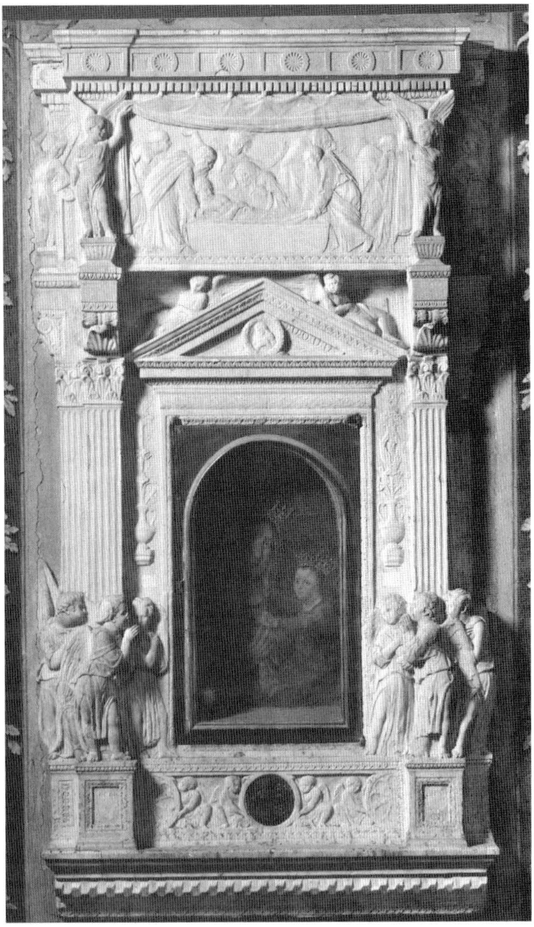

Fig. 35. Donatello, Tabernacle with relief of the *Entombment of Christ,* ca. 1433, Sagrestia dei Beneficiati, St. Peter's, Rome. (Photo: Alinari/Art Resource, New York.)

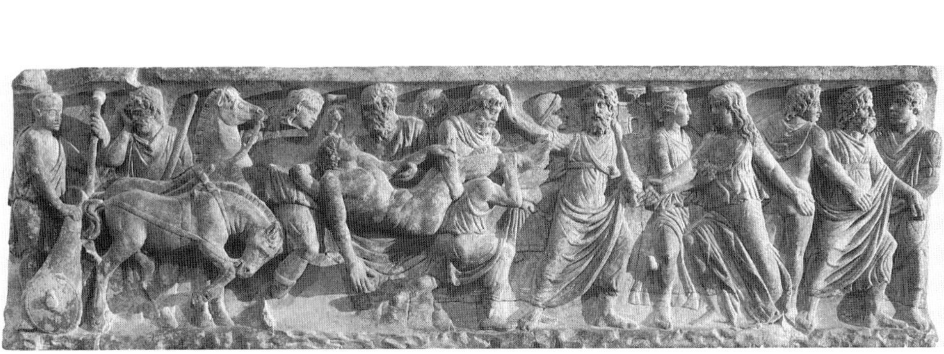

Fig. 34. Roman sarcophagus front, *The Return of the Body of Meleager to Kalydon,* ca. A.D. 220–30. (Courtesy of The Museum of Fine Arts, Houston; Funded by the Agnes Cullen Arnold Endowment.)

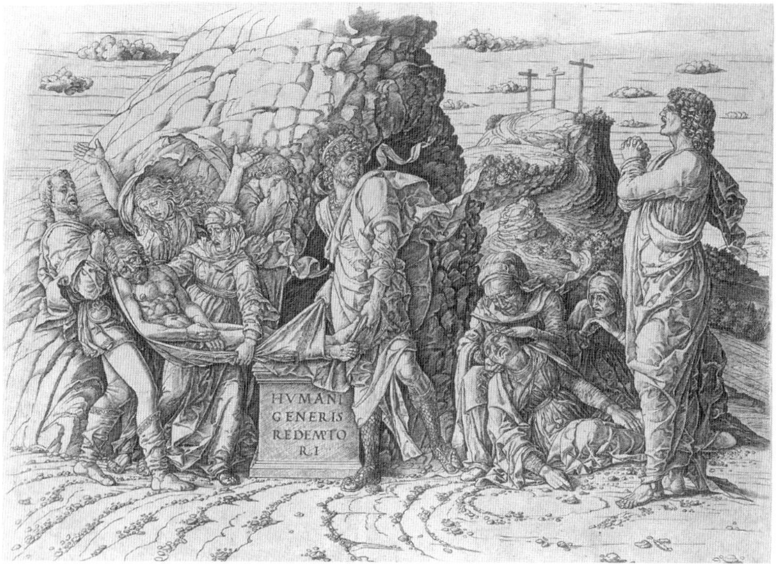

Fig. 36. Andrea Mantegna, Engraving of the *Entombment of Christ,* 1460s, Kupferstichkabinett, Staatliche Museen zu Berlin (Photo: Bildarchiv Preußischer Kulturbesitz/Art Resource, New York.)

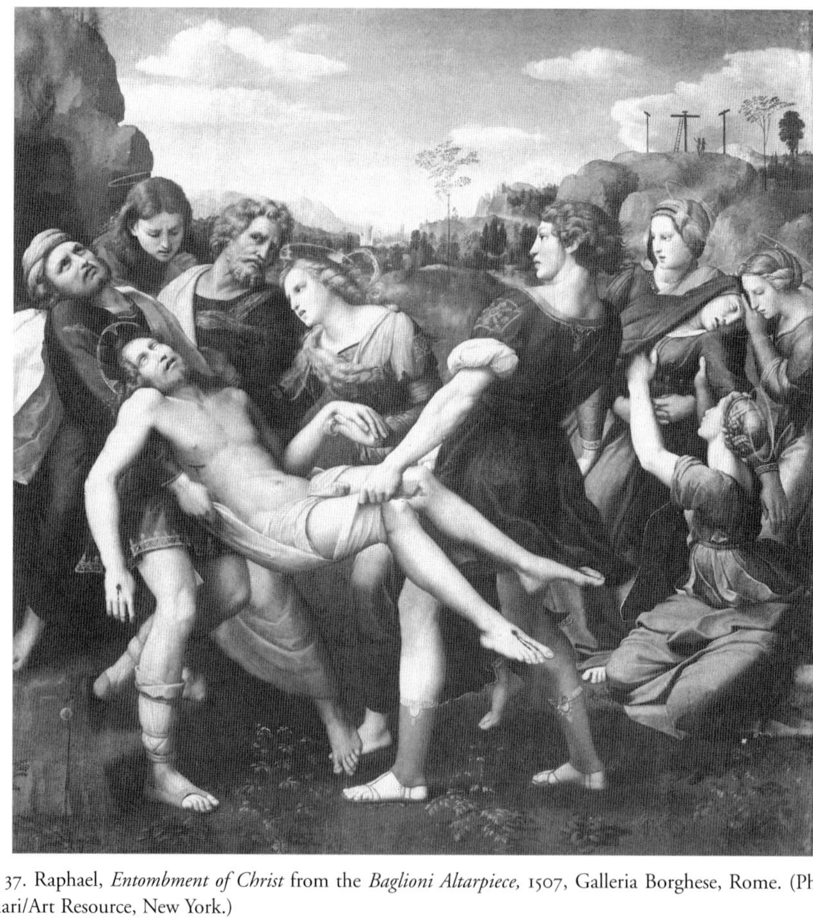

Fig. 37. Raphael, *Entombment of Christ* from the *Baglioni Altarpiece,* 1507, Galleria Borghese, Rome. (Photo: Alinari/Art Resource, New York.)

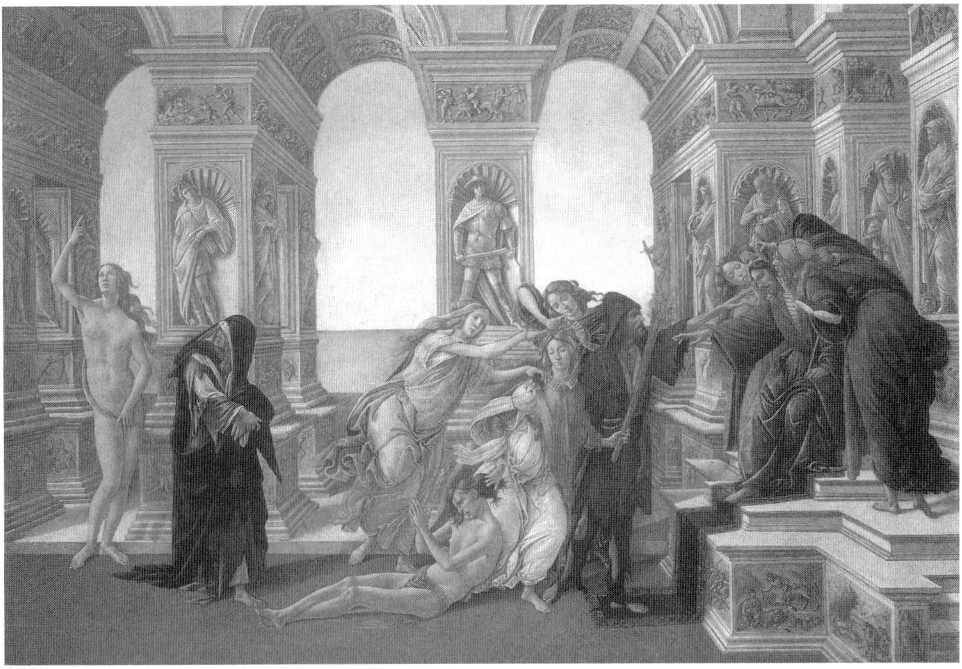

Fig. 38. Sandro Botticelli, *The Calumny of Apelles,* 1497–98, Galleria degli Uffizi, Florence. (Photo: Scala/Art Resource, New York.)

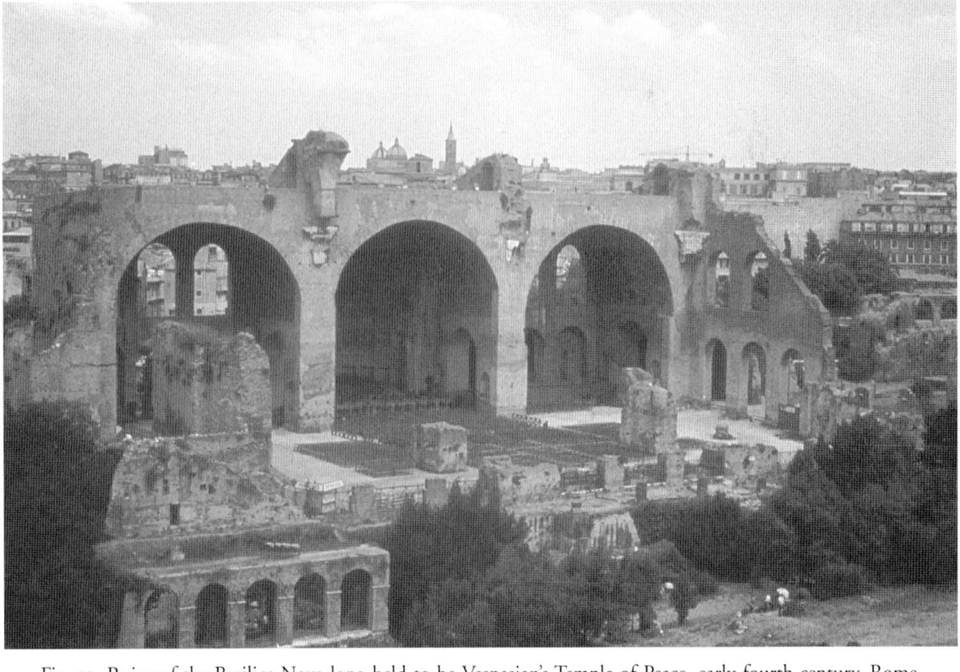

Fig. 39. Ruins of the Basilica Nova long held to be Vespasian's Temple of Peace, early fourth century, Rome. (Photo: author.)

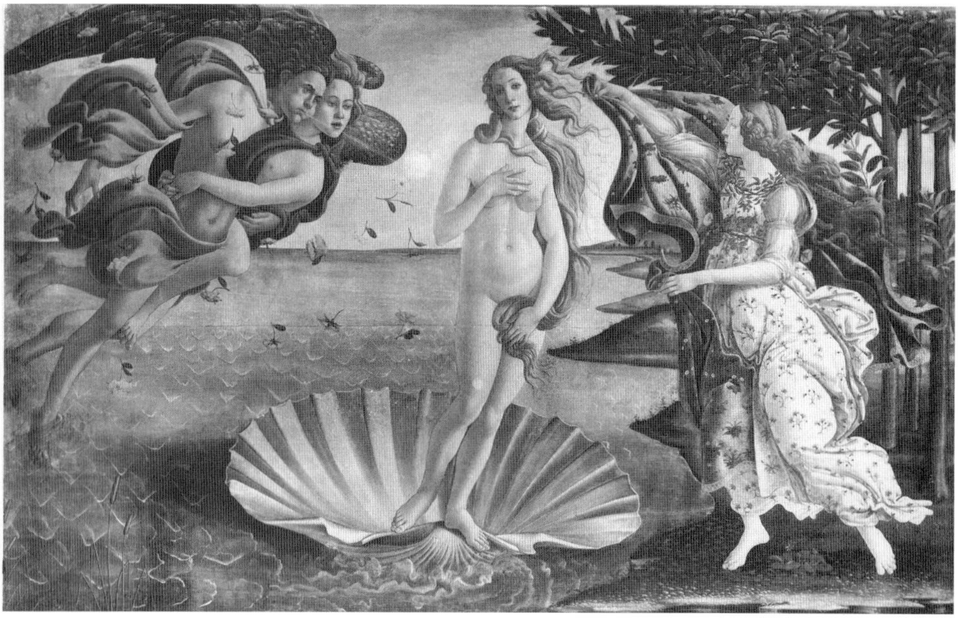

Fig. 40. Sandro Botticelli, *The Arrival of Venus,* 1481, Galleria degli Uffizi, Florence. (Photo: Alinari/Art Resource, New York.)

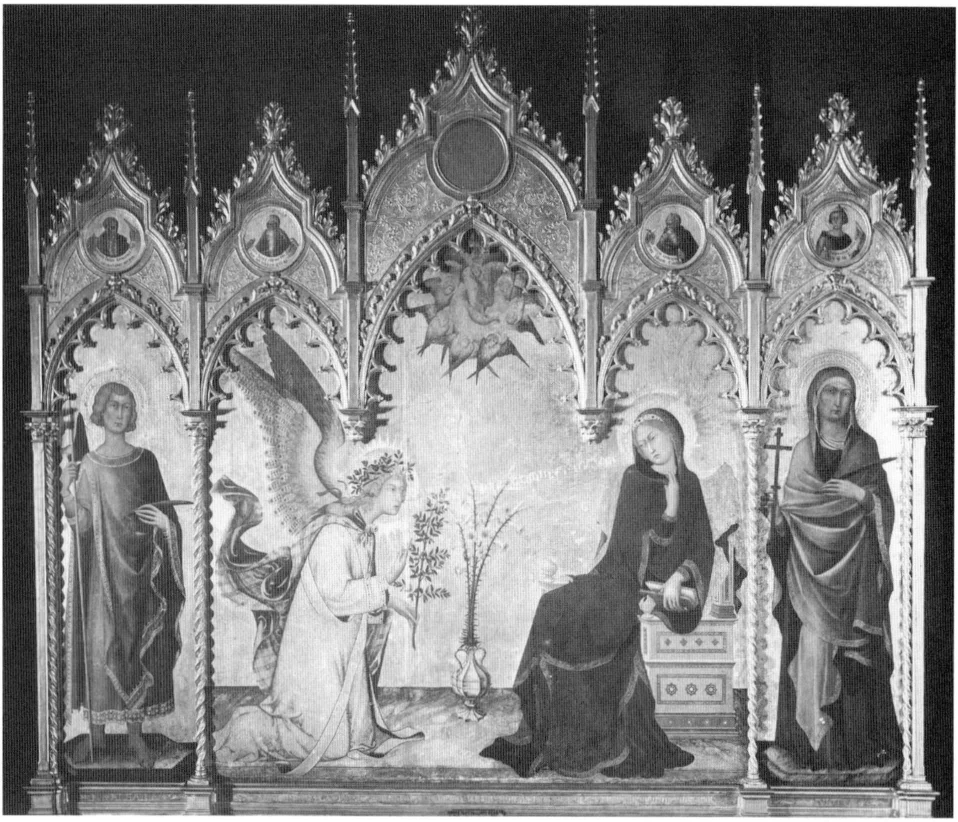

Fig. 41. Simone Martini, *The Annunciation,* 1333, Galleria degli Uffizi, Florence. (Photo: Alinari/Art Resource, New York.)

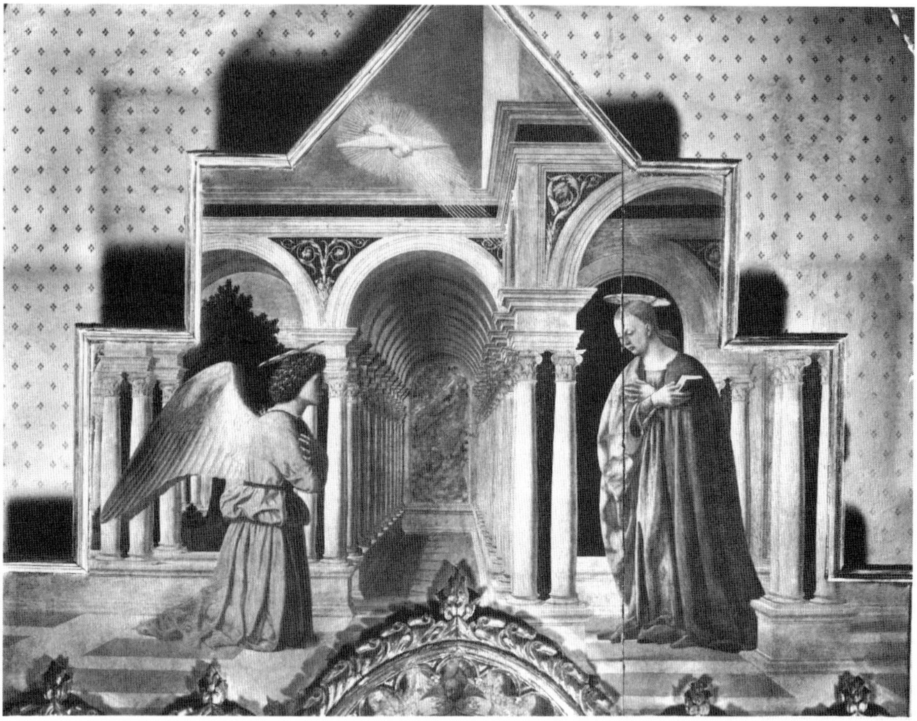

Fig. 42. Piero della Francesca, The *Annunciation Panel* from the *Perugia Polyptych*, 1460s, Galleria Nazionale dell' Umbria, Perugia. (Photo: Alinari/Art Resource, New York.)

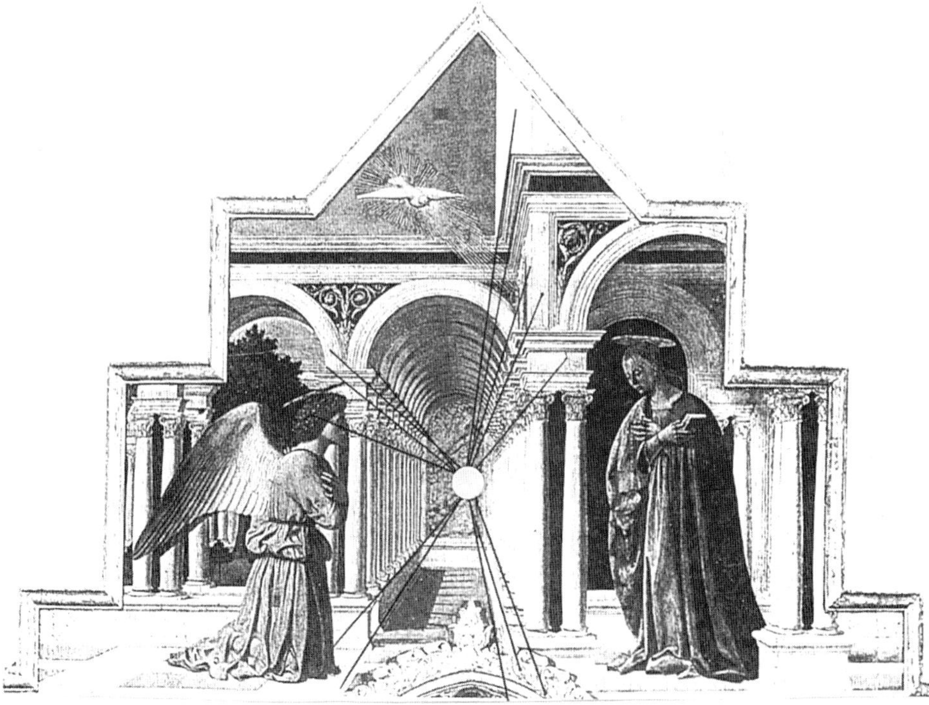

Fig. 43. Diagram of perspective scheme in the *Annunciation Panel* by Piero della Francesca. (Author.)

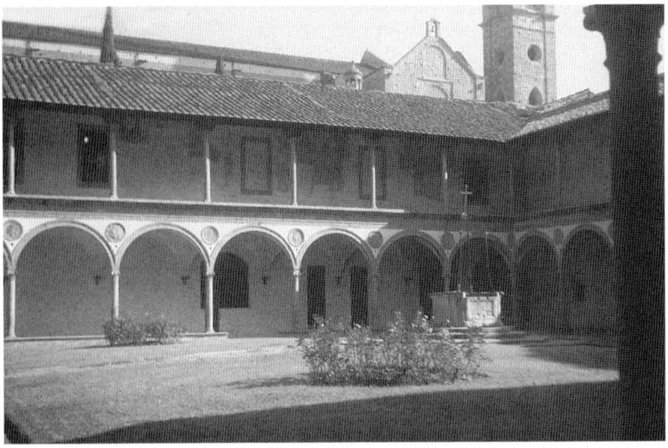

Fig. 44. Bernardo Rossellino, The Spinelli Cloister, 1446–53, Monastery of Santa Croce, Florence. (Photo: author.)

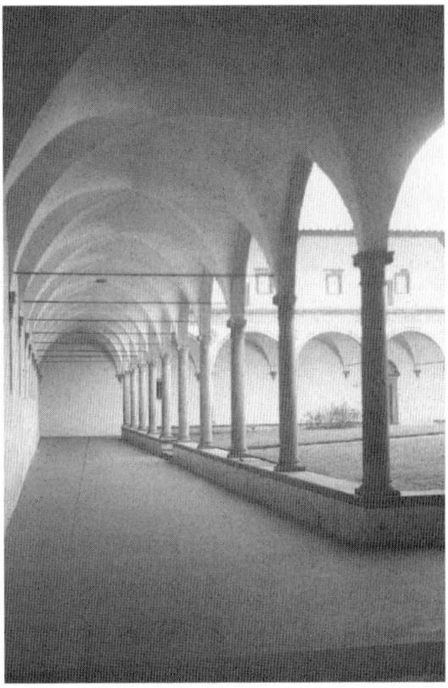

Fig. 45. Bernardo Rossellino, View along the east walkway of the Spinelli Cloister, Monastery of Santa Croce, Florence. (Photo: author.)

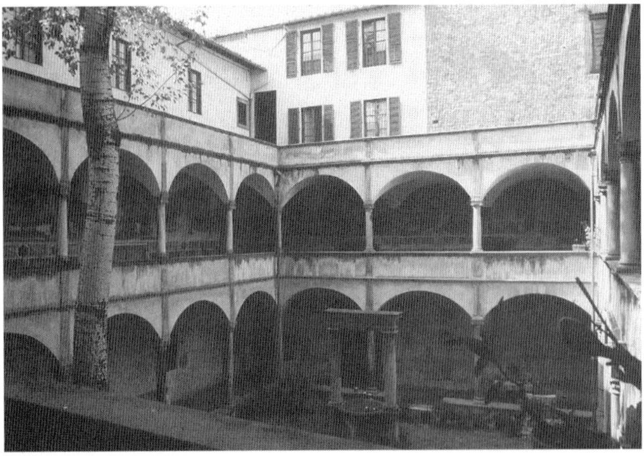

Fig. 46. Workshop of Antonio di Domenico, Cloister of the Oranges, ca. 1435, Badia Fiorentina, Florence. (Photo: author.)

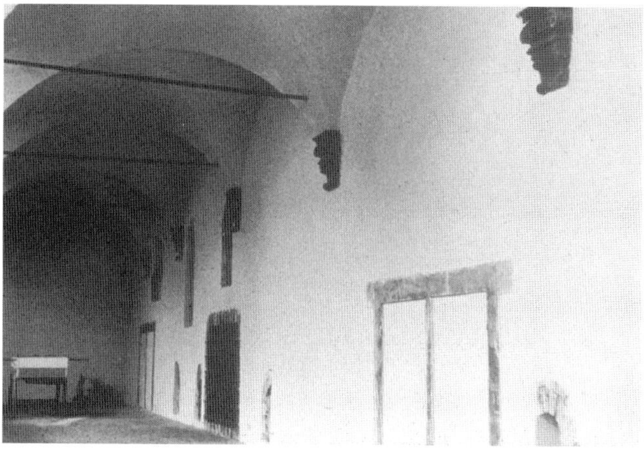

Fig. 47. Upper walkway of the Cloister of the Oranges in 1967 with frescoes by Giovanni da Consalvo removed for conservation, Badia Fiorentina, Florence. (Photo: author.)

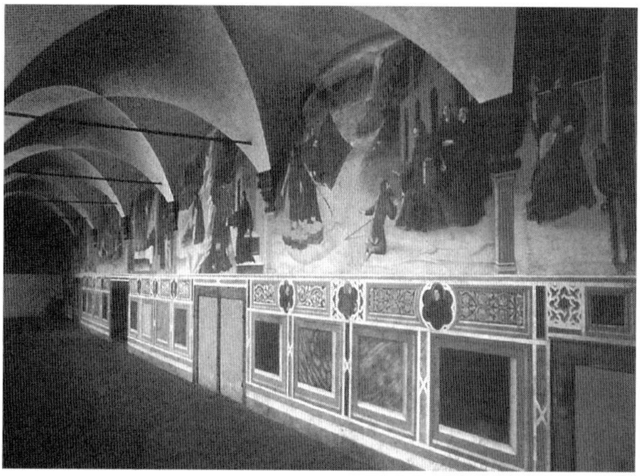

Fig. 48. Upper walkway of the Cloister of the Oranges in 1978 with the frescoes by Giovanni da Consalvo returned to their original locations, Badia Fiorentina, Florence. (Photo: author.)

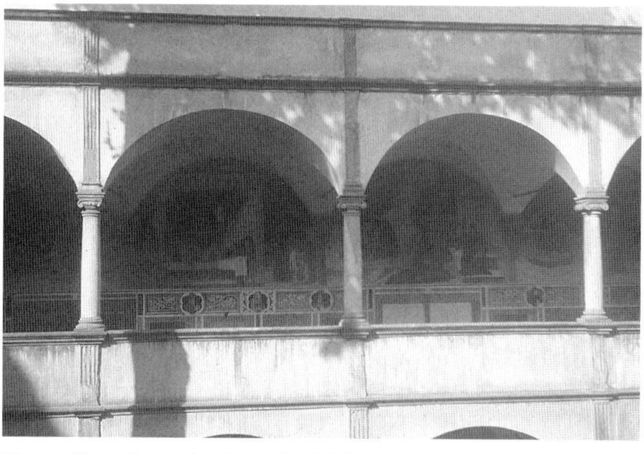

Fig. 49. View of upper loggia arcade with frescoes in place, Cloister of the Oranges, Badia Fiorentina, Florence. (Photo: author.)

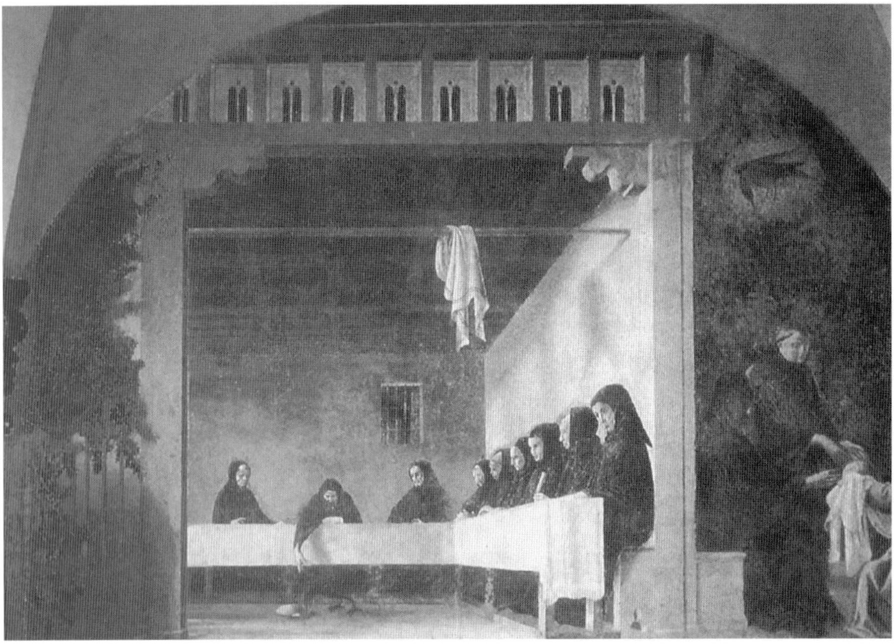

Fig. 50. Giovanni da Consalvo, *Miracle of St. Benedict*, 1436–39, Cloister of the Oranges, Badia Fiorentina, Florence. (Photo: author.)

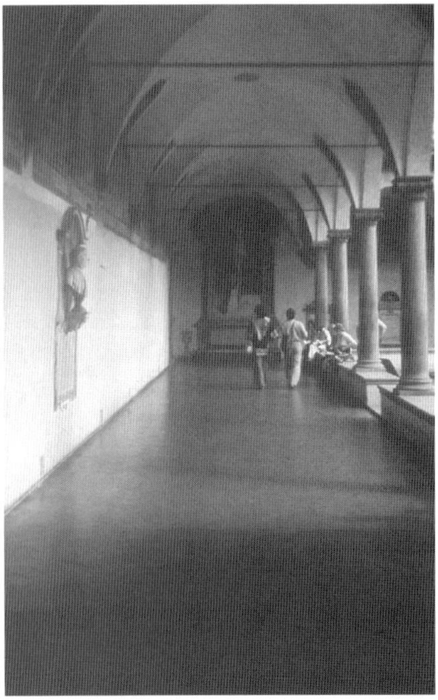

Fig. 51. View from entry along walkway of Michelozzo di Bartolommeo's First Cloister, ca. 1435, Monastery of San Marco, Florence. (Photo: author.)

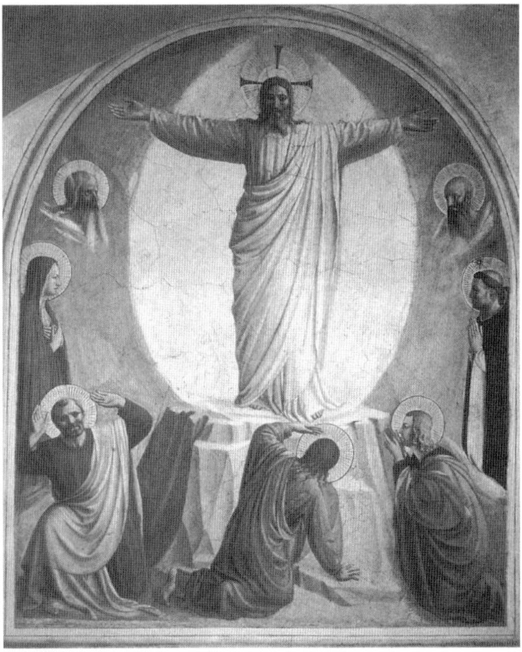

Fig. 52. Fra Angelico, *Transfiguration*, 1438–45, cloister dormitory, Monastery of San Marco, Florence. (Photo: author.)

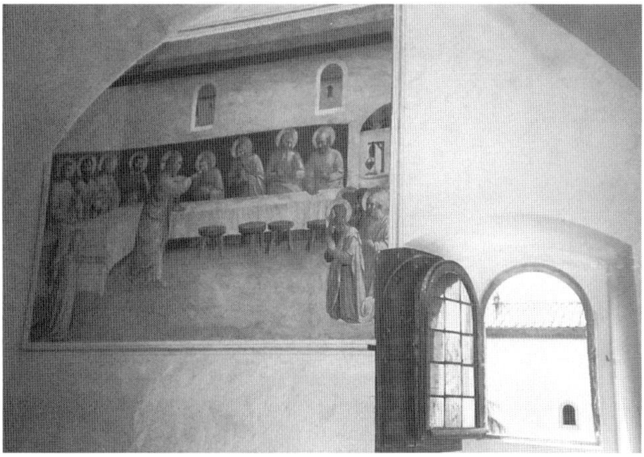

Fig. 53. Cell interior with real and fictive windows of Communion scene, 1438–45, Monastery of San Marco, Florence. (Photo: author.)

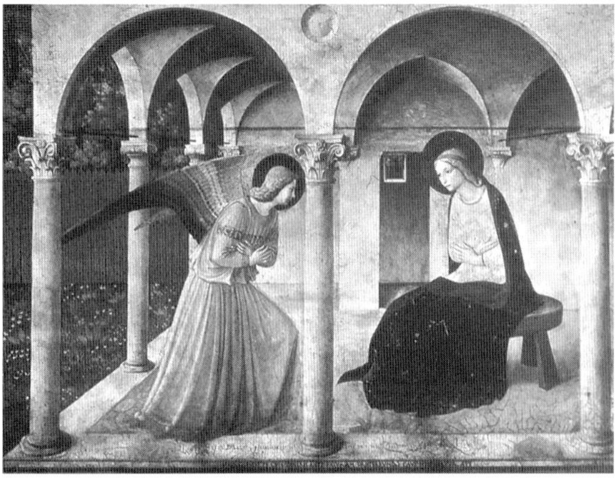

Fig. 54. Fra Angelico, Fresco of the *Annunciation,* 1438–45, Monastery of San Marco, Florence. (Photo: author.)

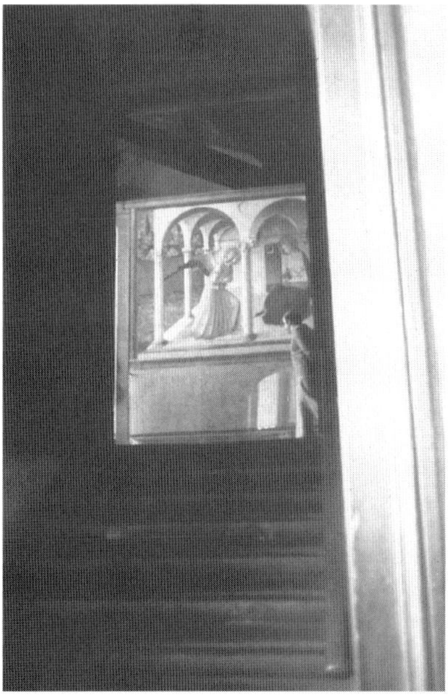

Fig. 55. View from staircase landing of Fra Angelico's *Annunciation,* Monastery of San Marco, Florence. (Photo: author.)

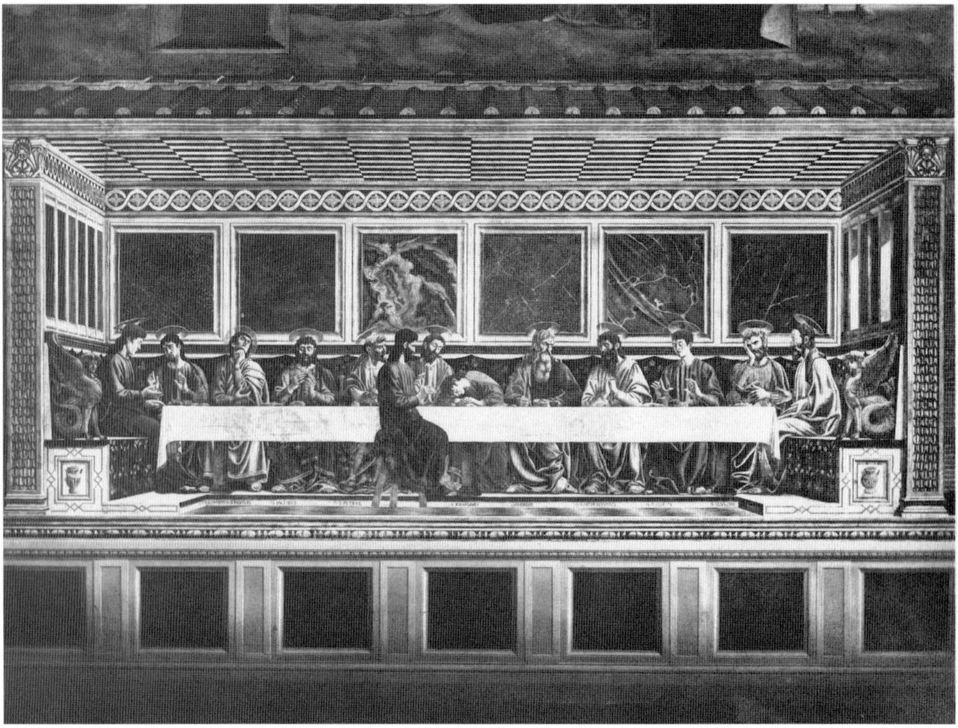

Fig. 56. Andrea del Castagno, *The Last Supper,* 1447, Refectory of the Convent of Saint Apollonia, Florence. (Photo: Alinari/Art Resource, New York.)

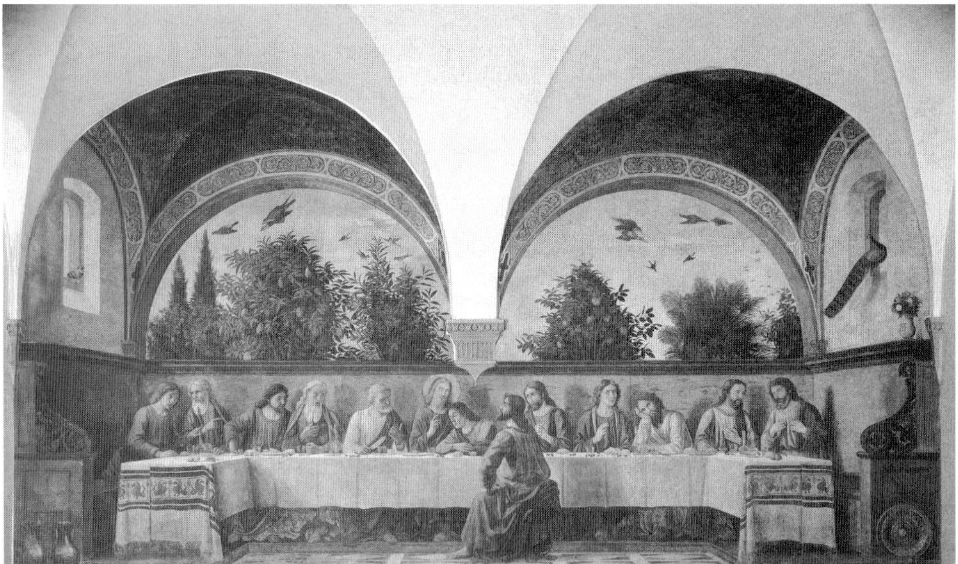

Fig. 57. Domenico del Ghirlandaio, *The Last Supper,* 1480, Refectory of the Monastery of Ognissanti, Florence. (Photo: Scala/Art Resource, New York.)

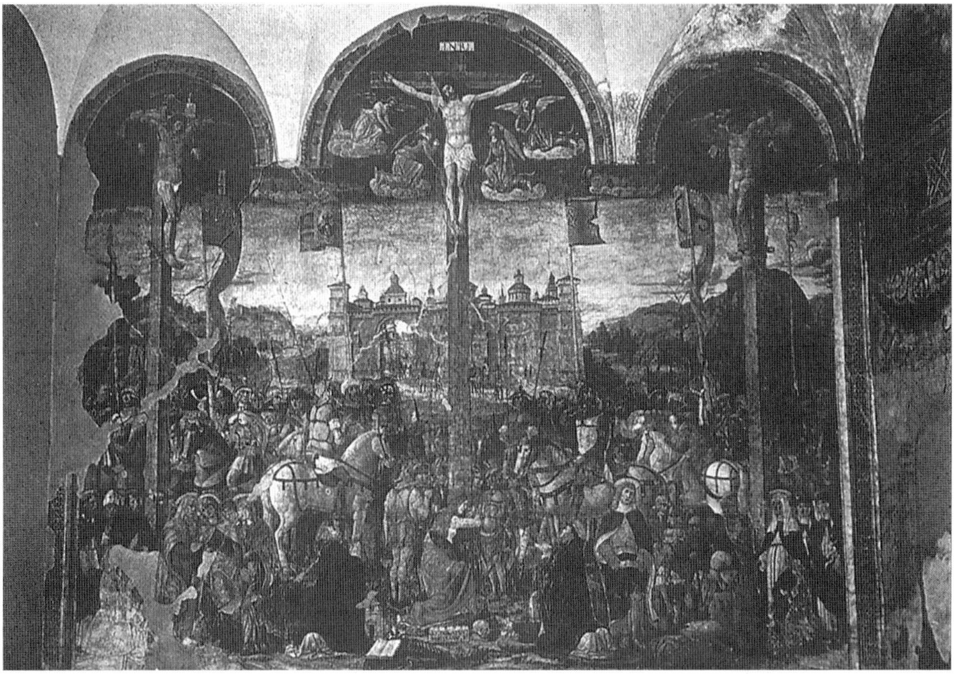

Fig. 58. Giovanni Donato Montofano, *The Crucifixion,* 1480s, Refectory of the Monastery of Santa Maria delle Grazie, Milan. (Photo: author.)

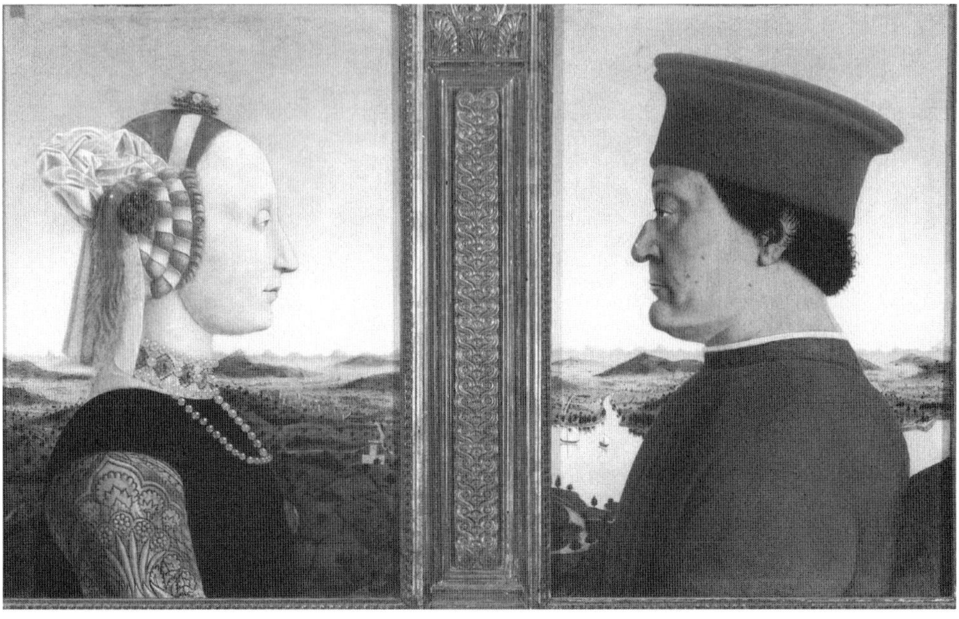

Fig. 59. Piero della Francesca, *Portrait Panels of Federico da Montefeltro and Battista Sforza,* ca. 1472, Galleria degli Uffizi, Florence. (Photo: Alinari/Art Resource, New York.)

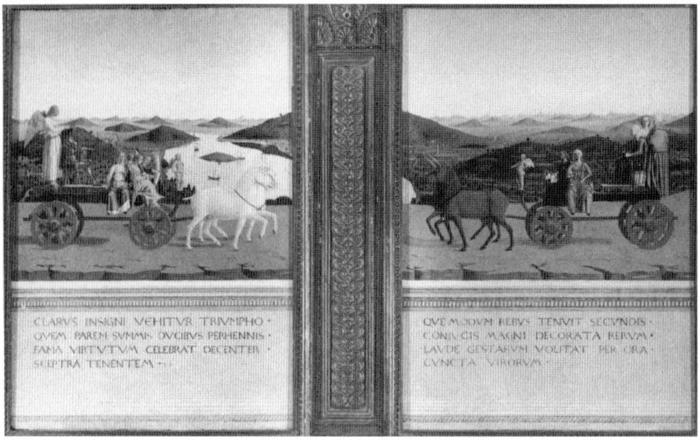

Fig. 60. Piero della Francesca, Reverse of the Montefeltro/Sforza Panels with triumphal carts before a continuous landscape, Galleria degli Uffizi, Florence. (Photo: Alinari/Art Resource, New York.)

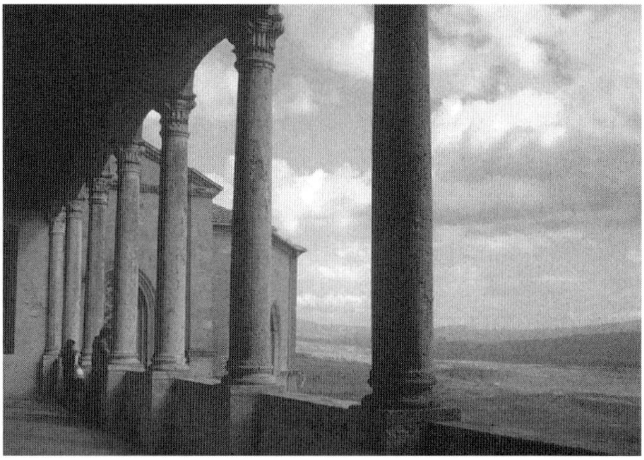

Fig. 61. The Orcia Valley as seen from the loggia of the Piccolomini Palace in Pienza. (Photo: author.)

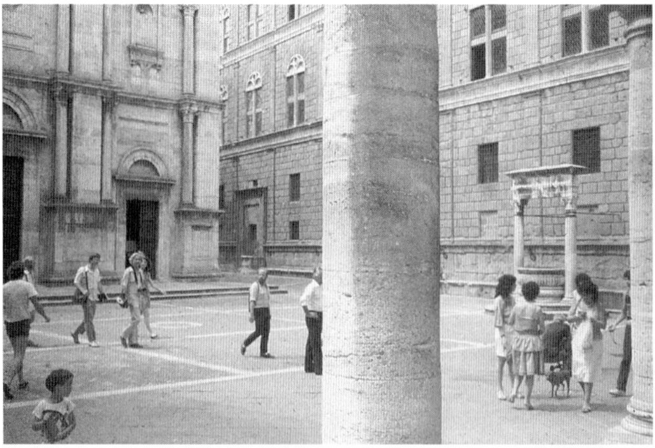

Fig. 62. View of the Cathedral square of Pienza showing grid pattern of paving. (Photo: author.)

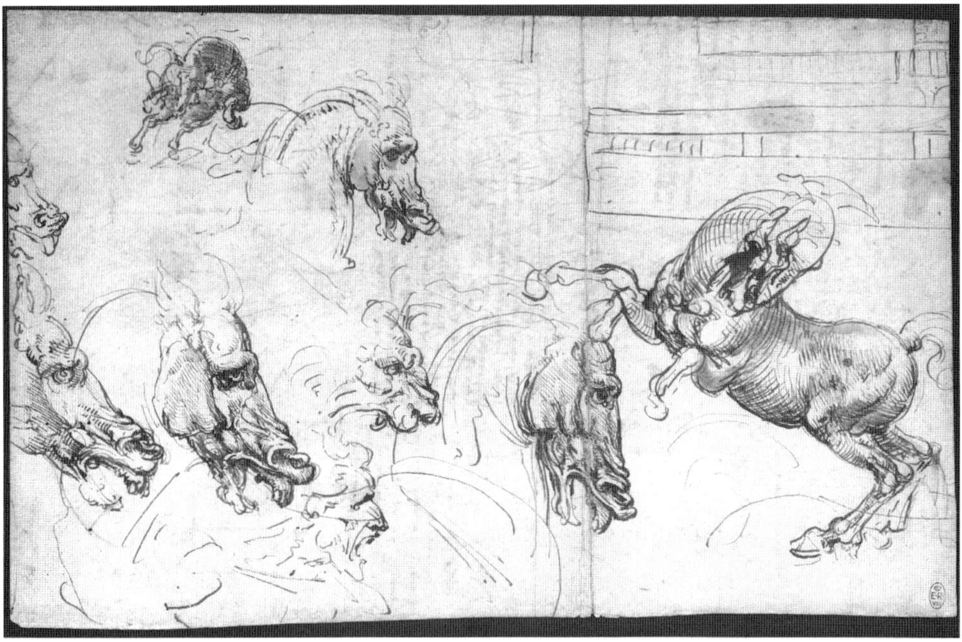

Fig. 63. Leonardo da Vinci, Preparatory drawing for his *Battle of Anghiari* showing human and equine ferocity, 1503–5, Royal Library, Windsor Castle, Great Britain. (Photo: The Royal Collection © 2004, Her Majesty Queen Elizabeth II.)

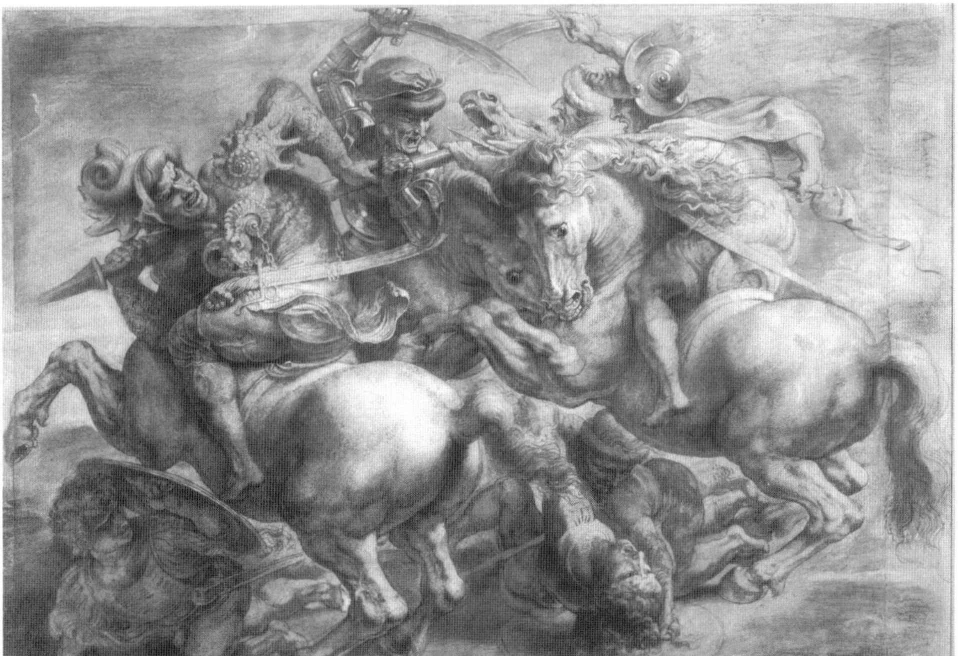

Fig. 64. Peter Paul Rubens, Copy after Leonardo's *Fight for the Standard,* ca. 1615, Cabinet des Dessins, Louvre, Paris. (Photo: Réunion des Musées Nationaux/Art Resource, New York.)

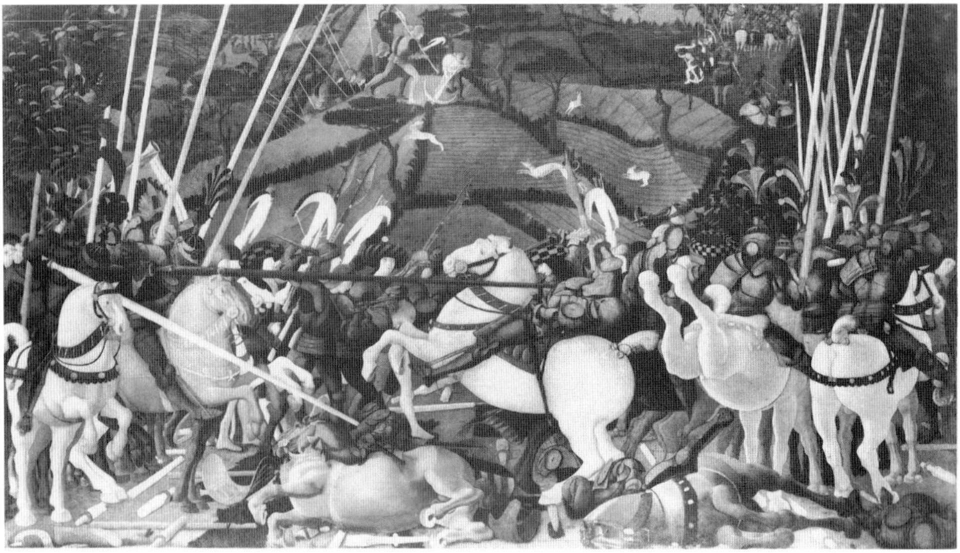

Fig. 65. Paolo Uccello, *Battle of San Romano,* 1430s, Galleria degli Uffizi, Florence. (Photo: Alinari/Art Resource, New York.)

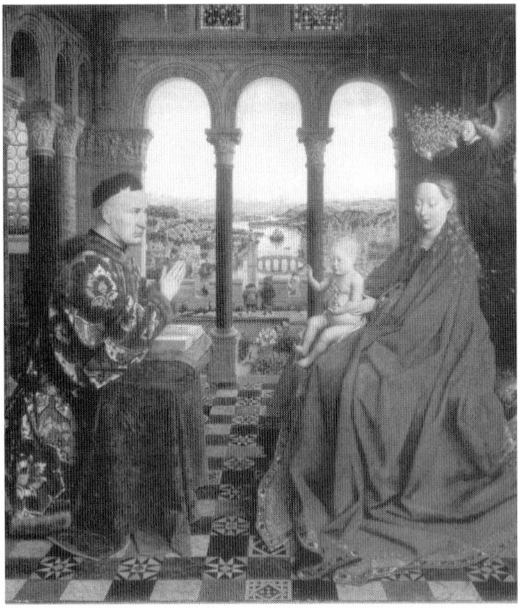

Fig. 66. Jan van Eyck, *The Madonna and Child with Chancellor Nicholas Rolin,* ca. 1435, Louvre, Paris. (Photo: Réunion des Musées Nationaux/Art Resource, New York.)

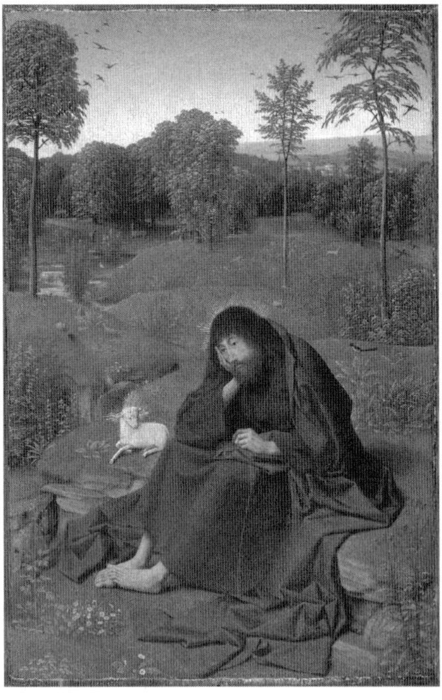

Fig. 67. Geertgen tot Sint Jans, *St. John the Baptist in the Wilderness,* 1490, Gemäldegalerie, Staatliche Museen, Berlin. (Photo: Bildarchiv Preußischer Kulturbesitz/Art Resource, New York.)

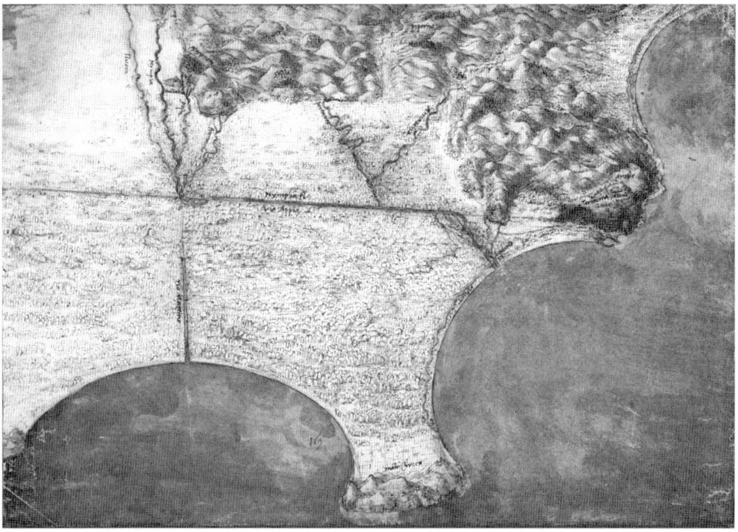

Fig. 68. Leonardo da Vinci, *Aerial View of the Italian Coast from Torre Astura to the Gulf of Terracina with Monte Circeo,* 1515, Collection of the Royal Library, Windsor Castle. (Photo: The Royal Collection © 2004, Her Majesty Queen Elizabeth II.)

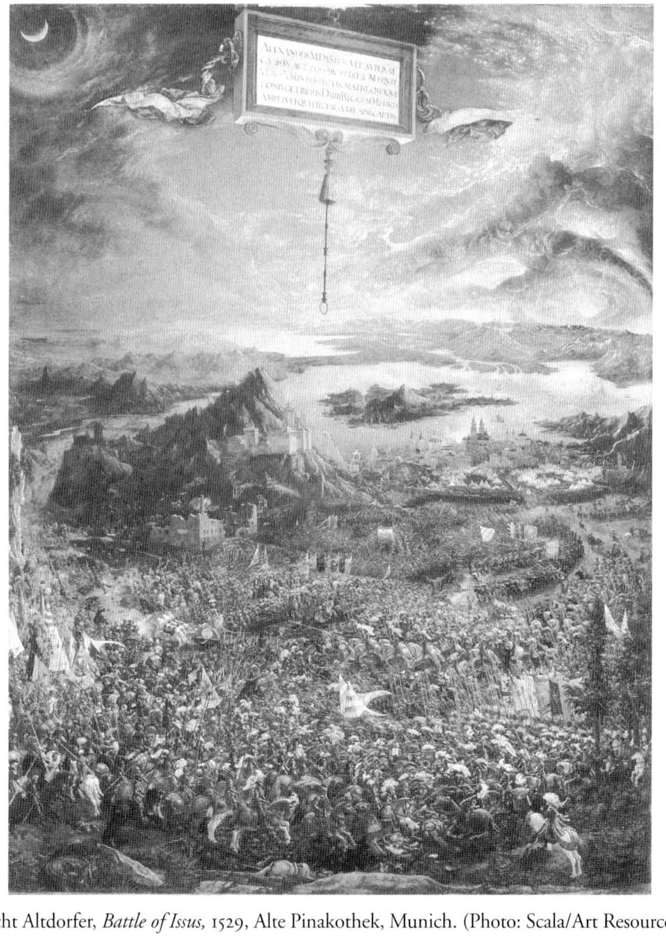

Fig. 69. Albrecht Altdorfer, *Battle of Issus,* 1529, Alte Pinakothek, Munich. (Photo: Scala/Art Resource, New York.)

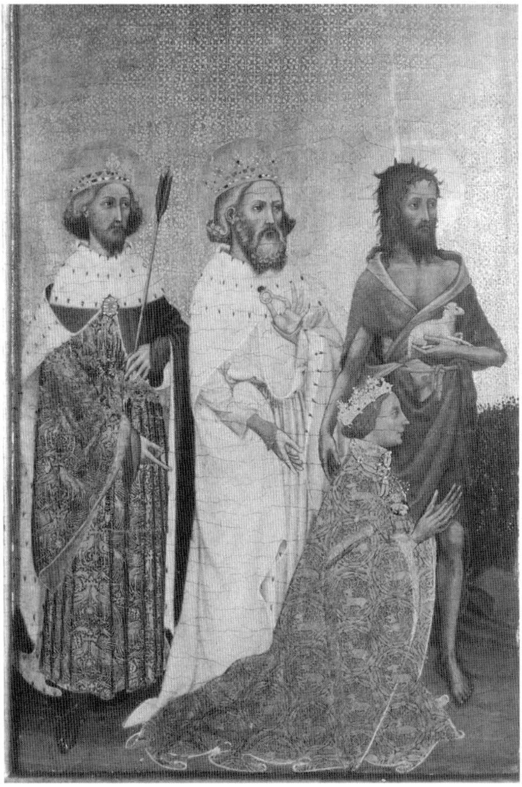

Fig. 70. Anonymous French artist, *Wilton Diptych,* 1395–1413, National Gallery, London. (Photos: Erich Lessing/Art Resource, New York.)

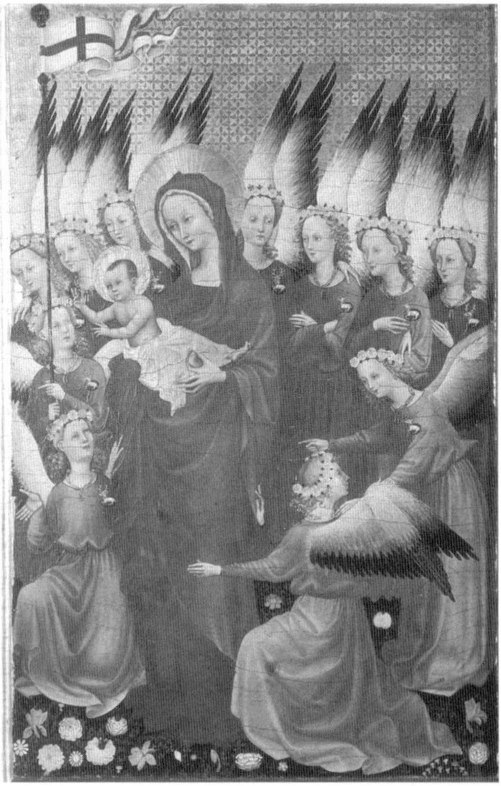

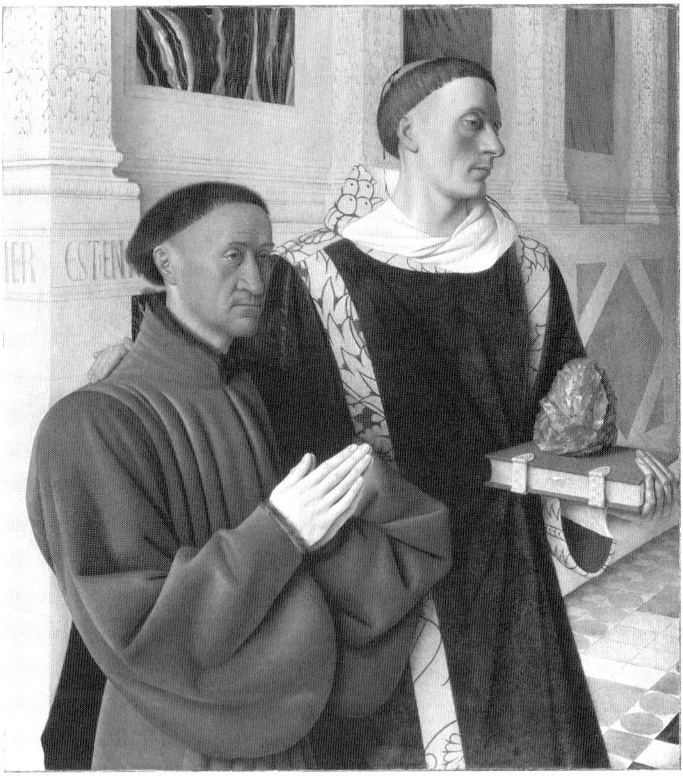

Fig. 71. Jean Fouquet, *Melun Diptych,* ca. 1455. Left panel, Gemäldegalerie, Staatliche Museen zu Berlin. (Photo: Bildarchiv Preußischer Kulturbesitz/Art Resource, New York.) Right panel, Koninklijk Museum voor Schoner, Kunsten, Antwerp. (Photo: Scala/Art Resource, New York.)

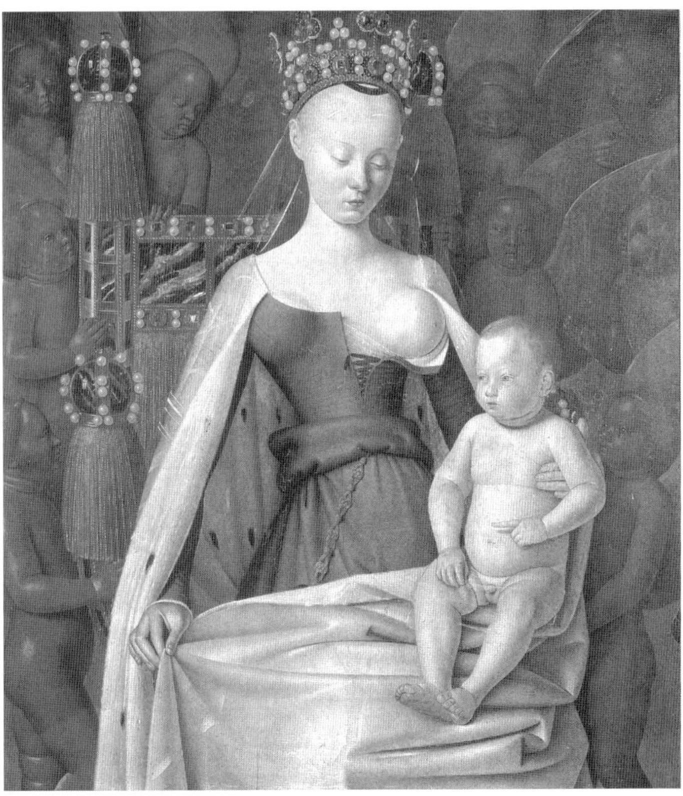

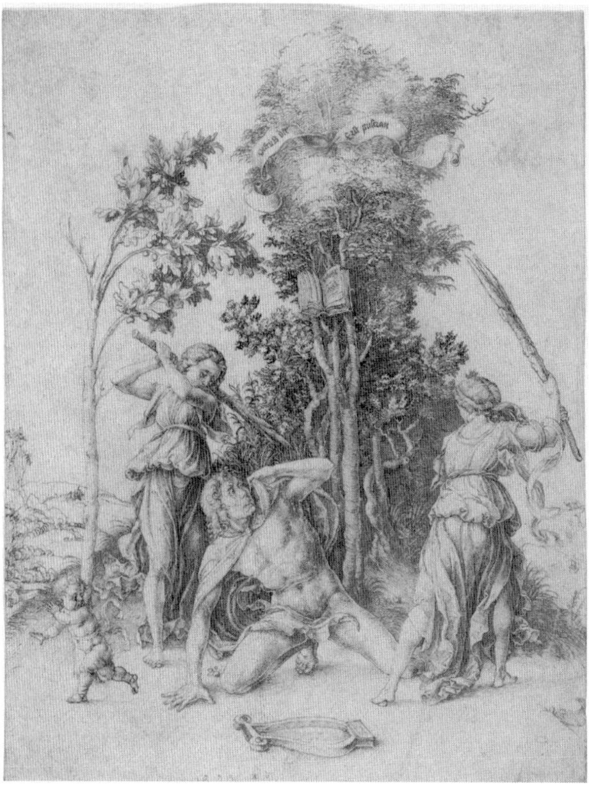

Fig. 72. Albrecht Dürer, *The Slaying of Orpheus,* 1494, Hamburger Kunsthalle, Hamburg. (Photo: Bildarchiv Preußischer Kulturbesitz/Art Resource, New York.)

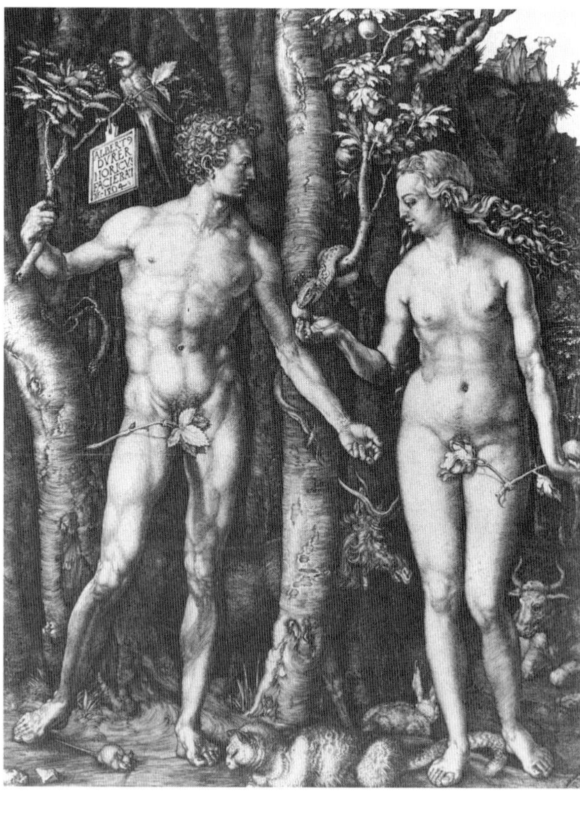

Fig. 73. Albrecht Dürer, *The Temptation of Adam and Eve*, 1504. (Photo: Foto Marburg/Art Resource, New York.)

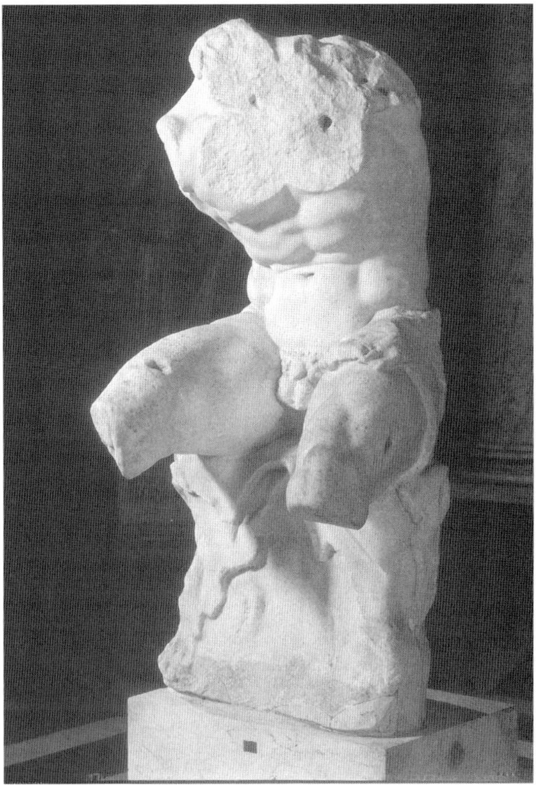

Fig. 74. Apollonius of Athens (?), *Belvedere Torso,* ca. 150–50 B.C., Museo Pio Clementino, Vatican Museums, Rome. (Photo: Scala/Art Resource, New York.)

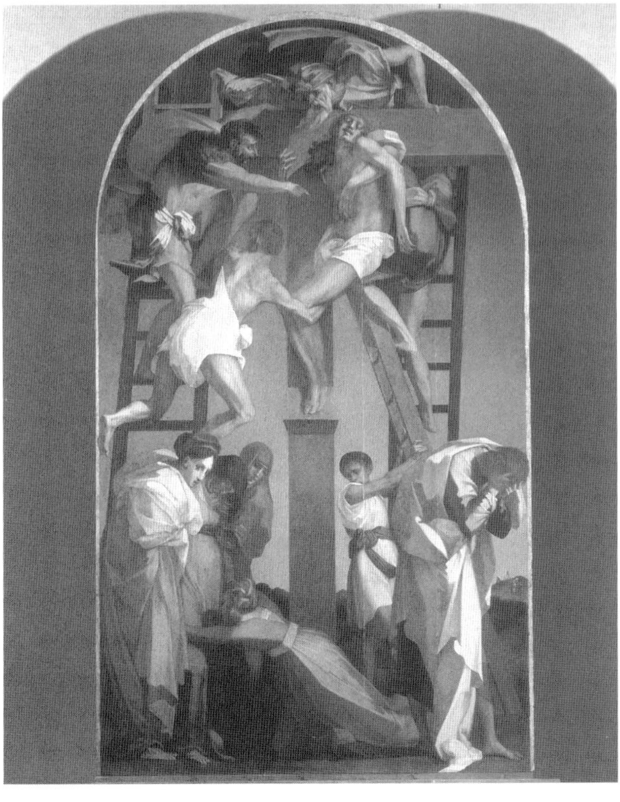

Fig. 75. Rosso Fiorentino, Detail of the Grieving St. John from the *Deposition,* 1521, Pinacoteca Communale, Volterra. (Photo: Scala/Art Resource, New York.)

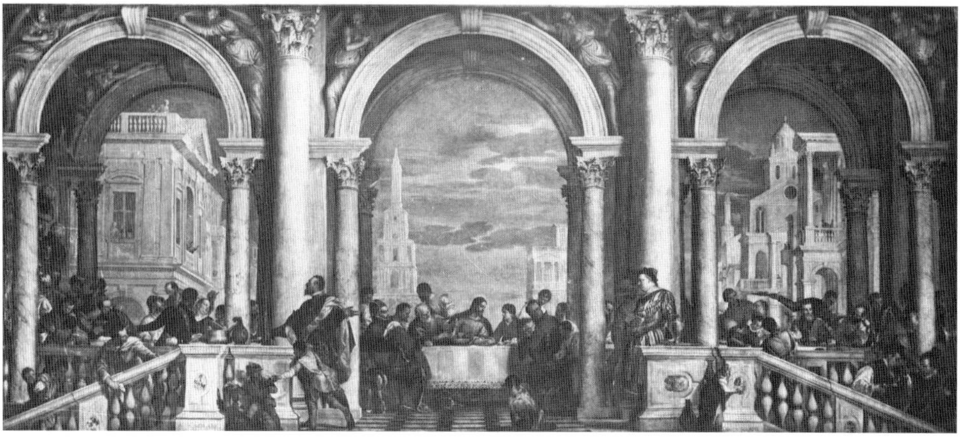

Fig. 76. Paolo Veronese, *Feast in the House of Levi,* 1573, Accademia, Venice. (Photo: Alinari/Art Resource, New York.)

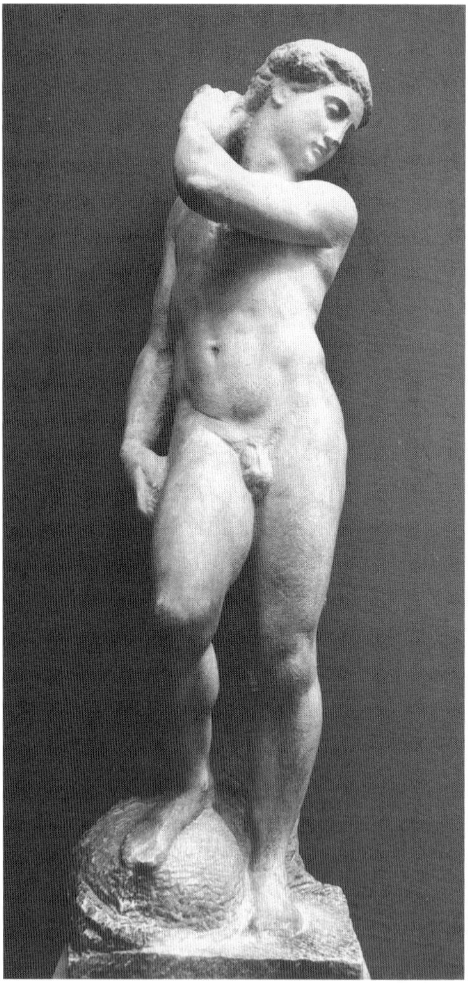

Fig. 77. Michelangelo Buonarotti, *David/Apollo*, 1527–32, Museo Nazionale del Bargello, Florence. (Photo: Alinari/Art Resource, New York.)

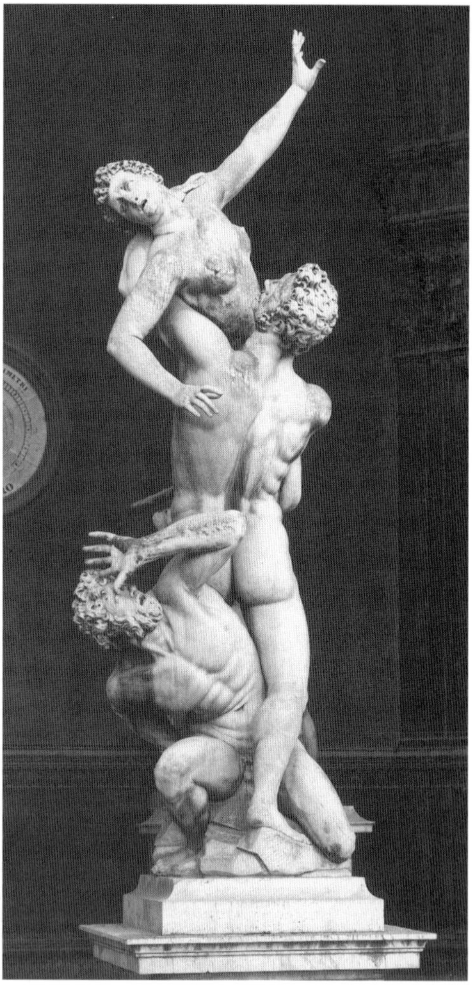

Fig. 78. Giovanni da Bologna, *Rape of the Sabine Woman,* 1581–82, Loggia dei Lanzi, Florence. (Photo: Alinari/Art Resource, New York.)